HISTORY
OF RUSSIA

Sergei Mikhailovich Soloviev

The
Academic International Press
Edition
of

Sergei M. Soloviev
History of Russia From Earliest Times

G. EDWARD ORCHARD
General Editor

Contributing Editors

HUGH F. GRAHAM

JOHN D. WINDHAUSEN

ALEXANDER V. MULLER

K.A. PAPMEHL

RICHARD HANTULA

WALTER J. GLEASON, JR.

WILLIAM H. HILL

G. EDWARD ORCHARD

LINDSEY A.J. HUGHES

NICKOLAS LUPININ

GEORGE E. MUNRO

DANIEL L. SCHLAFLY, JR.

ANTHONY L.H. RHINELANDER

PATRICK J. O'MEARA

PETER C. STUPPLES

T. ALLAN SMITH

MARTHA L. LAHANA

ANTHONY V. KNOWLES

HELEN Y. PROCHAZKA

ALEXANDRA S. KORROS

GARY J. MARKER

MARIAN J. RUBCHAK

RALPH M. CLEMINSON

CATHY J. POTTER

WAYNE D. SANTONI

SERGEI M. SOLOVIEV

History of Russia

Volume 13

The Reign of Tsar Fedor

Edited and Translated

By

Wayne D. Santoni

2002

Academic International Press

The Academic International Press Edition of S.M. Soloviev's
History of Russia From Earliest Times in fifty volumes.

Volume 13. *The Reign of Tsar Fedor.*
Unabridged translation of the text of Volume 7, Chapters 2-5 as
contained in Volume IV of S.M. Soloviev's *Istoria Rossii s
drevneishikh vremen* published in Moscow between 1959-1966,
with added annotation by Wayne D. Santoni.

ISBN: 0-87569-243-5

Composition by Janice Frye

Printed in the United States of America

A list of Academic International Press publications is found at
the end of this volume.

ACADEMIC INTERNATIONAL PRESS
Box 1111 • Gulf Breeze FL 32562-1111 • USA

www.ai-press.com

CONTENTS

Relations With the Caucasus and Persia—Ongoing Conquest
of Siberia

The Tsar's Administration—Finances—Trade—Protecting
the Frontier—The Army—The Code of Precedence—
Serfdom Emerges—Slaves—Migration—The Church—A
Muscovite Patriarchate—Other Church Matters—Morals and
Customs

The Mission of Riurik's Dynasty—Boris Accused of
Dmitry's Death—The Chronicler's Tale—The Investigative
Commission's Report—The Nagoys' Defense—Eyewitness
Accounts—Unsettling Questions—Resolution of the Case in
Moscow—Popular Opinion—Fedor's Death

WEIGHTS AND MEASURES

Linear and Surface Measure

Arshin: 16 vershoks, 28 in. (diuims) 72.12 cm
Chetvert (quarter): 1/4 arshin, 1/2 desiatina, 1.35 acres (sometimes 1.5 desiatinas or c. 4.1 acres)
Desiatina: 2,400 square sazhens, 2.7 acres, 1.025 hectares
Diuim: 1 inch, 2.54 cm
Fut: 12 diuims, 1 foot, 30.48 cm

Obza (areal): c. 10 chetverts, 13–15 acres
Osmina: 1/4 desiatina, 600 sq. sazhens, .256 hectare
Sazhen: 3 arshins, 7 feet, 2.133 m
Vershok: 1.75 in., 4.445 cm, 1/16 arshin
Verst: 500 sazhens, 1,166 yards and 2 feet, .663 miles, 1.0668 km
Voloka (plowland): 19 desiatinas, 20 hectares, 49 acres

Liquid Measure

Bochka (barrel): 40 vedros, 121 gallons, 492 liters
Chetvert (quarter): 1.4 bochkas, 32.5 gallons
Korchago (wine): Rus, unknown

Kufa: 30 stofy
Stof: Kruzhka (cup), 1/10 vedro, c. 1.3 quarts, 1.23 liters
Vedro (pail): 3.25 gallons, 12.3 liters, 10 stofy

Weights

Berkovets: 361 lbs., 10 puds
Bezmen: c. 1 kg, 2.2 lbs.
Chetverik (grain measure dating from 16th century): 1/8 chetvert, 15.8 lbs.
Chetvert (grain measure): 1/4 rad, 3.5 puds, 126.39 lbs., c. 8 bushels
Funt: 96 zolotniks, .903 lbs., 14.4 oz., 408.24 kg
Grivenka: 205 grams
Kad: 4 chetverts, 14 puds, 505.56 lbs.
Kadka malenkaia: 12th-century, small measure

Kamen (stone): 32 funt
Korob (basket): 7 puds, 252 lbs.
Osmina (eighth): 2 osmina to a chetvert (dry measure)
Polbezmen: c. 500 g, 1 lb.
Polosmina (sixteenth): 1/2 osmina
Pud: 40 funts, 36.113 lbs. (US), 40 lbs. (Russian), 16.38 kg
Rad: 14 puds, 505.58 lbs.
Zolotnik: 1/96 lbs., 4.26 grams

Money

Altyn: 6 Muscovite dengas, 3 copecks
Bel: Rus, pure silver coin
Chervonets (chervonnyi): gold coin of first half of 18th century worth c. 3 rubles
Chetvertak: silver coin equal to 25 copecks or 1/4 ruble (18–19th centuries)
Copeck: two Muscovite dengas
Denga: 1/2 copeck
Grivna: 20 Muscovite dengas, 100 grivnas equals 1 ruble, 10 copecks
Grosh: 10 peniaz
Grosh litovsky (Lithuanian grosh): 5 silver copecks
Kopa grosh: 60 groshas, one Muscovite poltina, 1/2 ruble
Kuna: 12th-century Rus coin comparable to Westerns denarii or Eastern dirhems. Varied in value by region. Replaced late 14th century by the denga or serebro (silver). Also a marten skin.
Moskovka: 1/2 copeck
Muscovite denga: 200 equals 1 ruble
Novgorod denga: 100 equals 1 ruble
Novgorodka: 1 copeck

Peniaz: 10 equals one grosh (Lithuania)
Poltina (poltinnik): 50 copecks, 100 dengas, 1 ruble
Poltora: 1 1/2 rubles
Polupoltina (-nik): 25 copecks, 50 dengas
Rezan: 12th century Rus coin. 50 rezan equals one grivna kuna
Ruble: 100 copecks, 200 dengas
Shiroky grosh (large silver coin): 20 Muscovite copecks
Veksa: 12th-century Rus small coin equal to one squirrel pelt (belka)

Foreign Denominations
Chervonnyi: c. 3 rubles
Ducat: c. 3 rubles
Dutch efimok: "lion dollar" or levok, 1 thaler, 2.5 guilders
Efimok: foreign currency, 1 thaler, .75-1 ruble, 1 chervonets or chervonnyi
Levok: Dutch silver lion dollar
Thaler (Joachimsthaler): c. 1 ruble, 1/3 chervonets or chervonnyi

Note: Weights and measures often changed values over time and sometimes held more than one value at the same time. For details consult Sergei G. Pushkarev, *Dictionary of Russian Historical Terms from the Eleventh Century to 1917* (Yale, 1970).

PREFACE

This book is an unabridged translation of Volume 7, Chapters 2-5, of the edition of Soloviev's *Istoriia Rossii s drevneishikh vremen* (History of Russia from Earliest Times) published in Moscow between 1959 and 1966. In the Moscow edition it is found in Book IV, pages 190-324. Chapter I follows Soloviev's Chapter II, pp. 190-199 in the edition of 1959-1966. Soloviev's third chapter has been divided into three. Our Chapter II consists of pp. 200-239 in the edition of 1959-1966, Chapter III to pp. 239-259, and Chapter IV, pp. 259-282. Our Chapter V follows Soloviev's fourth chapter, pp. 283-312, and Chapter VI corresponds to Soloviev's short final chapter, pp. 313-324. The Appendix consists of a translation of the lengthy discussion of views concerning the death of Tsarevich Dmitry, Note 131 to Vol. 7 of the original, which is found on pp. 338-341 of the 1959-1966 edition.

Soloviev's pages are featureless and interminable, one long and complex sentence treading Indian file after another. To make the text easier to follow, long paragraphs and sentences have been broken into shorter ones. The main consideration is to make his history as readable as possible consistent with accuracy. An effort is made to find English-language equivalents for the specialized terms that Soloviev employs (ranks, offices, titles, legal, administrative, and so on) in order to smooth the flow of the narrative for the general reader and to avoid cluttering the pages with untranslated words. The exception involves Russian words which have become common in English—boyar, tsar, cossack, khan and others.

Most of the subtitles are based on the descriptive topic headings clustered at the beginnings of the chapters in the Russian edition. These headings have been moved into the body of the text as subtitles to mark the transition from one subject to another. In some cases new subtitles have been added, but Soloviev's arrangement of the material has not been altered

Remarks in parentheses in the text are Soloviev's, as is the italicization of words or phrases for emphasis. Explanatory or interpretive information is supplied by the editor in footnotes placed at the end of the book. Where this appears in the text of the translation it is enclosed in brackets. The general policy followed in annotating is to identify prominent personalities at first mention and to give explanations and elucidations of obscure or uncommon terms and passages, assuming that many readers have relatively little familiarity with Russian history. Most of Soloviev's own notes are not included; their highly specialized archival, documentary, and bibliographic nature is of value to specialists who would prefer to consult the original Russian text. Similarly, most of the notes added by the editors of the edition of 1959-1966 also are excluded since they too are technical in nature, primarily supplying fuller bibliographic citations than Soloviev's notes. When the author's notes and those of the Soviet editors are included they are so designated. All other notes are those of the present editor. In the notes the reader is frequently referred to entries in the *Modern Encyclopedia of Russian and Soviet History* (MERSH), and its *Supplement*, a reliable and up-to-date reference source readily available in most university libraries.

Russian personal names are preserved in their Russian form except for Alexander, Alexis, Michael, Nicholas, Catherine, and Peter, which English usage has made familiar with respect to Russian historical figures. The names of prominent ecclesiastics have been recast into Latin or Greek equivalents. This applies to prominent individuals; less prominent figures retain their Russian forms. Certain other names and terms have been anglicized for the sake of clarity and because they are used widely, such as Casimir, Sophia, Danzig, boyar, rubles, versts, and Dnieper.

The editors of the edition published in 1959-1966 frequently added patronymics and other names, and these have been retained without brackets. Patronymics appearing in the original edition also have been kept. Plural forms in Russian for names and terms which might be confusing have been anglicized—Vologdians rather than Vologzhane, Voguls and not Vogulichi, the Dolgorukys not Dolgorukie, and so on; in a few cases the Russian plural form is used when it is common. The final "-iia" in feminine personal names has been shortened to "-ia," thus "Maria" and "Evdokia" instead of "Mariia" and "Evdokiia." Most Slavic surnames show gender, and this has been preserved. An "-a" at the end of a word usually signifies a female. For example, Golovkin's wife or daughter would be named Golovkina.

Non-Russian names, locations, terms, ranks and so on are spelled according to the language native to the person or particular to the city, region or culture where this can be determined. Confusion arises at times because the text is not clear about nationalities. An example is Lithuania where at least three languages intermingle. In such cases the context rules; the Russian rendering is the last resort. Individuals whose names were once non-Russian but were in Russian service for generations are named by the original spelling of the family name. Turkish, Tatar, Persian and other names and terms usually are spelled according to accepted forms in scholarly books. In some instances, if not otherwise ascertainable, they are translated from the Russian as given by Soloviev. The names of geographical locations conform to commonly accepted English usage, that is, Podolia, Moscow, Copenhagen, Saxony, and so on.

With respect to transliteration the translation follows a modified version of the Library of Congress system, omitting diacritical marks and ligatures, and rendering an initial "Ia-" and "Iu-" as "Ya-" and "Yu-" ("Yasnaia" and "Yury") and occasionally the initial "E-" as "Ye" (Yermak, Yevlev); the suffix "-yi" or "-ii" as "-y" ("Dmitry Poliansky" instead of "Dmitrii Polianskii"); and the form "-oi" has been replaced by "-oy" ("Donskoy" instead of "Donskoi"). The soft sign, indicated by an apostrophe in some transliteration systems, is dropped altogether ("tsar" instead of "tsar"), although in some cases an "i" has been inserted in place of a hard or a soft sign: "Soloviev" instead of "Solov'ev."

All dates, as in Soloviev's original text, except where otherwise specified, are according to the Julian calendar, in use in most of Western Europe in the sixteenth century until 1582; this in spite of the fact that Russians themselves at the time figured dates from the creation of the world (which they reckoned to be 5508 BC).

The term "the editor(s)" found in the Notes refers to the editor of 1959-1966 published in the Soviet Union.

A table of weights and measures is included at the front of this volume for the convenience of the reader.

This volume appears after an extraordinarily prolonged gestation, during which I have enjoyed the moral support, good advice and patience of many.

Ted Orchard's unfailing good nature and scholarly acumen ensured the translation would be completed. Southern Illinois University at Edwardsville provided some financial support and released time from teaching, and Veronique Zaytzeff of its department of Foreign Languages aided with several obscure passages. My mentors, George Yaney, Oswald Backus and Herbert J. Ellison shaped my love for Russian History and my respect for the undervalued craft of translation. My wife, Lana, provided her services as a reader, helping to shape rough hewn first drafts into their smoother successors. I finish as I started, with my parents, David and Josephine, who imparted in me the humor, tolerance and intellectual curiosity that enriches my life.

Wayne D. Santoni

INTRODUCTION

One obvious merit of Soloviev's *History of Russia* is its rich presentation of original sources, whether as direct quotations or in paraphrase. The History's interpretative framework is more obscure, hidden at least partly by its great length. Soloviev's clear and coherent interpretation of Russian history more easily is found elsewhere. It emerges more clearly in his public lectures or in the textbook he published based on the longer History, for decades a standard work for secondary school students in the Russian empire. In the full History his concepts usually ride subtly beneath the narrative, silently directing his emphases and conclusions. When they do surface occasionally it is in passages distinct not only in content but even in stylistic flavor.

Soloviev (1820-1879) of course formed his ideas in the context of the background, training and intellectual milieu within which he flourished. Born the son of a priest, he entered Moscow University in 1838, toured Western Europe during the summer of 1844, and by 1847 defended his doctoral dissertation. Soloviev differed from other priests' sons among his contemporaries in preserving his religious belief yet like most educated Russians of his generation he fell under the spell of Hegel. For him, therefore, Russian history unfolded through multiple dialectical processes, all played out within limits fixed by divine will, natural forces and human character.

I.D. Kovalchenko, writing an introductory essay to the first volume of the 1888 edition of the History, delineates several of its dialectical patterns. "Soloviev believed that most fundamental for all nations was the contradiction between Christian ideals as the ultimate end of historical progress and humanity's limitations in realizing them.... Soloviev considered the main underlying contradiction in Russia's historical development to be the distinction between familial and state relationships. In his opinion a major role also was played by the tension between 'forest' and 'steppe,' that is, between settlers and nomads, 'old' and 'new' towns, progressive bases of European civilization and obsolete forms and norms of social life, and so forth.... On one hand Soloviev viewed historical development as dialectic, but on the other he characterized this development as an evolutionary process. He did not recognize uneven, spasmodic revolutionary leaps in the historical process and considered revolutionary transitions which occur in history to be deviations from the normal course of historical evolution."[1]

Unlike Kovalchenko, most western critics would not consider evolutionary dialectical processes to be paradoxical, nor would they lament Soloviev's failure to see the importance of the class struggle and revolutionary leaps forward. Nevertheless, Kovalchenko's last observation leads directly to an important point, namely that Soloviev employed his emphasis on the constancy of certain processes of change, of certain contradictions and tensions, as the underlying theme essential to provide much-needed continuity to the History's many volumes. As George Vernadsky observes, "For Soloviev, the historical process was not only organic but continuous as well."[2] Dialectical change for Soloviev was the constant which lent continuity and unity to Russia's organic evolution.

This volume of the History demonstrates well Soloviev's talent at finding historical continuity. It describes the peaceful lull between two violent and tempestuous eras in Russian history, the reign of Tsar Fedor's father Ivan IV, and the Time of Troubles. Another historian might have stressed this relative tranquillity in order to differentiate Fedor's reign from those of Ivan or of Boris Godunov. Soloviev does in fact allude to this contrast at the outset of Chapter V, but elsewhere he holds to his emphasis on continuity. He casts his glance both forward and backward in time, reminding the reader of where his history has been and where it is going.

Ivan left a contradictory but basically negative legacy. Abroad, his reign commenced triumphantly with the conquest of Kazan and Astrakhan, Muscovy's two neighboring Tatar khanates, but ended badly with a sharp and costly defeat in Livonia at the hands of Poland's warrior king Stefan Bathory. At home, young and brilliant Ivan executed comprehensive legal and administrative reforms, then old, guilt-ridden and perhaps demented, Ivan died after presiding over a bloody, divisive and failed effort to carve from Muscovy a private and separate state ruled (and terrorized) by his personal administration, the so-called *oprichnina*, or crown estates. Historians differ widely in their explanation of the sources of Ivan's conduct. Some see in him a frustrated genius of state building, bedeviled by the archaic class pretensions and conservatism of a recalcitrant and powerful nobility. Others observe sanguinary propensities even in his younger halcyon years. For them, the later stages of his reign merely fulfilled an always present if sometimes latent impulse towards tyranny. Whatever their interpretation, historians agree with Ivan's contemporaries that his tumultuous and costly reign left both state and society weakened.

From this perspective Fedor's reign may indeed be portrayed as an interval of peace, stability and recovery. After his death his main adviser and the actual power behind his throne, Boris Godunov, was elected tsar. Godunov ruled only a handful of years in his own right before his reign ended in plague, famine and civil war, the "Time of Troubles." Soloviev describes these events, the sequel to our story here, in the next two volumes of this series, both translated by G. Edward Orchard: *The Time of Troubles. Boris Godunov and False Dmitry* (Academic International Press, 1988) and *The Time of Troubles. Tsar Vasily Shuisky and the Interregnum, 1606-1613* (Academic International Press, 1989).

Despite the nature of Fedor's reign as an interlude between successive epochs of upheaval and suffering, Soloviev chooses to stress those elements which are not exceptional but transitional. Three strains unify it with what came before and what follows: the personality of Godunov, a foreign policy determined by ominous threats and limited resources to meet them, and a profound and still unperceived social and economic crisis with its roots in Ivan's costly wars, the vastness of Muscovy's territories and the sparsity of its population. When the crisis materialized it exposed the underlying historical tension between forest and steppe which Kovalchenko mentioned above.

The original text of this volume comprises Chapters 2-5 in Volume 7 (Book IV) of the 1963 edition of this section of the History. Each chapter takes up a different historical theme, and each restates Soloviev's emphasis on continuity. His second chapter, Chapter I here, emphasizes the ongoing contradiction between familial and state power and, in the process, introduces Boris Godunov. It opens with the fundamental observation that Fedor's reign marked the end of the house of Riurik. This dynasty, starting as an extended family, had become by the sixteenth century the historical agency for collecting the Russian lands into a state. Like most of his contemporaries Soloviev viewed the "gathering of the lands" as historically progressive, and therefore looked favorably upon the house of Riurik as generator of the state principle. Now that Riurik's dynasty ended, other families struggled to create their own dynasties. In this process the familial principle was to express itself dramatically, to the detriment of the state principle. Soloviev alludes to the political and personal fate of those families laying claim to the Muscovite throne. He describes the triumph of the Godunovs and explicitly looks forward to the "storms" of the Time of Troubles when renewed strife destroyed them and threatened the very existence of the state over which the families had struggled.

Soloviev's third chapter, devoted to foreign affairs, takes up a lengthy eighty-three pages of the original text. I have broken it into three chapters—II, III and IV. Here Soloviev detects two constants, one much more recent than the other. These are the role of the Reformation in the domestic affairs of Muscovy's Western neighbors and the threat of Crimean raiders from the steppe for Muscovy, fundamentally a forest state. Chapter II deals with Russia's nearby Western neighbors, Poland and Sweden. It emphasizes how domestic problems in Sweden and Poland enabled a weakened Muscovy to recover its position somewhat but even to show new vigor upon Fedor's campaign for the Polish throne. The freedom of action Muscovy gained from the domestic problems of its western and northern neighbors made for success in encounters with the Tatars and their Turkish lords beyond the cossack steppe to the south and east. Soloviev's third chapter, my fifth, illustrates how Fedor, or more properly Boris, managed to bring relief from the stress, hardship and dislocation characteristic of Ivan IV's time.

This respite proved short lived. Fedor's peaceful rule gave way to cataclysm under Tsar Boris Godunov. By this stage Soloviev already has identified some causes of the catastrophe, all with roots in Ivan's reign or earlier, among them Boris's flawed character, the thrust of the Polish Counter-Reformation towards the East, ceaseless raiding from Crimea, and cossack propensity to insubordination or banditry. Soloviev's concluding chapter sweeps across Russia's past to unearth the deeper roots of the impending disaster. Russia's princes, he observes, always sought to balance or synthesize two antithetical cultures, one sedentary and molded by the forest, the other nomadic, shaped by the steppe. Now, with Riurik's line extinct and the legitimacy of the monarch Godunov in question, the tension between steppe and forest might explode. Only a spark was lacking. It was struck, as described at the end of this volume, by the mysterious death of Fedor's brother Dmitry at Uglich in 1591. The fire lit by this spark, suspicion of Godunov's complicity in the murder, smoldered until the appearance of a pretender claiming to be Dmitry then flamed into the Time of Troubles.

The present volume begins with the repressions at Fedor's accession and ends with the death at Uglich. Throughout, Soloviev manages to relate to this violence Boris Godunov, the dominant figure in his narrative. This theme, underscoring a propensity to political violence which marred Boris's otherwise admirable personality, lends continuity to the narrative and follows a tradition that Soloviev's predecessors established. It finds its origins in the chroniclers and in Karamzin and Pushkin, both of whom employed magnificent prose to fix Godunov's image as a flawed genius, a brilliant but sinful and guilty tsar-murderer. Such a portrait did not lack critics. Before Soloviev wrote, Konstantin Aksakov and Mikhail Pogodin already had reconsidered the question of Godunov's guilt. Soloviev addresses some of their arguments in an extended historiographical note (Note 131 in Chapter VI of the Russian edition), which constitutes my Appendix.

Caryl Emerson's *Boris Godunov. Transpositions of a Russian Theme* (Bloomington, 1986) rather provocatively discusses the genesis of this image of Boris. She traces it from the chroniclers, who felt moral repugnance for a murderer and enemy of the Romanov dynasty, through Karamzin's Romantic history and down to Pushkin's play and Mussorgsky's opera. The chroniclers' version, richly laden with images of sin and retribution, was hard for such artists to shun, and thus was taken at face value.

Soloviev occupies a transitional place in the evolution of history's appraisal of Godunov. He appreciates Boris's talents and frequently remarks on the chroniclers' hostility towards him. The History rises far more directly from the sources than do the works of Soloviev's predecessors. It is more sober, less of a colorful nationalist and dynastic narrative than Karamzin's earlier work. The extent and depth of Soloviev's discussion of the evidence bearing on the death at Uglich in Chapter VI demonstrates his awareness of how controversial the accepted version incriminating Boris had become.

For all this, Soloviev does retain Godunov and bloodshed as related central themes. The character of his Boris remains tragically flawed, however brilliant. Notwithstanding all Boris's many talents, for Soloviev he proved all too well humanity's frailty in the eternal dialectic tension between Christian ideals and human nature.

Subsequent historians have been kinder to Boris. Most exculpate him of the murder at Uglich. All judge his reign more in terms of his achievements and less in terms of his personal morality. Boris's rehabilitation started with the studies of S.F. Platonov, many of which are available in English. In his 1921 biography *Boris Godunov* (Academic International Press, 1973), translated by Rex Pyles, Platonov concluded that "it is the duty of historical scholarship to restore the true character of Boris Godunov." Over a half century later, in 1978, Ruslan Skrynnikov answered Platonov's call with another revisionist biography, *Boris Godunov* (Academic International Press, 1982). The translator and editor, Hugh Graham, provides a useful introductory essay to this volume in which he reviews the historians' treatment of Boris. Considering Platonov's and Skrynnikov's works in combination with George Vernadsky's *The Tsardom of Moscow, 1547-1682* (New Haven, Conn., 1969), Graham holds that history now views Godunov as one of "Russia's greatest rulers."

Besides Platonov and Skrynnikov there exists a less substantial biography of Godunov by Stephen Graham, *Boris Godunov* (New Haven, Conn., 1933). Some of Vasily Kliuchevsky's comments about Godunov are found in Volume III of C.J. Hogarth's translation of his classic *A History of Russia* (New York, 1960).

The reader interested in foreign policy, the topic which dominates most of this volume, may wish to review the reign of Ivan IV. The events are recounted in Vernadsky's work cited above. Yet it is Ivan's personal character that has been most studied. Not surprisingly, this colorful figure has drawn a parade of biographers: Kazimierz Waliszewski, *Ivan the Terrible* (Philadelphia, 1904, reprinted Hamden, Conn., 1966); Stephen Graham, *Ivan the Terrible* (London, 1933, reprinted Hamden, 1968); Jules Koslow, *Ivan the Terrible* (New York, 1961); Robert Payne, *Ivan the Terrible* (New York, 1975); Henri Troyat, *Ivan the Terrible* (New York, 1984) and Benson Bobrick, *Fearful Majesty* (New York, 1987). Joseph Wieczynski's translation of S.F. Platonov, *Ivan the Terrible* (Academic International Press, 1974), when read in conjunction with Vernadsky, best prepares the reader to understand the background to Fedor's reign. Platonov postulates the rationality of many of Ivan's policies even while conceding that the tsar suffered from some level of paranoia. Readers unwilling to embrace this opinion can find alternative verdicts on Ivan in Platonov's own chapter assessing the work of his predecessors, or they can peruse Richard Hellie's essay introducing Wieczynski's translation, which more strongly stresses Ivan's pathology. Hellie not only weighs Platonov's conclusions but also considers those of his Soviet successors. Finally, there is a sensitive consideration of Ivan's political ideology in terms of sixteenth-century norms and with reference to Platonov's views in Bjarne Norretranders, *The Shaping of Tsardom Under Ivan Groznyj* (Copenhagen, 1964).

Soloviev recounts the ebb and flow of Moscow's complex foreign policy through the traditional narration of diplomatic exchanges. Because this perspective naturally focuses on Muscovy the reader may wish to consult works concerning Moscow's neighbors. An overview of Polish affairs, the major subject of Chapter II, is found in the appropriate parts of Norman Davies, *God's Playground* (New York, 1984) and in the earlier *Cambridge History of Poland* (Cambridge, 1950), edited by W.F. Reddaway and others. Nevertheless, no study in English does justice to sixteenth-century Poland's domestic affairs or to its role in Europe.

The reader of this and other volumes of the History soon notices Soloviev's lengthy quotations from diplomatic exchanges between the Muscovites and their neighbors. Traditional formulas, usages and claims at that time were crucial to diplomatic intercourse and in a sense provided a certain constancy of discourse patterns in a shifting pattern of proposal and reply, threat and conciliation. Some motifs emerge readily. The Muscovites broadcast Godunov's praiseworthy qualities with pride, while others do the same in hope of thereby gaining his favor to their own ends. Christian princes claim to do God's work and exhort other Christians to emulate them. The size of Muscovite "gifts" to Tatar princes reflects their place in the Crimea's aristocratic hierarchy. Such patterns do lend a certain continuity to Soloviev's narrative, but for Soloviev true permanence is found in those deeper forces underlying Muscovy's relationship with the outside world.

A full history of how the struggle between the Reformation and Counter-Reformation affected Russia has yet to be written, still Soloviev does provide some insights. The significance of religious questions in the complex politics of king-making. Both in Sweden and Poland forms one theme of Chapter II. Soloviev observes the extent to which religious fervor caused both Bathory and Sigismund Vasa, Fedor's Polish contemporaries and adversaries, to contribute to the eventual weakening of Poland-Lithuania. Their efforts to control or crush Poland's Protestant and Ortho-dox communities and thereby restore unity of faith served in the long run only to undermine Poland's unity. The West's religious struggle affected Moscow in other ways, less noted by Soloviev. It contributed to Europe's general willingness to bear the price of larger mercenary armies using the new equipment of the gunpowder era. This raised the cost of king-making in Poland, as Soloviev observes, and also meant that sooner or later capital-poor Muscovy faced increased military expenditures. Soloviev shows the role of mercenaries in Poland's election of a king. Their participation in Western military intervention in Muscovy during the Time of Troubles made that experience even more devastating. Finally, religious controversy in Muscovy's western borderlands was bound sooner or later to demand an Orthodox Russian defense against Protestant and Catholic ideas. Defining Orthodoxy's traditionally loose theology and liturgy in turn gave rise to potentially divisive controversy within Russian Orthodoxy. None of this could be clear to Fedor's contemporaries, who on balance may have profited from Western religious divisions, as Soloviev argues, but Muscovy could not remain unscathed by such a profound historical movement. Once again Soloviev's theme is transition. In this instance Fedor's reign lies along a road leading from the peaceful disputation between the Jesuit Possevino and Ivan IV to the occupation of Moscow by the pretender with his Polish mercenaries and priests.

The reader seeking a fuller exposition of this story may start with the introduction and the first two chapters, "The meeting of Rome and Moscow (1472-1533)" and "Echoes of the Reformation and Catholic Reform (1533-1613)," in Donald Treadgold's *The West in Russia and China. Religious and Secular Thought in Modern Times. Volume 1, Russia, 1472-1917* (Cambridge, Mass., 1973). A stimulating interpretation of the multiple consequences of Western religious controversy for Russia and its eventual role in the seventeenth-century crisis of Russian culture is found in chapters two and three of James H. Billington's, *The Icon and the Axe. An Interpretative History of Russian Culture* (New York, 1968). Once again, Platonov provides a fine introduction to the topic in his *Moscow and the West* (Academic International Press, 1972), translated by Joseph Wieczynski, which includes a very useful introductory essay by Serge Zenkovsky. Paul Fox's *The Reformation in Poland* (Westport, Conn., 1971) describes Polish Protestantism; Oscar Halecki's *From Florence to Brest (1439-1596)* (Hamden, Conn., 1968) describes Catholic activity in Muscovy's borderlands from a decidedly Catholic perspective.

A weakened Muscovy managed to secure peaceful relations with its immediate neighbors thanks to their religious problems. Relations with more religiously united and distant Western states, England and the Habsburg empire, form the subject of Chapter III. Russo-English relations revolved around trade under Fedor as they had under Ivan. Here the English-language reader has the advantage of access to Soloviev's sources, the accounts of English merchants, travelers and ambassadors, many of which are found in the extensive *Hakluyt Society Collection.* They can be used in conjunction with T.S. Willan's *The Early History of the Russia Company, 1553-1603* (Manchester, 1956).

Relations with Habsburg Austria, like those with England, followed a pattern established under Ivan. When Henri of Valois was elected Poland's king in 1574, Ivan proposed that Austria and Muscovy join to partition Poland-Lithuania. During the next interregnum in Poland, following Henri's return to rule France, Ivan supported an Austrian candidacy. Soloviev picks up this thread after Stefan Bathory's death in his extended discussion of Muscovite-Habsburg diplomacy aimed at electing to the Polish throne either Fedor or the Austrian Archduke Maximilian. As Soloviev notes, this commonality of interest reflected both immediate and long-range ends. In the short term Austria, by gaining Poland, could reinforce both Habsburg power and that of the Catholic cause for which the dynasty stood. Muscovy might gain all or part of Lithuania and bring Poland under more friendly control. In the long term Austria and, beyond, the papacy hoped to achieve that grand alliance sought for decades for uniting the Habsburg possessions, Venice, Poland-Lithuania, Muscovy and, by Fedor's time, Persia and the small Christian states of the Caucasus. The target of that alliance was, of course, the Ottoman empire and its vassal state, the Crimea.

When Austrians looked south they saw the Balkans, the mountains where they hoped to reverse the Ottoman thrust into Europe. For Muscovy, this thrust came from the steppe. To Soloviev, the steppe represented one of the two dialectically opposed Russias, the northern forest Russia and the southern steppe Russia. He saw both areas as subject to incessant external threats. Like all Russian historians he appreciated the dangers that Muscovy faced from steppe nomads, Crimeans and cossacks a danger enhanced during this time by the very great power of the Ottoman empire. Most of Chapter IV is devoted to relations with Tatars and Turks. The threat from Poland-Lithuania, in the forest zone, held a cultural component, the western borderlands of mixed Roman Catholic, Eastern Catholic,

Orthodox and even small Protestant populations. The menace from the steppe was more clearly military. It ranged from almost annual slave raids and banditry to infrequent but potentially devastating Crimean invasions that reached the very gates of Moscow, such as the one described here. Events followed diplomatic and military patterns rooted in the past: the giving of "gifts," interference in the Crimean Horde's complicated domestic disputes, mobilization of cavalry sent to watch for Crimean raiders on "river banks watch" and construction of a network of forts connected by regular patrols. Cossacks played an ambiguous role in this drama, sometimes treacherous and dangerous, sometimes reliable and useful, and always complicating relations with Crimea, Poland-Lithuania, and Austria.

A brief treatment of both Tatars and cossacks considered within in the wider context of the entire steppe as an ecological zone appears in William H. McNeill's *Europe's Steppe Frontier, 1500-1800* (Chicago, 1964). In addition, there are Philip Longworth, *The Cossacks* (New York, 1969) and the fourth chapter of *Eastward to Empire. Exploration and Conquest on the Russian Open Frontier, to 1750* by George Lantzeff and Richard Pierce (Montreal, 1973). The literature is less satisfactory as regards the Crimea, although Alan Fisher's *The Crimean Tatars* (Palo Alto, Cal., 1978) does offer a brief history of the khanate and a sketch of its institutions. Soloviev also sketches in Chapter IV Muscovy's first tentative relations with Georgia, for the history of which two standard English works are W.E.D. Allen, *A History of the Georgian People* (New York, 1971) and Ronald Suny, *The Making of the Georgian Nation*, (Palo Alto, Cal., 1988). Siberia, which Soloviev also discusses briefly in Chapter IV, can be studied in three monographs, Benson Bobrick's *East of the Sun* (New York, 1992), W. Bruce Lincoln's *The Conquest of a Continent* (New York, 1993), and a collection of essays edited by Yuri Slezkine and Galya Diments, *Between Heaven and Hell* (New York, 1993). All three treat the entire expanse of Siberian history but provide information for a reader interested only in the earliest period, discussed in this volume.

Soloviev's fourth chapter in the original Russian, my Chapter V, defies easy characterization. It gathers disparate topics in domestic history not addressed elsewhere. These include state finances, the code of precedence, organization of the army including more information on the cossacks, trade and commerce, the rise of serfdom, peasant customs, the status of the church and the establishment of the patriarchate. Of these, I shall concentrate here on the establishment of serfdom, which Soloviev considered most crucial, and concerning which some English works exist.

Among these, Richard Hellie's *Enserfment and Military Change in Muscovy* (Chicago, 1971) stands out on two grounds. It offers an excellent introduction to the historiography of the question of serfdom in Russia, and therefore provides a context within which to place Soloviev's views. Hellie's own argument echoes some aspects of Soloviev's interpretation, dividing the historians of serfdom into those who believed that the institution was imposed by decree and those who argued that it arose organically from various aspects of peasant life, most notably the debt caused by crop failure. Soloviev clearly belongs to the first school. He is certain that serfdom was imposed by a decree during Fedor's reign although in Chapter V he must concede that he cannot cite the decree and can rely solely on circumstantial arguments for its existence. Like Soloviev, Hellie considers Fedor's reign an important stage on the path towards enserfment, and shares with Soloviev an emphasis on the Muscovite government's need to maintain the military service class and on Godunov's desire to use this class as a political weapon against the landed aristocracy. Hellie even refers to one of Godunov's decrees as "a demagogic move to win the support of the servicemen in his drive for the throne."[3] Even more than Soloviev, Hellie argues that Fedor's reign was characterized by peasant unrest and flight to the borderlands in reaction to the imposition of serfdom, a vital theme we shall return to below. Besides Hellie's work the reader may consult Jerome Blum, *Lord and Peasant in Russia from the Ninth to the Nineteenth Century* (New York, 1964) and R.E.F. Smith *The Enserfment of the Russian Peasantry* (Cambridge, 1968). The latter, a collection of decrees, contains one from Fedor's reign used by Soloviev.

Soloviev's fifth chapter, here translated as Chapter VI, serves two seemingly distinct but ultimately connected purposes. Its first section analyzes the role of the house of Riurik in Russian history. Soloviev takes this occasion to summarize the meaning of his History up to the end of the sixteenth century and to expound his historical interpretation. The mission of the house of Riurik, he argues, shifted when the ecological setting of its major activity, the creation of the Russian state, moved from the south to the north, from the steppe to the forest. This argument naturally hearkens back to a theme suggested earlier, in Chapter IV, the dialectical tension between the steppe and the forest, between the nomad and the settled cultivator, between Riurik's heirs in the South as representatives of a great and ever mobile clan and in the North as sedentary property owners, the "gatherers of the Russian land." This is history on the grand scale, what one might call macro-history, with a pronounced Darwinian tone and with passages which presage the geographical emphases, bordering on determinism, of twentieth-century French *Annalistes* like Fernand Braudel. Chapter VI then abruptly turns to micro-history, concluding with an analysis of the evidence surrounding Dmitry's death at Uglich. For all the suddenness of the shift, the connection between the two parts of the chapter is clear. The first lays bare a root cause of the Time of Troubles; the second exposes its immediate antecedents.

Concerning the history of Russia's frontiers the reader can consult the book by Lantzeff already cited. Soloviev's emphasis on the importance of ecological determinants along the steppe frontier also permeates McNeill's work, cited above. In *The Russian Frontier. The Impact of the Borderlands upon the Course of Early Russian History* (Charlottesville, Va., 1976), Joseph Wieczynski offers a broad overview of the role of the Southern frontier in Russian history, comparing and contrasting it with the American frontier experience as described in the famous Turner thesis. Wieczynski's assertion that "the triumph of the Russian state over the spirit of the Russian frontier was, as we shall see, one of the most significant victories won by the princes and Tsars of Moscow" echoes Soloviev's last sentence in the first part of Chapter VI, "The state waxed strong; the vagabond cossack would not overcome the landed man."

The most intriguing of the theses concerning the frontier is found in S.F. Platonov's *The Time of Troubles* (Lawrence, Kan., 1970), translated by John T. Alexander. Like all Russian historians Platonov (1860-1933) deeply felt Soloviev's influence. *The Time of Troubles* brings together some broad themes from the present volume of Soloviev's History. According to Platonov, Ivan's reign precipitated a profound social crisis. The state's incessant hunger for land to support military servitors compelled it towards two policies. On one hand, as observed by Soloviev, it imposed serfdom; on the other, as Platonov stressed, it exploited the conquered lands on the southern and eastern frontier as sources of military service estates. Platonov characterizes Fedor's reign as a period of internal unrest and migration, if not outright rebellion, a description which, as we saw above, Hellie later reinforced. So, during Fedor's supposedly tranquil reign the peasantry of the central provinces actually fled bondage. Naturally they migrated to the yet relatively uncontrolled borderlands only to have the crown with its attendant promise of serfdom follow and overtake them. The draining of rural population from the center brought decline to many old urban centers, further diminishing the state's income. When revenue dried up, the expansive new lands on the frontier seemed an ever more attractive alternative to money as a means of maintaining and rewarding servitors. Consequently the state turned its attention towards the new lands of the south and east, thereby alarming those peasants who had fled to them. It is interesting in light of this thesis to read in Chapter V Soloviev's rather contorted attempt to minimize or negate the English visitor Giles Fletcher's portrayal of declining revenues from trade under Fedor. Godunov's policies of upholding the rights of military tenure estate holders and expanding steadily into the steppe and bolstering there the network of frontier fortifications only served to bring a greater sense of potential security and to lure peasants to the borderlands, thereby exacerbating the process. Disaffected, apprehensive and embittered migrants, ever wary of enserfment, filled the borderlands.

Soloviev speaks in Chapter VI of the "anachronistic representative of another epoch" who "found the new society uncongenial" and "fled to the open steppe and there awaited his chance to struggle against that new order which he judged to be so hostile." Platonov's genius lays in arguing that this population was but recently arrived and, more important, received its impetus to push outward from the center from the very policy the central administration depended upon to defend the frontier. It was this population, he argues, that exploded in rebellion and provided support for the various popular risings of the Time of Troubles. Such a splendid example of the dialectical process.

Soloviev's primary sources may be divided into five headings: (1) documents gathered from published collections, (2) unpublished archival material, (3) chronicles, (4) foreigners' accounts and (5) narrative histories written by contemporaries, or "tales."

During the decade before Soloviev's birth Minister of Foreign Affairs Nikolay Rumiantsev initiated a process leading to the creation of a Russian archaeographical commission attached to the Academy of Sciences. This body, led by the indefatigable P. M. Stroev, ultimately published several rich collections of documents used by Soloviev: *Acts Collected in Libraries and Archives of the Russian Empire by the Archaeographic Expedition of the Academy of Sciences; Juridical Acts; Historical Acts, and Supplement to Historical Acts.* Rumiantsev himself earlier published the *Collection of State Charters and Treaties Held by the State College of Foreign*

Affairs, which Soloviev also consulted. In addition, Soloviev employed published sources emanating from the Russian Historical Society and the Moscow Historical Society, as well as documents from *Russian Library*, a collection published by the late eighteenth century dissident Nicholas Novikov. Soloviev drew his unpublished sources for diplomatic history largely from the foreign affairs repository of the Central State Archive of Ancient Acts.

One chronicle used regularly by Soloviev, the Chronicle of Many Rebellions, has been discussed by G. Edward Orchard elsewhere in this series (see below, Chapter I, Note 26). Chapter I also sees Soloviev use the first part of the Morozov chronicle written in either the late seventeenth or the early eighteenth century, which described events starting with Ivan IV and ending with the Time of Troubles. This chronicle included parts of an another work, *The Tale of the Reign of Tsar and Grand Prince Fedor Ivanovich*.

Books of degrees were sixteenth-century outgrowths of the chronicles, a sort of intermediate step in the evolution of historical works. They combined information from Russian chronicles, chronicles of world history and other sources, ordering them in such a fashion as to serve as a guide to the larger corpus of chronicles. Chronographs, also sometimes cited by Soloviev, served a similar purpose. The term "degrees" refers to their common arrangement, passing down the line of heredity from Vladimir, founder of the Russian state, to Ivan IV. The *Latukhinsk Book of Degrees*, compiled late in the seventeenth century by the monk Tikhon, served Soloviev as a source for uniquely valuable information concerning Boris Godunov. Platonov argued that the original author, clearly no partisan of Godunov, nevertheless must have had access either to documents or to tales about him which had since been lost. Soloviev also relied heavily on Siberian chronicles. He cites a title and date of publication which indicate that he used the Stroganov chronicle as opposed to others available to him. This chronicle, composed at the behest of the wealthy and powerful Stroganov family, glorifies them and their hireling Yermak. Soloviev further cites works by the historian Müller which contained material from other chronicles to lend some balance to his account.

English accounts are by far the most cited among the various foreign sources employed by Soloviev. Not only does he cite them extensively when describing diplomatic relations with England, he also he relies on Horsey, Fletcher and Bowes when narrating Godunov's rise to power (Chapter I) and analyzing the structure of Muscovy's civil and military administrations (Chapter V). Soloviev uses as well accounts by the Swedish Peer Peerson de Erlesunda (Petreius), the Prussian Reinhold Heidenstein, the Austrian Nicholas Warkotsch and the French Jacques Margeret, but their role is minor compared to that of the English. The issue sometimes must be raised of the reliability of such sources. I have commented on it in my endnotes.

Most important among the "tales" cited by Soloviev is that by Avraamy Palitsyn, which he uses as a source of evidence concerning Godunov's responsibility for the death of Dmitry at Uglich (Chapter VI). Palitsyn (1555-1627), from a family of crown servitors, fell into disgrace and took monastic vows in 1588, possibly for playing some role in the efforts of Boris Godunov's enemies, the Shuisky family, to have Fedor divorce Boris's sister Irina (see Chapter I). He later participated in negotiations with the Poles during the Time of Troubles. Thereafter, around 1620, he produced his Tale, the first part of which, a history of events from the time of Ivan IV to the coronation of Boris Godunov, Soloviev used for this volume. It bears mention that Soloviev used the second recision of Palitysn's Tale, which was far more severe than the first in its condemnation of Godunov, underlining his role in Dmitry's death, emphasizing his violence towards the Nagoy family, and blaming him for the subsequent fire in Moscow.

Soloviev infrequently referred to secondary sources, that is, to the works of his predecessors. In the discussion of the death at Uglich he comments critically on the studies written by Pogodin and Aksakov. Elsewhere, Soloviev occasionally cites Karamzin's History, which was the most extensive general history of Russia written previously, although its value for the historian resided more in its extensive footnotes than in its elegantly written prose. Some Polish works are cited in Chapter II when describing events there. On the whole, however, Soloviev depended upon primary sources when writing his History, to which we shall now turn.

HISTORY OF RUSSIA

Volume 13

The Reign of Tsar Fedor

I

THE RISE OF BORIS GODUNOV

THE RULING FAMILY AND ITS FUTURE

Strictly speaking, Ivan the Terrible was the last of the house of Riurik to rule in Moscow. Gathering the Russian lands, elimination of ancient ties of kinship among the princes and of the status of the princes' retinues, rooted in those bonds, could not be managed without violent and bloody scenes.[1] Such events grew ever more savage, ultimately attained terrifying dimensions, and bore their fruit. The collateral lines of descendants of Vasily the Dark[2] came to a sudden end. Their princes met a violent death or wasted away in dungeons, leaving no heirs. Finally Ivan the Terrible,[3] driven by his frightful habit of lashing out in anger, fatally struck his eldest son[4] and thus, as they say, tore the grandchild from its maternal womb.[5] His despair at murdering the youth must have mounted as he pondered the circumstances in which he had left his posterity. Fedor, the younger son, was incapable of ruling. Ivan had another son, Dmitry,[6] by his fifth wife,[7] but this one was in swaddling clothes when his father died.

Ivan's death thus found the realm in a situation analogous to that which prevailed at the death of his father.[8] Although Ivan's son Fedor mounted the throne as an adult, he remained childlike in his abilities. This necessitated a guardianship, a regency, and opened the field for contestants. Since Fedor's minority was permanent, and since he would die without a natural heir, the struggle among the boyars assumed new meaning during his reign. The struggle summoned the participation not only of the most powerful boyar clans, but even of future dynasties. Two of them perished in the struggle, in the storms of the Time of Troubles.[9] A third secured a foothold on the throne as a member of the house of Riurik.[10]

The Mstislavskys were the most prestigious among princes of the house of Gediminas.[11] Prince Ivan Fedorovich Mstislavsky[12] ranked first among the boyars, yet members of this family never displayed remarkable talents or energy. The Golitsyns, a cadet line of the famous Patrikeev family,[13] were far more outstanding in this regard. Their representative, Prince Vasily Vasilievich, sought the throne during the Time of Troubles.[14]

Riurik's princely offspring were numerous, both the southern branch from the clan of Sviatoslav of Chernigov[15] and the northern from that of Vsevolod III of Suzdal,[16] but these princes lost their importance during the conflict with Alexander Nevsky's junior line,[17] the rulers of Moscow. Common kinship and descent from a single ancestor were overlooked when these princes called themselves slaves of the Muscovite sovereigns. The princes keenly recalled their old prominence, but the people had forgotten it. We have seen how tenuously these princes were connected with the lands which their forefathers once ruled, and how Ivan the Terrible used confiscation by the treasury and exchange of patrimonial estates in an effort to sever this link completely.[18] Among the people even the title "prince" no longer evoked an image of descent from Russia's first rulers, for alongside princes of the house of Riurik now stood Lithuanians from the house of Gediminas and newcomers from the Horde and from the Caucasus, bearing the same title.

As before, familial traditions, dynamism and outstanding achievements placed the Shuisky first among princes of the house of Riurik. The disfavor which befell this family during Ivan's majority could not crush it. Prince Peter Shuisky played an eminent role as a military commander. Although he fell ingloriously at the second battle of Orsha,[19] his son Prince Ivan Petrovich[20] more than restored the family's merit through his illustrious role in the defense of Pskov. The public is notorious for cherishing a lone success among many failures and for holding dear him whose heroic exploits uphold the national honor just when others betray it. It is therefore not surprising to find that Prince Ivan Petrovich Shuisky enjoyed special favor among Moscow's townsmen, merchants and commoners.

Alongside the princely families springing from the house of Riurik and Gediminas stood the Romanov-Yurievs and the Godunovs, who had drawn near the throne through kinship with the tsars. Of course, neither the heirs of appanage lines symbolizing obsolete antiquity nor Lithuanian newcomers could make such an historical claim to succeed the gatherers of the land, the Muscovite sovereigns, as could these two families, representatives of that ancient and true Muscovite boyar elite which so zealously served the gatherers of the land in their task. No family of devoted boyars so steadily held such high rank, so constantly participated in Moscow's mission of creating the realm, as did the Romanov-Yurievs.[21]

The Godunov name enjoyed less prominence. Boris Fedorovich Godunov[22] first entered Tsar Ivan's inner circle by marrying the daughter of the tsar's favorite and infamous crown servitor Maliuta Skuratov-Belsky,[23] and became closer to the ruling family when his sister Irina[24] wedded Tsarevich Fedor. Boris's own merits enabled him to preserve and strengthen the influence he gained through these marital bonds.

All sources concur that the dying Ivan entrusted his sons Fedor and Dmitry to several of his closest advisers, but they differ sharply over the name and number of these magnates. Some cite only the two senior members of the boyar council, Princes Ivan Fedorovich Mstislavsky and Nikita Romanovich Yuriev,[25] whereas others name the latter and Prince Ivan Shuisky. According to some accounts Ivan commended Fedor to Shuisky, Mstislavsky and Nikita Romanovich, but others vaguely refer to four chief advisers. Finally still others specify five names, adding Bogdan Belsky and Boris Godunov to the three above. At first the tsar's uncle Nikita Romanovich[26] held the greatest influence among these dignitaries, but he was reported gravely ill by August 1584.[27]

DISTURBANCES AT FEDOR'S ACCESSION

Fedor did not assume the throne unchallenged. Just as when Grand Prince Vasily died, sedition started around an appanage prince,[28] so now the opposition rallied around Fedor's younger brother Dmitry, although this appanage prince was still only a child. The plot must have originated during Ivan's life because on the very night of his death, March 18, dignitaries supporting Fedor accused of treason Fedor's maternal family, the Nagoy, ordered them arrested, and placed them under guard.[29] Numerous other favorites of the dead tsar were seized and exiled to scattered towns. Some were cast into dungeons and others held under arrest. Their homes were destroyed and their patrimonial estates and service lands given away. The court dignitaries and the townsmen grew restless. To preserve the peace patrols scoured the streets, and cannon stood in the squares. Then Dmitry, his mother, her father and her relatives the Nagoy family were sent off to the family appanage estate at Uglich.[30]

Foreigners write that the chief instigator of the plot around Dmitry was Bogdan Belsky,[31] a man famed for his intellect, skilled in all affairs, restless, ambitious, and inclined to sedition. After Dmitry left for Uglich Belsky remained in Moscow and continued the conspiracy, which led boyars hostile to him, along with the populace, to besiege the Kremlin with artillery and compel his surrender. The Russian chroniclers also speak of a popular uprising in Moscow against Belsky. In their version a rumor flourished that Belsky and his confederates murdered Tsar Ivan and now sought to crush the boyars and kill Tsar Fedor, after which Belsky would rule Muscovy. The excited commoners aroused the soldiers, many of whom came to the city bearing arms. The Kremlin gates could only just be shut against them. Men from Riazan, the Liapunovs[32] and the Kikins, as well as other junior boyars from the provinces joined the mob.[33] They trained a cannon on the Frolov (Savior) gates, meaning to blast them open. Then Tsar Fedor sent to the crowd the boyars Princes Ivan Mstislavsky and Nikita Romanovich Yuriev, and the crown secretaries the Shchelkalov brothers,[34] with orders to persuade them gently that those hoping to spill Christian blood had aroused them needlessly, and to learn why and after whom they had come to town. This question evoked the resounding cry "Give us Bogdan Belsky! He wants to uproot the ruling stem and the boyar families." The tsar then had it proclaimed that he had exiled Bogdan Belsky to Nizhny Novgorod and the crowd, hearing the tsar's words and seeing all the boyars, dispersed to their homes.[35] According to other information, widespread popular rumors held that Belsky intended the Muscovite tsardom for his associate Boris Godunov, and that the Shuisky princes inspired the Liapunovs and Kikins of Riazan to instigate the troubles.

Lastly, one source attributes the unrest to the following circumstance. The boyars had formed two factions with Princes Mstislavsky, Shuisky, Golitsyn, Romanov, Sheremetev, and Golovin belonging to one, and the Godunovs, Trubetskoys, and Shchelkalov (?)[36] to the other. Bogdan Belsky wished to be ranked above[37] the treasurer Peter Golovin. Prince Mstislavsky supported Golovin, while Godunov stood firmly behind Belsky. The first group set out to kill Belsky, who barely managed to flee to the tsaritsa. Just then a junior boyar galloped from the Kremlin to the marketplace shouting that the boyars were beating the Godunovs to death. The people rioted and headed for the Kremlin. The sight of its barred gates fired their passions and they dragged cannon toward them. The boyars resolved their differences, rode out and talked the crowd into leaving. Several accounts state that twenty men died and about a hundred suffered injuries in this affair.[38]

Whatever the case, Fedor's supporters certainly feared the hostile designs of Dmitry's partisans. Likewise, Bogdan Belsky's ambitious urges surely aroused against him the intense hatred of a numerous and potent faction within the boyar council, to which he had to succumb because of a popular uprising, either spontaneous or generated by his enemies.

The chronicler[39] states that Boris Godunov, avenging the attack upon Bogdan Belsky, arrested and exiled to scattered towns and dungeons the Liapunovs, Kikins, and other junior boyars, as well as many townsmen, but we know how the chroniclers relished ascribing all sorts of vile deeds to Godunov. They also accused him of the arrest of the Nagoy immediately after Tsar Ivan's death. We know too that at that time he scarcely wielded the power he later commanded.

In the words of the chronicler, eminent men came to Moscow from all the towns and tearfully besought Tsarevich Fedor to take the crown of Muscovy and become tsar. This is a most curious report. Why were these distinguished delegates from the towns in Moscow? Did such prominent representatives customarily visit the capital to congratulate a new tsar, and why did they now, alarmed by the tumult, implore that Fedor hasten to take the throne?[40] Either the situation was quite turbulent and dangerous, or a question actually arose as to whether the mature but feeble-minded Fedor or the minor Dmitry should reign. Did Dmitry have so many adherents that the boyar council felt compelled to summon notables from the towns? The Englishman Horsey,[41] then in Moscow, does speak of an assembly on May 4, attended by the metropolitan, the archbishops, bishops, abbots, and the entire service nobility.[42]

FEDOR'S CORONATION

Fedor was crowned with the customary ritual on May 31, 1584. Metropolitan Dionisy read the sermon.[43] He admonished the tsar to stand fast by the holy churches and the righteous monasteries, to obey him, the metropolitan, and all his devout clergy, for honor rendered to an ecclesiastical leader rises to Christ himself, to love and honor his brother,[44] to favor and cherish the boyars and the court dignitaries in accordance with their lineage, while being accessible, gracious, and affable toward all greater and lesser princes, the junior boyars, and all military men, to protect, favor and care for all Orthodox Christians with his whole heart, to stand manfully and majestically for those offended, to do no harm through the courts and the law, to spurn flattery and empty rumor, to disregard slander and distrust the wicked, to love wisdom and heed the wise because God dwells in them as on a throne, to distribute honors without recompense, for he who purchases power gives bribes, and so forth.

In April 1586 the boyar Nikita Romanovich died.[45] In his place, the chronicle states, the tsaritsa's brother Boris Godunov became ruler. As

TSAR FEDOR IVANOVICH, 1584–1598

Basil Dmytryshyn, *Medieval Russia. A Source Book, 850–1700.*

shown earlier, even while Nikita Romanovich lived Boris fully exploited Nikita's illness, never missing a chance to strengthen steadily his influence over the tsar through his sister. Contemporary witnesses[46] observed that Irina knew well how to exert her own influence and to transmit that of her brother, yet Godunov naturally could not rest secure in his place as regent without contending with those who felt more entitled to the post.

BORIS DEFEATS THE SHUISKYS

Discord reigned among the boyars, say the chroniclers. They broke into two factions. One included Boris Godunov with his brothers and uncles, joined by some princes, boyars, crown secretaries, clergy and many servicemen. The other consisted of Prince Ivan Fedorovich Mstislavsky, the Shuiskys, Vorotynskys, Golovins, Kolychevs, other servicemen and Moscow's populace. Reportedly Godunov first attracted Prince Mstislavsky to his side. The prince even called Boris his son. Then the Shuiskys, Vorotynskys, Golitsyns, other boyars, the servicemen and Moscow's common people set out to convince Mstislavsky to join them in eliminating Boris. Having demurred for some time, Mstislavsky endorsed their scheme to assassinate Godunov during a banquet at Mstislavsky's home. The story is credible. We know how the Shuiskys behaved during Ivan's minority.[47] His subsequent terrible reign certainly offered them no occasion to lose the habit of violent and bloody deeds. The hereditary characteristic of the Mstislavskys, namely inherent lack of character, also rings true. At first Prince Ivan balked, then agreed to the murder of one whom he once had called son.

Whatever the case, the sources concur that this time the struggle with Godunov was waged in name of the ranking boyar Prince Mstislavsky, and that Godunov allied with the crown secretaries the Shchelkalovs, invoked their patronage and overpowered his foes.[48] Prince Ivan Mstislavsky was seized and tonsured in the St. Cyril monastery.[49] The Vorotynskys, Golovins and numerous others were banished to various towns, some being cast into dungeons. Mikhail Golovin, hearing of the fate of his relatives, fled from his estate at Medyn to the Lithuanian king Stefan Bathory.[50]

Nevertheless the Shuiskys, artfully acting through others, remained untouched. Godunov and his advisers were enraged with them. For their part they opposed him and yielded nothing. All the leading merchants[51] and Moscow's common traders rallied round the Shuiskys, and supposedly wanted to stone Godunov, thus driving him to seek peace with the Shuiskys. Metropolitan Dionisy sought to mediate. Summoning both

Godunov and the Shuiskys before him, he implored them to make peace, but while the boyars were at the metropolitan's palace a crowd of tradesmen gathered before the Palace of Facets.[52] Prince Ivan Shuisky, leaving the metropolitan, approached the merchants to inform them that the Shuiskys had settled their differences with Godunov. Two merchants stepped out of the crowd and told him "You bought peace at the cost of our heads. Forsake Boris, or we too shall perish." That very night these merchants were arrested and exiled to an unknown place.

Such aggressive participation of Moscow's tradesmen in the Shuiskys' struggle with Godunov is interesting. It must reflect the consequences of the policy of Ivan the Terrible who, hostile toward the boyars, raised the status of Moscow's urban residents, inviting them to the council,[53] and laying before them his complaint against the boyars upon his departure for Alexandrov village.[54]

Of course Godunov's reprisals against the merchants rendered unworkable his agreement with the Shuiskys, who devised a most opportune method for eradicating the source of Godunov's power. They would induce Fedor to imitate his grandfather, divorce the childless Irina and remarry. Prince Ivan Petrovich Shuisky and other boyars, Moscow's wealthy merchants and all the traders sanctioned and confirmed a petition to the tsar about the divorce. The metropolitan, whose voice carried the greatest weight in this matter, also consented to cooperate with them.

Godunov had learned of his enemies' plan and tried to dissuade Dionisy from initiating proceedings. Incidentally, Godunov is said to have suggested to the metropolitan that it would be preferable that Fedor remain childless lest a civil war erupt between such children and their uncle Dmitry of Uglich. Having deflected this misfortune, naturally Godunov could not leave the Shuiskys at leisure to concoct yet another scheme against him, neither could the Shuiskys remain quiet for long.

The chroniclers record that Boris did not soften his heart against the Shuiskys. He persuaded their servants, Fedor Stary and his companions, to accuse their masters of treason. This led to the arrest of the Shuiskys in 1587. Prince Ivan was apprehended on the road to his hereditary estate at Suzdal. Along with the Shuiskys, their friends Princes Tatev, Urusov, Kolychev and Baksakov also were taken. Their servants suffered various tortures and blood flowed freely. Fedor Nagay and his friends, Moscow leading merchants, also endured severe torture but confessed to nothing. When the investigation ended Prince Ivan Shuisky was banished under guard to his patrimony, the village of Lopatnichi. From Lopatnichi he was sent to Beloozero and strangled. Prince Andrei Ivanovich Shuisky[55] was exiled to Voskresensk village and thence to Kargopol for strangling. They sent Prince Ivan Tatev[56] to Astrakhan and Kriuk-Kolychev to the stone jail in Nizhny Novgorod. The Baksakovs and other nobles were scattered about in exile, while the Moscow leading merchant Fedor Nagay and his six companions were beheaded at the stake in Moscow. Other tradesmen received sentences of life imprisonment or exile to various towns.

Are the chronicles fully credible concerning the fate of the two Shuisky princes, Ivan and Andrei? Were they in fact strangled, and on Godunov's order, or was this just a rumor? The case of the Romanovs should make us cautious.[57]

It is interesting how the government, that is Godunov and his faction, tried to represent this affair to foreign powers. Ambassadors sent to Lithuania were instructed "If you are asked why the sovereign laid his disgrace upon the Shuiskys[58] or why he executed townsmen, answer that the sovereign bestowed a substantial grant upon Prince Ivan for his services and gave him as maintenance the revenue from Pskov with its bytowns, including tolls and sureties. The sovereign never before endowed a single boyar with such a maintenance. Ivan's brother Prince Andrei and his other brothers behaved faithlessly and treasonably before the tsar, and plotted many evils with trading peasants. Prince Ivan indulged them, stood by them, and bore false witness before the sovereign. Little wonder, then, that the crown favors the good and executes the wicked. Our sovereign is gracious. When he succeeded to his father's lands he showed his great mercy and generosity to all men, but the trading peasants, relying upon the tsar's clemency, set out to steal, meddled in others' affairs and joined idlers. The sovereign investigated this and put to death those five or six peasant thieves who committed such idle deeds. He banished Prince Andrei to the countryside for having associated with such idlers, but placed no disgrace upon him. Prince Andrei's brothers Princes Vasily, Dmitry, Alexander and Ivan are in Moscow, and Prince Vasily Fedorovich Skopin-Shuisky,[59] he who was living on a grant at Kargopol is now, we believe, also in Moscow. The boyar Prince Ivan Petrovich departed voluntarily for his new patrimony at Kineshma, an estate given to him by the tsar. He owned a large town on the Volga, with which the sovereign rewarded him for his heroism during the siege of Pskov. All the townsmen and peasants live as before.

"Should you be asked why the Kremlin was readied for siege and posted with a strong guard, deny this and assert that some scoundrel said it. A state of siege prepared against peasants? Besides, the watch on the gates and within the city was also no novelty, merely an old routine. The guards, supervised by junior boyars who live at the gates, are there for the protection of all."[60]

BORIS CONQUERS THE CHURCH

Blood flowed in the torture chambers and poured out on the block. Blood spilled in civil strife among the boyars. Metropolitan Dionisy recalled his duty to care for the sorrows of others. Seeing such murder and shedding of innocent blood, he and Archbishop Varlaam of Krutitsa[61] apprised the tsar of Godunov's many lies, yet what affect could the speeches of prelates have on a child still tied to his nurse? Godunov, reports the chronicler, slandered the hierarchs to the tsar. Dionisy and Varlaam were overthrown and cloistered at monasteries in Novgorod. Archbishop Job of Rostov, a man utterly devoted to Godunov, became metropolitan.[62]

Metropolitan Dionisy is said to have been an aspiring, intelligent and eloquent man who collaborated with the Shuiskys against Godunov out of frustrated ambition and because he perceived that Boris had hampered his influence over the devout tsar.[63] Dionisy may have been learned and an orator—many chronographs call him "the wise grammarian"—but not a shred of contemporary testimony maintains that he competed with Godunov out of ambition. He first acted as an intermediary between Godunov and Shuisky. Then, when immediately following the reconciliation Godunov rekindled the animosity by banishing Shuisky's followers to unknown places, the metropolitan supported Shuisky. Even then Dionisy let Boris dissuade him from pursuing the question of Fedor's divorce, for this matter must have been deeply troubling for the churchman's conscience. He could not help but remember how much censure was heaped upon Metropolitan Daniel for his part in the divorce of Grand Prince Vasily.[64] Finally when, as the chronicle asserts, Boris spilled much innocent blood in his pursuit of the Shuiskys, Dionisy openly exposed his lies before the tsar and suffered for doing so. The human soul is murky. Dionisy might have acted from various impulses, but it is impermissible for an historian to impute immoral motives to a historical figure in the absence of any evidence.

Godunov was now free of rivals. After the fall of the Shuiskys and the removal of Dionisy and Varlaam none dared challenge the omnipotent ruler, who was recognized as such both at home and abroad. Godunov assumed the titles of master of the horse[65] and grand privy boyar, lord lieutenant of the tsardoms of Kazan and Astrakhan. Foreign governments were made to understand that obtaining concessions from Muscovy required the good offices of the tsar's brother-in-law, whose requests the tsar never failed to fulfill. Godunov corresponded and exchanged gifts with the Holy Roman emperor, the queen of England, the khan of the Crimea and the grand vizier of Turkey. He received ambassadors. Foreigners present in Moscow relate that Boris was the nominal ruler of the land with the actual power of a tsar. His annual income, including salary, exceeded 93,700 rubles. He gleaned revenue from the Vaga region, from Riazan and the lands of Severia, from Tver and Torzhok, from Moscow's steam baths and bath houses, and from apiaries and meadows along both banks of the Moscow river for thirty versts upstream and twenty downstream. Godunov and his family were said to be capable of mustering a hundred thousand armed men from their estates within forty days.[66]

We have observed how Boris gained the status of a ruler and the means he employed to dispose of all his enemies. Now we should turn to his administrative activity, first glancing at the personal features of both tsar and the ruler as their contemporaries portrayed them.

Fedor was short, stocky and swollen. His nose was aquiline and his gait staggering. He was heavy and lethargic, but always smiling; simple and dull witted, but very affectionate, calm, gracious and extraordinarily pious. He customarily arose around four in the morning. While he washed and dressed his confessor brought a cross for him to kiss. Then the tsar's chaplain carried into the apartment the holy icon venerated on that day, before which Fedor prayed for about a quarter of an hour. The chaplain again entered with holy water and sprinkled the icon and the tsar with it. The tsar then sent to inquire whether the tsaritsa had slept well, and shortly thereafter he went to greet her in the middle of a room between their chambers. Thence they went together to church for matins, which lasted about an hour. Returning from the church, the tsar sat in the great hall where those boyars enjoying his special favor came to salute him. About nine he attended mass, which lasted two hours. Having relaxed after the service, he dined. He slept after eating, usually for three hours, sometimes only for two if he went to bathe or watch a boxing match. After resting he attended vespers and returned to pass time with the tsaritsa until supper. There jesters and dwarfs of both sexes entertained him with somersaults and songs. This was his favorite entertainment, his other diversion being bear baiting. Every week he made a pilgrimage to some nearby monastery. Should someone request something of him as he emerged, he set aside worldly matters and tiresome questions and referred the supplicant to the great boyar Godunov.[67]

Contemporaries say that this great boyar blossomed with splendor and surpassed all men in appearance and wisdom. A marvelous and eloquent man, he established numerous exceedingly praiseworthy things in the Russian realm. He hated bribery and tried to eradicate brigandage, thievery and drunkenness, but he failed. He was enlightened, benevolent and compassionate to the poor, but he lacked military talent. He flowered like a date palm with the foliage of virtue, and had not the blackthorn of envious spite darkened his flower he might have been likened to the tsars of old.[68] Rage led him to give credence to slanderous accusations against the blameless, and thus brought down on himself the indignation of the leading figures of the whole Russian land. Hence the many disastrous evils that welled up against him and suddenly snipped off the vibrantly flowering blossoms of his reign.

II

POLISH AND SWEDISH AFFAIRS

POLAND AT THE BEGINNING OF FEDOR'S REIGN

Just when Riurik's last descendant took the crown in Moscow and before his eyes struggled two families, Godunovs and Shuiskys, both destined to sit on the throne briefly before floundering in the tempests of the Time of Troubles,[1] Europe prepared to resolve the great religious controversy that rose in the sixteenth century. The Southern peninsulas, Appenine and Pyrenean, remained faithful to Catholicism. In the North, on the contrary, in England, Scotland, the Netherlands, Denmark and North Germany, Protestantism prevailed. In Sweden too, despite King John's vacillation,[2] Protestant victory seemed certain. In Central Europe the struggle continued. The ruling Valois line ended amidst bloody upheavals in France but Henri of Bourbon, having entered the struggle under the Protestant banner, soon had to recognize the need to defer to the Catholic majority. Germany anticipated the Thirty Years War, which would leave upon it the stamp of religious division. Catholicism prevailed in Poland, where Bathory's reign came to an end.[3]

Bathory ranked among those historical figures who, drawing upon their personal dynamism, choose to stand out against the established order of things, to confront the work of centuries and of whole generations, and who momentarily manage to divert the flow of irresistible events. Such individuals show how significant one great man can be at a given moment, yet simultaneously they prove the inadequacy of a single individual if he stands in the path of what sooner or later must be. Fortuitously placed on Poland's throne, Bathory decided to undertake the task of confirming Polish power and crushing the Muscovite state, and he seemed to have achieved his goal. He vanquished and humiliated Ivan IV, stripping from him the Baltic coasts, domination of which was a prerequisite for Muscovy's ongoing prosperity, for its power. Nevertheless when he set out to strike a telling blow at Moscow he found within his own land that obstacle which the centuries prepared and which he could not surmount. This was the power of the magnates, each of whom pursued his private ends and agreed only on one aspiration—not to see the monarch's power enhanced.

Bathory did not act alone. He attracted, in the office of hetman and chancellor, Jan Zamoyski, Poland's most talented and erudite magnate.[4] Yet even the combined forces of these two remarkable men came to naught.

The affair of the Zborowskis,[5] reminiscent of the Romans Catiline, Clodius, and Milo,[6] provides a clear understanding of the state of Poland in this period. In 1574, under King Henryk,[7] two enemies, Samuel Zborowski and Jan Teczyński, clashed at the king's castle. Each was supported by his personal retinue. At Teczyński's side stood his friend Andrzej Wapowski, who was injured fatally in the fray. Zborowski was banished forever from Poland for this offense, but he exhibited scant regard for the decree.[8] Having recruited a mercenary band, he roamed with it through districts of Poland where local administrators either did not dare or did not wish to detain him. He stayed in contact with his brothers Krzysztof and Andrzej who, seeing Bathory's and Zamoyski's disfavor toward them, and on the verge of ruin because of their extravagance, openly displayed hostile intent toward the king and his hetman. Twice Bathory came to know of the Zborowskis' plots against his life.

Such was the state of affairs when Zamoyski rode to Cracow to exercise his judicial functions as prefect there. While on the road he got word that Samuel Zborowski also was approaching Cracow by a different route, and was boasting publicly that he would make his entrance into the city the same time as Zamoyski. When Zamoyski lodged at Proszowice, a place already within the Cracow prefecture, Zborowski stopped at Podolani, about a mile away, and at sunset rode to Pieczma, to visit one of his relatives. Meanwhile in Cracow a crowd of unruly youths gathered to fall upon Zamoyski when he entered the city, just as Zborowski struck him from the rear. Having learned that Zborowski was alone at Pieczma, Zamoyski dispatched a squad of infantry under reliable officers to arrest him there at night. This having been accomplished easily, Zamoyski invoked his authority as prefect to enforce the courts' verdicts, and had Zborowski executed. The death penalty was mandatory when the case involved violation of a sentence of eternal banishment.[9]

The chancellor's deed stirred up a frightful storm. The Zborowskis enjoyed a large following, and besides them many others were displeased with the king and Zamoyski. Doubt was cast on Zamoyski's right to have Samuel executed. It was argued that although King Henryk had condemned Zborowski to perpetual exile he did not revoke his aristocratic privileges, and therefore his immunity from capital punishment still held. In opposition it was retorted that if one under perpetual banishment could not be threatened with death, what would deter him from returning to the homeland? Indeed banishment was applied to precisely those malefactors whose crime came close to meriting the death penalty.

The Zborowskis also managed to draw to their cause Stanisław Górka,[10] governor of Poznań, who exerted a strong influence in Great Poland. Until then Górka was an enemy of the Zborowskis and a friend of Zamoyski, then grew vexed and shifted his allegiance to the Zborowskis when, on his brother's death, he petitioned the king for the Jaworowo prefecture, only to see Zamoyski ask for and receive it.

As the Sejm drew near turmoil marked the district dietines.[11] Krzysztof Zborowski came from Moravia to the dietine at Proszowice. When Zamoyski's kinsman Mikołaj Zebrzydowski[12] strode into the church shots rang out. As soon as the sessions began Zborowski and his comrades railed loudly against Bathory. Indignantly they pointed to Zamoyski's power, lamented Samuel Zborowski's death, and characterized his trial as an unprecedented tyranny by which the government threatened the two other Zborowskis. Krzysztof Zborowski bluntly charged Zamoyski with an attempt to have him poisoned, but the man whom Zborowski labeled as Zamoyski's would-be assassin, having escaped Zborowski's control, declared that Zborowski used blandishments, threats and tortures to make him confess his guilt and to have him implicate Zamoyski as instigator of the crime. At the dietine in Great Poland the Gniezno castellan Jan Zborowski heaped abuse upon Zamoyski. When Canon Petrowski of Cracow defended the chancellor, Górka, the governor of Poznań, interrupted him. An outcry of support erupted from the Zborowski partisans, and shots were fired. Other dietines experienced similar upheaval.

As a consequence, fully armed crowds congregated at the Great Sejm as if for war. The king came escorted by Zamoyski's retainers, most of Lithuania's senators, and Prince Konstantin Ostrozski.[13] A court began to judge Krzysztof Zborowski, who considered it better not to appear in person. As well as the attempted regicide already mentioned, it indicted him for collusion with the Muscovite court to the harm of Poland and for similar relations with the cossacks. Jan Zborowski and Jan Niemojewski,[14] the accused's self-appointed defenders, performed so poorly that the court sentenced Krzysztof to loss of aristocratic privileges, of rights enjoyed by the gentry, and of his property. Of course this verdict did not pacify but merely served to incense the Zborowski faction.

LEO SAPIEHA IN MOSCOW

Despite domestic turbulence Bathory remained undeterred from his plan to strike a decisive blow at the Muscovite realm, to wrest from it at least Smolensk and the land of Severia. He believed that the accession of the weak Fedor and the immediately evident sedition and discord among the boyars offered a splendid opportunity. His ambassador Leo Sapieha,[15] with an eye to intimidating Muscovy's new administration, announced that the sultan was preparing for war with Moscow. He demanded that the tsar pay the king twelve hundred thousand zlotys[16] to ransom Muscovite prisoners and that he liberate without payment Lithuanian captives in Muscovy. The king's prisoners, he argued, were nobility, whereas the tsar held only commoners. Furthermore Fedor must satisfy every complaint put forth by his Lithuanian subjects, and must strike from his title any reference to Livonia.

The new regime in Moscow inherited from its predecessor a profound aversion to war with Bathory, and employed every means to prolong the truce. In honor of Fedor's coronation the tsar and the boyars decided to release their Lithuanian captives of whatever rank without compensation, but to leave the Russian prisoners in Polish hands at King Stefan's disposal. Should the king not reciprocate this gesture the tsar would be the more righteous ruler, as all neighboring states must see. If Stefan wished to sell the prisoners, they would be ransomed. Sapieha was informed of this decision, and of the fact that nine hundred prisoners already were freed in anticipation of a like concession from Stefan. Recent petitions from Fedor's Lithuanian subjects would be remedied but complaints from the time of Ivan IV were old business, unworthy of consideration. Russians too had suffered wrongs at Lithuanian hands, yet the tsar would not allude to them.

Sapieha further was advised that Fedor's title to Livonia was inherited from his father, along with the tsardom. The ambassador departed, having concluded only a ten-month prolongation of the truce. The news he carried to the king could hardly make him more desirous of peace.

Sapieha wrote a letter from Moscow to the papal legate Bolognetti[17] on July 10, 1584 in which he appraised the personality of the new tsar and the situation in Moscow. "The grand prince is small in stature. He speaks softly and most slowly. He has but little intelligence, or as others state and as I have witnessed, none at all. When at the time of my audience he sat enthroned in all his regal finery, gazing upon the scepter and orb, he laughed the whole time. Among the court dignitaries the bickering and quarreling is ceaseless. This very day I heard that relations among them draw nigh the point of bloodshed, and the sovereign is not such that he might prevent it. The Cheremiss[18] have cast off the yoke and the Tatars threaten an attack. Rumor has it that the king of Sweden is mustering his army, although none is so feared here as is our king. Arson is constant in the city itself, undoubtedly the work of the brigands who abound here." Reports reached the king that discord reigned among the four great dignitaries whom the dead tsar had named as regents, and that they often squabbled over precedence[19] in the presence of the sovereign. Prince Mstislavsky, first in rank of the boyars, was said to be very well disposed towards the king of Poland, and should Nikita Romanovich from the opposing faction die, for he seemed unlikely long to survive his serious illness, the king would gain many supporters among the boyars.

IZMAILOV'S EMBASSY TO BATHORY

Even before Sapieha departed Ambassador Andrei Izmailov[20] was sent to Bathory with the announcement of Fedor's accession. Izmailov's orders were to comport himself with great restraint, to yield on points of ceremony. He was not to appear before the lords, instead he was to convey his message to the king alone. Should the lords prove stubborn, should they forthrightly demand that he come before the Senate, he might comply but was not to deliver speeches or present his diplomatic credentials. Earlier ambassadors were enjoined to address the throne and present their documents first, before approaching the king's hand, even so now Izmailov was permitted to consent to approach the king at once. If the king did not inquire about the tsar's health or rise at Fedor's greeting Izmailov was to declare that Tsar Ivan Vasilievich had stood up for King Stefan's salutation,

Izmailov must observe[21] "Tsar Ivan Vasilievich rose for the king's greeting. If King Stefan does not stand, he knows that thus he acts against custom," and must say no more.

In fact the king did not rise for the tsar's name and salutation. After Izmailov spoke as ordered the king stood and removed his hat. Izmailov presented a safe conduct permitting high-ranking Lithuanian diplomats to journey to Moscow for the conclusion of a treaty, which the lords of the council[22] rejected. "It does not please our king," they said, "to dispatch envoys to your sovereign for this cause. Leo Sapieha, the ambassador of our sovereign, is even now with your sovereign in Moscow, and he is sorely confined. His residence is hemmed in with a high fence and even the tiniest crack is sealed so that not only can none be seen, not the slightest breeze can stir. No one can go out of the Lithuanian compound, and the provisions are wretched. Lithuania's ambassador is constrained worst of all. No one wishes to undertake an embassy to such a land, and our sovereign will not compel anyone to go."

"Some rogue," replied Izmailov, "has borne this tale. The ambassadors of various realms who now stay in Moscow reside at antagonistic courts and strict watch is placed over them lest they quarrel. Were ambassadors of other lands not present in Moscow your ambassador would be at complete liberty. The Crimean ambassador and couriers dwell at some distance from the city where they occupy a special residence erected for them, and they may not leave it to go anywhere."

One lord, the young Sierotka Radziwiłł,[23] spoke with vehemence. "Our sovereign's ambassador now is in Moscow," he said. "Your tsar must give him leave and dispatch after him his own envoy to the king. Our sovereign will take counsel with all the lords and with the land, as to how to conduct future dealings with your sovereign. Your sovereign is young, but ours is old. It behooves your tsar to write our king in the manner of a younger brother. Further, your sovereign should relinquish to our sovereign Smolensk and the towns of Severia." Izmailov replied that such intemperate speeches were unseemly.

After all the lords retired the old man Haraburda[24] remained. He approached Izmailov with these words. "I saw how these young lords very nearly left matters in shreds. They will not heed their elders." Izmailov commented that older men should direct the younger towards the worthy cause, towards peace, yet should the king, listening to the younger lords, spurn peace, Fedor would put his faith in God and prepare for war.

Haraburda, knowing well the disposition of opinion among the senators and the lesser nobility, assured the ambassador that peace would prevail, although the king continued to display his hostility to Moscow.

At his departure Izmailov was told that Bathory would neither accept the safe conduct, nor commission new ambassadors for peace talks in Moscow. The king did not invite Izmailov to dine, giving as an excuse the pressure of affairs. Izmailov reported to his court that the king wanted to declare war on Moscow immediately after the death of Ivan IV, but the council dissuaded him. Because of the crop failure in Poland the country could provide only half of Bathory's military expenses.

Stefan released to the tsar only twenty Muscovite prisoners. Luke Sapieha, the emissary who delivered them to Moscow, was chided by the boyars. "Tsar Fedor set at liberty nearly nine hundred Lithuanians," they said, "yet the king sent him twenty of the most low-ranking servitors. Only one of them, Prince Meshchersky, has any seniority, and even he comes from the ranks. There is not even one worthy junior boyar among them." Sapieha responded that the king would liberate all his captives later, holding only thirty for ransom. "Hereafter," the tsar wrote Bathory about this matter, "let neither of us suffer Christians to be sold from captivity for Russian dengas and Polish zlotys."[25] He cited as an example his conduct at his father's death.

Bathory conceded nothing. Moscow also did not wish to yield but had no desire to irritate the king and hasten a dangerous break in relations. The Muscovite bailiff escorting Luke Sapieha was handed such instructions. Should Lithuania's emissary speak of discord and war he was to comment "It is not wise to stir up trouble. It is better to act worthily. There is nothing worth boasting in that which causes Christian blood to flow on both sides. Moscow now is not feeble. In Moscow many youths yearn to fight and shred decrees of peace, what profit is there in having Christians on both sides shed their blood?"

EMBASSY OF PRINCE TROEKUROV AND BEZNIN

Unable to count on receiving ambassadors from Bathory the Muscovites dispatched to him early in 1585 their high ambassadors led by the boyar Prince Troekurov[26] and the conciliar noble Beznin,[27] with these instructions.[28] Do not approach the king's hand before the formal greeting. If compelled, comply while protesting "This is an innovation, and at variance with previous custom." Shun contact with everyone so as to utter nothing to anyone, save to the bailiffs and to those bringing responses. Do not embellish speeches to such intermediaries, rather speak with reserve so as to get to the point. If they reproach the tsar, say God judges those who rebuke the tsar, and step back for a moment. Gather information. Have the Germans of Riga heeded the king, and are the king's men now in Riga? Who are they, and how many, and what have the people of Riga conceded to the king? How thoroughly has Stefan organized the Livonian land, and how does he intend to administer it in the future? When asked about the king of Sweden, answer "Our ruler will work against the king of Sweden insofar as the help of God permits."

As for their main mission, the conclusion of a treaty, the ambassadors were instructed "Secure a truce of like duration to that which was ratified under Tsar Ivan. If the lords speak in a haughty manner, respond with equal arrogance. Say that Moscow is not now as it was in the past. Its sovereign will not purchase peace and he stands ready to resist the king. This is *most crucial*.[29] Behave thus only when you are certain that the king has quarreled with the lords. Should you judge that the king and the lords do not differ much and that the lords cannot be swayed by this initial stratagem, have recourse to some other measure so as without fail to obtain a truce from the king. If you cannot negotiate by any other tactic, demand a diplomatic communication so that you can exchange messengers with your sovereign concerning the matter. Should they not consent to a communication and dismiss you, have recourse to extreme measures to be sure to ensure a truce, even if only for a short term." The ambassadors further were ordered to try induce Timofey Teterin[30] and other Muscovite émigrés to return home under safe conduct, except for a certain Golovin,[31] who fled recently because of Godunov's victory over the Shuiskys.

This Golovin's calumny seriously impeded the embassy's labors from the outset. He worked to convince the king, whose belligerence needed no nourishment, that Moscow, with a feeble tsar and contentious boyars, was in such a sad state that the king's armies would meet no resistance from any quarter. "No one," he contended, "will raise a hand against him. The boyars are sorely divided, the people lack order, and no man cares to serve and to fight for such discord and chaos." Golovin also assured the king that Troekurov and Beznin were sent to make an armistice completely to Stefan's liking. These speeches inspired the king to claim from the ambassadors Novgorod, Pskov, Smolensk, Velikie Luki and Severia, and to add "Your sovereign's father at first did not deign to acknowledge me, yet eventually he did so, and your present tsar does not acknowledge me, but he too will do so. When I have his recognition I will make peace with him, but since now he takes no notice of me why ought I to settle with him?"

Bathory again encountered opposition in the Senate and in the Sejm. "The king," reported Troekurov and Beznin to Moscow, "requested mercenaries and money from the lords of the council and the district deputies. 'Do not bring harm upon yourselves,' he said, 'give me leave to do battle against the Muscovite. God will deliver a realm into your hands at no cost.'"

The district deputies refused to make appropriations. Moreover, Troekurov and Beznin floated the rumor that Golovin was untrustworthy, an agent purposely planted with Bathory by the boyars. The lords and the lesser nobility, who already lacked any inclination towards war, were quick to believe this tale. According to the report of Troekurov and Beznin the district deputies told the king "Why put faith in such nonsense, that wherever the king goes, all will be his? What has become of Moscow's men? Had Golovin fled to you under the old tsar we might give him credence, for the old tsar was cruel, but why desert the present tsar? The sovereign they now have is kind. You should seek peace now, bearing in mind that if it is found that Golovin spoke the truth you shall not escape a later war with the Muscovite sovereign." Bathory fumed against the district deputies and was vexed with the Muscovite ambassadors. He did not accept their gifts, he did not summon them to dine, nor did he send them dishes from his table. They stayed far from the city in cramped quarters. For all that, he had to assent to a two-year truce.

Luka Novosiltsev,[32] sent by way of Poland to the Holy Roman emperor, reported that the primate Archbishop Karnkowski,[33] who entertained him during his journey, said over dinner "Our King Stefan sought no peace with your ruler and heeded the words of Mikhail Golovin. Yet I have heard from Lithuanian prisoners that your tsar is pious and benign, that the tsaritsa is judicious and benevolent towards her own people, and likewise merciful to captives. Your sovereign granted freedom to all his prisoners, and released them without ransom. I and the deputies of all the districts[34] refused to supply the king with requisitions from our lands with which to hire men at arms. 'Should you wish to do battle with Moscow,' we said, 'expend your personal fortune on mercenaries.' We prevailed upon him to set free the prisoners, as did the Muscovite sovereign, but many are captives on the manors of lords who in their avarice ignore the king. Our king will not last. We eventually favor joining with you under the rule of your sovereign, because he is Christian and godly. Our prisoners told us that there is in Moscow the tsar's brother-in-law, Boris Fedorovich Godunov, the ruler of the land and a most generous benefactor. He took pity upon our prisoners, bestowed abundant charity upon them, gave them food and drink at his own expense when they were set free, and granted them clothing and money. While they were in prison he lavished bountiful alms upon them. We feel that it honors such a great sovereign to hold privy such a sage and kindly councilor. Your last tsar had Alexis Adashev.[35] He too ruled over the Muscovite realm." "Alexis was intelligent, but he is more than another Alexis," replied Novosiltsev. "This is an exalted man, a boyar and master of the horse, the tsaritsa's brother. God has filled him with all knowledge. He cares deeply for the whole land." The official escort advised Novosiltsev that the king felt insecure and unloved throughout the country, and had lost affection for the queen. Now he was growing ill, having opened old wounds in his foot. The doctors dared not treat him, for the treatment was as likely to kill as to cure.

A HABSBURG ON THE MUSCOVITE THRONE?

At this juncture a new circumstance intensified the pacific disposition of the lords and gentry toward Moscow, and must have influenced even the king. In the past Moscow had to follow closely the election of kings in Poland, to worry about the unification of [European] crowns [with Poland], or at least, the election of a hostile monarch.[36] Now Poland and Lithuania in turn assumed the same posture with respect to Muscovy. Spreading through Bathory's domains was the rumor, a very strong rumor, that the Austrian archdukes were working assiduously to see that Maximilian,[37] the Holy Roman emperor's brother, replace the incompetent Fedor on the Muscovite throne. Supposedly the Muscovite boyars dispatched to the emperor a mission concerning the matter. Bathory learned from sources in Danzig that the Habsburgs were striving to this end, also that the electors of the empire had assembled in Regensburg to confer on how Maximilian might procure the Muscovite throne.[38] Should this cause succeed Poland would be threatened with encirclement by possessions of the house of Austria. Then, when Bathory died, Poland would almost be compelled to select some prince from this family, an outcome undesirable to Bathory, Zamoyski and many others. Therefore it was decided to send to Moscow the familiar and welcome Orthodox lord, Haraburda. He would bring proposals aimed at counteracting the pretensions of the Austrian princes.

HARABURDA IN MOSCOW

Haraburda opened the talks with grievances against the oppression suffered by Lithuanian merchants in the Muscovite realm and the tsar's
failure to free captive Livonian Germans. The Russians retorted with
complaints. King Stefan had released only men of lesser rank such as
junior boyars, musketeers and plowmen. As for the Livonians, some
entered the tsar's service and lived on military service estates.[39] Others,
who were tradesmen, trafficked alongside Muscovite merchants. It made
no sense to talk of liberating either group.

When peace negotiations began they commenced with the usual preliminary claims, and then Haraburda stated "I can forgo further claims on
Novgorod and even on Pskov, but our sovereign stands firm for Smolensk
and the Severian land." "Such words often have been uttered in the past,"
commented the boyars, "but later these speeches were put aside. Our
sovereign will not part with even the roof tiles from one city."

After this formality Haraburda set about accomplishing the main purpose. "The lords of the council," he told the boyars, "entrusted to me this
letter for the most reverend father Metropolitan Dionisy, and for you, the
tsar's council.[40] 'Words fly between us about cities and about rural districts,' this letter reads, 'but these speeches are fruitless. Why is this? Can
you not concede to us without bloodshed what we seek from you? Certainly we cannot yield without bloodletting what you demand of us. So let
us on both sides be done with speech making, and let our sovereign and
yours end it thus: what each now holds, that shall he keep. No man shall
seek from another what cannot be taken without killing. Better that brother
not ask of brother that which would cause slaughter. May the Lord bless
both sovereigns with long reigns but should He come for King Stefan, and
none of his offspring remain, the Polish crown and the grand principality
of Lithuania will join Muscovy under the tsar's sway. Cracow will equal
Moscow, and Wilno will equal Novgorod.[41] Should God take the soul of
your tsar, the Muscovite realm will come under the sway of our ruler, and
you will seek no other. I am empowered to negotiate this weighty matter
and to seal the documents.'"

"We deem it improper," answered the boyars, "even to consider such
words as you have uttered concerning our sovereign. This proposal can
have no good end." The boyars reported these discussions to Fedor. His
council advised that he ratify a peace with Stefan securing the current
boundaries, whereas talk of the sovereign's death was unseemly.

Haraburda nevertheless did not abandon his proposal, and instead began altering its conditions, probably having concluded on the spot that Fedor would not die soon. "Should God send for your tsar's soul, Muscovy would unite with the Polish kingdom and the grand principality of Lithuania, and be one under the rule of our king as distinct realms but with a single head. Should King Stefan perish, we Poles and Lithuanians will be at liberty to choose your sovereign or be free to reject him." "We have not discussed this with you," the boyars replied. "Why are you talking thus to us about our sovereign? We have had hereditary rulers from time immemorial, and we have been their hereditary slaves, but you Poles elect your monarchs. Your king is whomever you choose. Now you have exceeded by far your proposal of the day before yesterday. Your words have taken another form, and we shall talk no more about this. We presented your ideas to the metropolitan and the entire consecrated assembly, and they have forbidden us under pain of anathema to consider them. How dare we even conceive this of our tsar, let alone say it? We have no wish to speak of it even concerning your sovereign, yet you would discuss and ponder this about him. You, the ambassador of a great king, come to our mighty sovereign and voice such unfit words about their majesties' deaths? Who shall not condemn us when we, in the sovereign's presence, beholding him in good health, utter such words? "

"I see that you are angry," Haraburda replied. "You state that the metropolitan and the priests forbid you from addressing the matter I have presented you, still I am only relating what is my charge. If you will not entertain my suggestion, I have been ordered to seal no agreement without concessions on your part." Reiterating the tsar's refusal to part with even a shingle, the boyars claimed for the tsar his ancient patrimony consisting of Kiev with its districts and related towns, and his other hereditary domains. Filled with emotion, they chided Haraburda. "If your only business is what you have presented," said they, "you should not have bothered to come. If an ambassador is not straightforward, what are we to believe?" The official escort cautioned Haraburda "Moscow is not now feeble. It is not Polotsk or Livonia, instead it is Wilno that now must be shielded from Moscow."

Haraburda sensed failure but also could see that flattery evoked a change of tone from the Muscovite boyars and the bailiff. In order to show some result he proposed that a conference of high ambassadors meet at the border to arrange a permanent treaty. The boyars, who sought every opportunity to play for time, agreed to the meeting provided that the term of the truce be extended. "Mikhail," they told Haraburda, "this is a grave matter for all Christendom. Our sovereign must consult the entire land about it. First the metropolitan and the entire consecrated assembly, then the boyars with all the councilors, every commander and the whole realm. Such an assemblage must congregate from distant places." Haraburda protested that he lacked authority to prolong the truce, leading the boyars to retort "Is this how you manage affairs? You came with nothing and you will leave with nothing." In fact Haraburda returned empty handed. He did tell the boyars of the rumor that the throne had been offered to Archduke Maximilian. In reply the boyars wrote to the lords "We are sorely vexed that some traitorous malefactor has started such villainous talk."

TROEKUROV AGAIN BEFORE BATHORY

Nonetheless Moscow still judged it necessary to extend the truce. Prince Troekurov made a second journey to Bathory, whom he found in Grodno. Now the lords in turn upbraided the boyars for spurning their proposal to unite the countries. They assailed Troekurov with abusive speech. "We gave bread to your tsar's boyars, your brethren, and they cast stones in return. Judge for yourself, is this not a stone? We zealously intercede with our sovereign and, at our behest, for a time he shuns battle with your tsar. Henceforth we wish well of your sovereign, the boyars and the entire land. Yea, the entire land. Yet the boyars write that the tsar is girding up against the aggressor. What is more, they urge that our king yield to your sovereign his ancient and eternal patrimony, which he has just recovered. After writing these articles, they would have us induce our king to eternal friendship with you! Judge for yourselves, can we place such a document before our sovereign?

"We marvel among ourselves at such a missive. How can the boyars not perceive what has befallen your realm on account of its sins? Your sovereign has no offspring. We know his nature. There is godliness in him, but that will not serve to restrain his foes. Likewise we know how things are in Moscow. It is depopulated, while those who remain are impoverished, disorderly and filled with discord. The boyars hope to protect themselves, yet they only defeat their own purposes. We long have been aware in our land that your boyars have dispatched an ambassador to the emperor's brother, but did the emperor embrace your realm? The emperor cannot even help himself. Many lords, observing this communication with the emperor's brother, covet your land and scheme to gain it. The Turk wants

Astrakhan and Kazan from you. The Perekop[42] constantly wage war on you and will continue to do so. Even your Cheremiss[43] are hostile. Are your boyars stupid? They write that your tsar stands ready against every foe, yet it does not shame them to make entreaties. Your speeches to our king were fruitless, they only weighed on his heart. Now not only will we not beg the king to keep peace with your sovereign, we will remind him that he has sworn a solemn vow to win the lands wrested from his predecessors. Not only will we provide him with money for mercenaries but we too, with all of our commanders from both lands will be ready to ride with him. You therefore will leave with that with which you came."

"It ill behooves you to grow vexed at the boyars' statement," the ambassador answered, "and you need not bring it up. By custom both sides refer to bygone matters when bargaining. Then they turn to what pertains to matters at hand, and consider subjects leading to a settlement. Your reasoning astounds us. You display neither fear before God nor shame before men, giving voice to that which ought not even be imagined. You recount the fate of our sovereign's domain because of its transgressions. We see no such sin upon our kingdom, only divine grace and prosperity. You have not yet spoken with God, neither to man is it given to know the future. It has been written that he who maligns the tsar shall perish. Our sovereign is a sturdy lord, wise and fortunate. He holds sway over his realm with his father's blessing, sees personally to its order, and is steeled against all foes, as were his father, grandfather and great-grandfather. He has many men, twice as many as before, for he shows them clemency and lavishes many gifts upon them, not sparing his treasury. They serve with exceeding zeal, and thus yearn to serve hereafter, willing to sacrifice their lives against all his adversaries. There is no dissension among them. Traitorous dogs have delivered such vain speeches before you. It does not suit you to indulge such men, and it is wrong for you to utter perfidy. There is much that we might say about your sovereign, your kingdom and you, but in accordance with the tsar's command we will not speak. We have been sent on worthy business, not for strife. Our tsar shall not buy peace from your king. Should your sovereign wish an honorable settlement, thus will ours. If your sovereign does not desire it, our tsar stands ready"

Of course, when discussion turned to mutual claims on certain territories, no agreement was possible. Again the Poles insisted that dignitaries confer at the frontier whereas the Russians, in keeping with their purposes, demanded in return for this conference an extension of the truce for one year. "We shall not ratify a truce for even half a year," replied the lords.

"You are not suggesting a conference seriously, merely to gain time. Why must you have a full year's additional truce before a conference?" The ambassadors asserted that consultation with the entire land required much time, to which the lords objected. "We know your customs," they said. "Your tsar and boyars deliberate and abide by their decision, without involving the land." The ambassadors had to accept most reluctantly an extension of the previously concluded truce for just two months. Simultaneously they arranged for a meeting of high ambassadors, to convene between Orsha and Smolensk. This conference would consider whether both realms might come under a single ruler if one or the other sovereign died, and how to define their borders should they not wish to unite.

BATHORY'S DEATH

Bathory did not live to see the conference. He died on December 2, 1586 without managing to complete even one of his undertakings, foreign or domestic. His conquest of the Baltic coast retarded only temporarily the development of the Muscovite state. Ultimately he failed to crush its power and restore Lithuania to its boundaries of Vytautas's time.[44] Limited resources, restricted royal authority and the powerful magnates' suspicion towards a warlike king prevented that. Nor could Bathory bridle the power of the magnates, curb anarchy or institute hereditary rule, or at least establish a better method of electing the king. Finding his realm wracked with religious controversy Bathory, not by nature a fanatic, undertook no persecution of dissidents. Still, he did foster the consolidation of the Jesuits because this illustrious order promised him energetic assistance in his projected domestic reforms.

The nature of this Jesuit aid and the sort of inspiration which youth educated by the Jesuits always received from them pervades the sermons of their most talented pupil, Piotr Skarga of Powno,[45] who thundered against the current state of affairs in Poland. On one hand he preached the subordination of secular to ecclesiastical authority, of king to Pope. On the other hand he underscored the need for resolute and unhampered royal power. "The natural order," he said, "is that one head governs the body. Should a state have not one but many heads, this signifies a grave, fatal illness." Skarga asserted that the Roman empire attained its fullest extent only when monarchical rule was firmly implanted. He took issue with the delegates to the Sejm because they assumed authority detrimental to monarchical and senatorial power. They transformed salutary monarchy into democracy, the most pernicious form of government, particularly in a kingdom as vast as Poland-Lithuania. Skarga identified as the source of brigandage, treason and the like the law which forbade arrest of members of the lesser nobility not convicted of a crime.

All these reprimands remained futile. The Jesuits could not reshape the political structure of Poland and Lithuania. They could achieve the one goal which Bathory, of course, did not desire. They inflamed the Catholic population of Poland and Lithuania with religious intolerance, which caused the maltreatment of dissident creeds, especially the Orthodox Rus. This persecution drove Little Russia to secede, inflicting a vital blow on Poland.[46] Thus a weapon forged to undergird the fortress, the power of Poland, became an instrument for its downfall.

CONTEST FOR POLAND

Events late in Bathory's reign foreshadowed the grave disturbances following his death. Hatred between the Zborowski faction and Zamoyski's partisans now could run rampant. Disturbances erupted at the district dietines. Even at Lvov, where Zamoyski's influence was so strong, there were supporters of the Zborowskis, among them Mikołaj Jazłowiecki,[47] prefect of Sniatyń. Jazłowiecki proclaimed that the time had come to limit the exaltation of one man above all others, and that everyone knew of Zamoyski's schemes to place a member of the Bathory family on the throne, no matter what the cost. To safeguard the realm, he argued, Zamoyski must be stripped of the hetmanate[48] because every administrative officer must vacate his post at the death of the king. Zamoyski retorted that he had earned all his distinctions and honors through righteous service to the fatherland. The rumor about his designs on behalf of the Bathorys was a slander. To assert that all governmental functions must cease with the monarch's death was nonsense, for precisely during an interregnum the kingdom could least afford to dispense with its military leader, the hetman.

Zamoyski carried the day at Lvov but lost at the convocational Sejm in Warsaw. Archbishop Primate Karnkowski of Gniezno, who ranked first in the kingdom during an interregnum, completely succumbed to the influence of the Zborowskis and Górka. At their urging he wrote Zamoyski that the security of the kingdom's frontier necessitated Zamoyski's remaining in the field, and thus he must not leave the army. Zamoyski's absence gave the Zborowskis an advantage in the Senate, where Andrzej Zborowski came to demand justice against him. When one senator, Liesniowolski,[49] rose to defend Zamoyski, Zborowski's supporters drowned out his voice with shouts and threats. One even trained a pistol on Liesniowolski and asked the Zborowskis whether he should fire. Beyond the walls of Warsaw as well, political strife approached the level of civil warfare. Finally, the date of the electoral Sejm was set for June 30, 1587.

The Zborowskis attended the election with ten thousand soldiers, among whom were not a few French, German, Italian, and Czech mercenaries. This crowd was hired with Austrian money, for the Zborowskis, supported by the papal nuncio Annibale di Capua,[50] hoped to elect Archduke Maximilian, brother of the Holy Roman emperor Rudolph II.[51] Zamoyski relied mainly upon the gentry, and drew from the coffers of Bathory's widow, Queen Anna. He favored her nephew, the Swedish prince Sigismund,[52] son of King John and Katarzyna Jagiellonica. Zamoyski, and Górka with the Zborowskis, each settled into armed camps at designated places on the Wola plains around Warsaw. Each faction prepared to support its candidate with weapons in hand if necessary. Near Kamionka, on the opposite bank of the Vistula, stood the special encampment of the Lithuanians, who had their own candidate, the Muscovite tsar.

FEDOR'S CANDIDACY

Moscow learned of Bathory's death on December 20, 1586. Recent experience demonstrated the importance for Muscovy of the election of a king in Poland. Ivan IV had declined to campaign vigorously for the Polish throne, and let Bathory acquire it. He had lost the Baltic coast and was compelled to sign a shameful peace with Lithuania.[53] At the time of that election Ivan was still unaware of Bathory's character and he could scorn this petty Transylvanian prince, so lacking in resources. Now Fedor's boyars could not help but discern the awful danger threatening their realm should the Swedish prince win[54] Poland's throne and bring under one head two neighboring kingdoms hostile to Moscow. Accordingly they resolved to work strenuously to gather supporters for Fedor in Poland, and especially in Lithuania.

RZHEVSKY'S MISSION TO LITHUANIA

The nobleman Rzhevsky[55] departed for Lithuania by January 20, 1587, bearing the tsar's appeal to the lords, "You, lords of the council," it read, both secular and ecclesiastical, having taken counsel amongst yourselves and with the entire land, must be solicitous of the welfare of Christians, seek our favor and desire us as sovereign over the Polish crown and the grand principality of Lithuania, that both realms may rest under the tsar's mighty hand in mutual love, union and concord. We will in no manner violate your rights and liberties, and even more than before we will add to your honors and estates, and heap grants upon you." Besides this general statement the tsar sent separate messages to every magnate. He wanted each to advocate his election with his brothers, nephews and entire family. Then each boyar addressed a similar proposal to a Lithuanian lord of corresponding rank.

"If the Lithuanian lords," Rzhevsky's instructions read, "assert that they long for the tsar as ruler but that the Polish lords do not so desire, and therefore they ask if the tsar will stand by them should they separate from the Polish kingdom, answer 'You know that the Poles differ from Orthodox Christians in faith, while you Lithuanian lords of the council and all Lithuania are of one creed and one rite with our land. How could you not desire our sovereign, a Christian ruler? Were Lithuania to cleave to Muscovy, how could our sovereign not shield the Lithuanian lands? Let both states be as one against all foes, and the Polish land must perforce be united with Moscow and Lithuania. This prospect enhances our tsar's fervor to count the grand principality of Lithuania among his lands. How could the tsar not support this? The original Kievan state belongs to our tsar by hereditary right and now, involuntarily, it has been torn from Lithuania for the Polish crown.[56] The Poles took even more than Kiev from you, Lithuanian lords, and they joined it to the Polish land by force. Why ought not our sovereign strip all this from Poland and secure it for you, and for the Muscovite realm?'"

"Meet Timokha Teterin, David Belsky, Murza Kupkeev[57] and others who have deserted to Lithuania," Rzhevsky was instructed. "When they inquire whether the tsar has outstanding charges against them, urge them to seek the tsar's grace, serve him, and wish him well, but let them doubt not that in their flight to Lithuania they offended him and displayed insolence towards him. The sovereign will remit their guilt should he come to rule Poland and Lithuania, and he will favor them in everything, as in their native land. He will put aside military patrimonial holdings and service tenure estates for those wishing to stay in Muscovy, and will have them established there according to their merits. Let them now render service to the tsar. Have them seek knowledge of the opinions of the lords of the council, learn which lords would have him as sovereign and which would not. Having learned this, let them tell the ambassadors and show good will to the tsar. Should the lords argue for the tsar to place over their realm his brother Tsarevich Dmitry, answer 'This is a different matter. The tsarevich is yet a youth, only four years old. You will fare better under the tsar's protection, living by your own ways and managing your affairs as it pleases you.'"

In reply to Rzhevsky's proposals the Lithuanian lords observed that the election could be decided only at the Sejm in Warsaw, where the tsar should dispatch his ambassadors. Luke Mamonich, a rich Lithuanian trader with mercantile connections in Moscow, spoke to Rzhevsky on behalf of three lords, Mikołaj Radziwiłł, Leo Sapieha, and Tadeusz Skumin.[58] "These noblemen think highly of your tsar," said he, "and advise him to be quick to send his most august delegates to the electoral Sejm. He must write to the lords of the council and the knighthood of both lands lovingly and affectionately, and not haughtily, for the Polish lords are angry and stubborn men who must be approached with sweetness. What does a great prince lose thereby? Write to the knighthood that the sovereign favors them, and from his coffers will meet the grants left unpaid by King Stefan. The money will not be much, five or six thousand and, indeed, the knights will not take the money. Nevertheless inscribe this promise in the charters so that they will support your tsar. King Stefan swore to honor his debts to the knighthood and took an oath, but they got not a penny[59] from him. Your sovereign also must bestow something upon the lords. The emperor and other lesser princes bidding for the realm heap blandishments and rich gifts upon them." Rzhevsky responded that the tsar found it inappropriate to have his ambassadors sent to the Sejm.

CZERNIKOWSKI AND OGIŃSKI

This did not end all relations. Lithuania did not fear from Fedor what it dreaded from Ivan, and it yearned all the more to elect the Muscovite tsar. Furthermore the Lithuanian lords wanted no break in negotiations with the tsar lest he exploit the interregnum by dispatching an army across their borders. This explains why, as early as April of the same year [1587], two distinguished Lithuanian envoys, Czernikowski and Prince Ogiński,[60] brought to Moscow a request to extend the truce through 1588.

The boyars greeted this overture warmly saying "We, the tsar's boyars and councilors, join the entire land in hoping and praying God that the Muscovite, Polish, and Lithuanian states come under the tsar's rule. Not long ago Lithuanians leaving their country came to us in Pskov and related that some lords, for the money the queen disburses, acclaim the Swedish prince. These nobles proclaim in their writings the lavish profit which the Swede will bring Poland and Lithuania, but a voice for the Swedish prince diminishes Christendom. It is unprofitable, for blood will flow as it did under King Stefan. No sooner will the Swede be elected than blood will be shed between us and you, and indeed amongst all Christians a great bloodletting will begin, and it shall not end."

The ambassadors, recalling that Stefan's wars had not harmed Poland, asked "What evil happened under King Stefan?" "We shall recount for you the truth about Stefan," was the reply, "and about his benevolence towards your realm, but do not grow angry. We, you and all Christendom will benefit from the election of our tsar, for our sovereign is Christian, god-fearing, merciful and gracious toward all Christianity. Other *ordinary* sovereigns are chosen in a realm but have no love for it, like for example, King Stefan. He vowed to the sultan that he would make the Poles and the Lithuanians subject to the Turk. In secret messages he wrote to the sultan to raise a host against the Polish and the Lithuanian lords. He wrote to the effect that there are wealthy men in Poland and Lithuania with fortunes reaching five hundred thousand gold efimoks[61] and limitless treasure. These riches, he held, must be shaken loose so that the wealthy will cast off their inordinate pride, for they are now very haughty. Yet our tsar possesses his own unlimited wealth and will not spare his treasury to shelter both the Muscovite realm and Poland-Lithuania from the Tatars and Turks. From the Crimea to the Don, Donets and Dnieper he will post his men, create towns, and advance upon the Crimea that henceforth none of the pagans will raid Podolia, the land of Volhynia, Poland or Lithuania.

"The sovereign cares not to partake of the royal revenues and profits. He promises to deliver all this to the lords of the council and the entire knighthood. Indeed, from his own purse he will increase this sum for the Polish and Lithuanian lords of the council and for the entire knighthood, and he will establish towns in the steppe in his realms, and will make grants of land to the men of Poland and Lithuania. Because of the sins of all Christendom you hate us so, and this hatred harms all Christians, destroying the peace and loving unity of them all. You, all the lords, must counsel that which most benefits the whole of Christianity, and you will stand innocent of Christian blood before Almighty God.

"Can that which furthers the friendship of Christian and pagan befit any Christian? Should you combine your realms with our sovereign's Orthodox tsardom, the pagan overlords will lose heart. They will have to protect themselves at once, and no longer enslave Christendom. Moldavia, Wallachia, Bosnia, Serbia and Hungary, which now belong to the Turks, will fall to Poland and Lithuania, while Moscow will incorporate what is closer to us, namely the Crimea, Kaffa, Azov, the Cherkassians and the lands of the other Hordes. Even now three Crimean princes with many men stand ready in Astrakhan for our sovereign. Should the Swedish prince be chosen, these same Tatars instead of attacking the Crimea from Astrakhan and from beyond the Volga will turn on Lithuania. If you elect our tsar he will confront the Muslims *in person* and with all his host. He will aid with his treasury. In no way will he infringe the customs and the liberties of the lords, nor will he ask anything from them. The sovereign will transfer to the lords of the council the revenues collected in the Lithuanian and Polish lands. They shall have the treasury of past kings, what has been added to it of late, and what was imported from Hungary, for our tsar needs none of it. His coffers are full. No realm is blessed with such riches as his. Our sovereign has no need of the many assemblies which have burdened Poland and Lithuania. He will come with his own provisions and his own revenues, and will require of you nothing save your affection. Our sovereign comes to you with his own treasury, that from it he may provide for all the local people."

FURTHER MUSCOVITE ELECTORAL EFFORTS

The possible union of Poland and Lithuania with Sweden profoundly disturbed Moscow. No longer did it seem inappropriate to send high ambassadors to the Sejm, Stefan Vasilievich Godunov[62] and Prince Fedor Mikhailovich Troekurov,[63] both boyars, with the illustrious crown secretary Vasily Shchelkalov.[64] Lithuanians also longed for Fedor's success. Messages to the tsar from the residents of Wilno were intercepted, but Fedor's advocates in Lithuania understood clearly the major obstacles to his election in the Polish Sejm. Lithuania's crown treasurer Tadeusz Skumin told the Muscovite ambassador Rzhevsky "I am a Christian of your Greek faith, as were my mother and father, so I speak to you as a co-religionist. We all are eager to join with you in perpetuity, making your sovereign lord over our aristocracy, yet God must deign that we surmount three objections which the lords of the council hold and will express. (1) Your sovereign must take the crown among us, in Cracow. (2) He must list first among his titles those of king of Poland and grand prince of Lithuania. (3) He must change his faith. You insist that to convert is unthinkable for you, let alone for your sovereign. That is just, and I have asked the lords of the council how a Christian can be expected to abjure his faith. If, God willing, we cross these three bridges, we will be united with you forever."

Godunov and Troekurov carried concessions to the Sejm exceeding those already offered to the Lithuanian envoys in Moscow. The tsar would disburse from his personal treasury up to a hundred thousand Hungarian gold pieces for the back pay of Bathory's mercenaries. Once the Swedes were driven from Estonia all its cities save Narva would be annexed to Poland and Lithuania. Polish and Lithuanian merchants would enjoy free access to every region of Muscovy and beyond to all the Oriental countries. Unimpeded freedom of communication and marriage would be granted residents of the united realms. As for the tsar's sojourn in Poland (a fourth bridge, forgotten by Skumin) the ambassadors were to suggest that Fedor, after lingering briefly in Poland and Lithuania, would return to Moscow and reside there, in the first of his realms. The lords of the council would administer Poland and Lithuania, maintaining existing customs, laws and liberties. Ambassadors who arrived with less important matters would be referred to the lords of the council, after consultation with the sovereign. Those bearing business of great concern to all three lands would dwell with the tsar in Moscow, where two lords of the council and a scribe would represent the interests of Poland and Lithuania.

Should the Sejm reject Fedor the ambassadors were to recommend the election of Maximilian, the emperor's brother. "That would please the tsar because Maximilian, the son of a great sovereign, befits such exalted kingdoms. Do not choose the Swede or any other monarch from the maritime regions. These rulers lack concern for Christianity and always seek the spilling of Christian blood." Eager as Muscovy was to block the election of Sigismund of Sweden, it found it difficult to develop a formula for ruling two realms which would not yield to one another in either prestige or income. This dilemma inspired the Muscovite administration to propose full autonomy for Poland and Lithuania if only they acknowledged the Muscovite tsar as their titular sovereign. "It matters not," said the orders for Troekurov and Godunov, "whether they elect us as sovereign or recognize our suzerainty and govern themselves. Agree, provided only that they ally firmly with us against any enemy. Just labor for this, prove your zeal and dedication, that God will vouchsafe you do not return without accomplishing your mission."

Lithuania rejoiced that Moscow's sovereign consented to strive resolutely for the crown of Poland and Lithuania, and that he agreed to appoint a high embassy to the Sejm. These emissaries behaved most courteously, shunning the usual haggling over details of ceremony. The Lithuanians who rode out to meet them said "We greet you now, high ambassadors of the Orthodox tsar. God grant that we and the whole land welcome your sovereign among us. In the Lithuanian land, in every township, all the knighthood and the whole nation have ruled that they wish to accept your sovereign as lord." "You have shown ample flexibility toward the traditional rituals," said the bailiffs to the ambassadors. "Earlier, when official escorts from the king approached the envoys of your tsar, your envoys began an argument about caps. They did not remove their caps immediately upon hearing the royal name, now you, eminent ambassadors, have doffed your hats for the speeches of your brethren, the lords of the council, who accept this as a great courtesy on your part."

The Lithuanians shortly realized that Moscow's ambassadors, as in the past, differed from the other embassies attending the Sejm to plead their monarch's candidacy. As before, the Muscovites came without money. The Lithuanian lords of the council sent a scribe to advise them. "You must plan," he said, "to expend about twelve hundred rubles at once to attract everyone away from the Zborowskis, Governor Górka of Poznań, and Chancellor Jan Zamoyski, and turn them toward your tsar. When the knighthood and their followers see the color of your tsar's money[65] they will all desert the Zborowskis and the chancellor for us. Success is impossible without money. 'What sort of ambassadors are these,' they will say of you, 'who cannot produce money!'"

The Muscovites proposed to discuss everything personally with the lords of the council, at the embassy. Then, at night, Governor Jan Hlebowicz of Troki, accompanied by the crown table attendant Prince Vasily Pronsky, secretly visited them, declaring "I wish to prove my service to your tsar. I am striving to convince the governor of Poznań and the Zborowskis to join with us in choosing your sovereign, and I have already induced them, but they have mercenaries whose payment draws near. The governor of Poznań and the Zborowskis need help, a subsidy with which to pay the soldiers and resist the chancellor." The ambassadors replied that they lacked instructions, and in any case had brought no funds.

Despite this deficiency in money, that most potent resource at an electoral Sejm, the Muscovite party remained strong, not only in Lithuania but even among the Poles, for a majority viewed Fedor's election as the most viable alternative to a clash between the rival factions, the Zborowskis and Zamoyski. When three standards were raised in a field, a cap for the Muscovite, a German hat for the Austrian, and a herring for the Swede, an overwhelming majority gathered under the cap. On August 4 Godunov and Troekurov carried out their mission at the lower house of the diet, before the assembled knighthood.[66] A bench for the ambassadors was placed before the most eminent aristocrats, around which sat the lords of the council and district delegates. Having seen the bench prepared for them and that the lords and the district delegates were seated, Moscow's delegates began their address to the lords of the council. "In no country is it customary," they said, "that ambassadors coming from their sovereign sit while speaking. How can we perform our duty to the tsar while seated? We will deliver our message from the sovereign while standing, and you too should stand and hear from us our sovereign's speech."

"We," responded the lords, "are telling you what is our custom. Do not bicker about it. Fulfill your mission from the bench, and we will arise at your sovereign's name." The ambassadors continued to object, and finally the lords said "We are informing you of our practice here. You take no heed, so do what you wish. We will sit, and you will carry out your embassy as you please." Then the lords sat, and the ambassadors delivered their speeches while seated.

A village near Warsaw, Kameniec, was where the fifteen ecclesiastical and secular lords appointed to meet the Muscovite ambassador came to discuss with them the details of Fedor's election. Here those obstacles that Skumin considered so insuperable emerged from the lords' questioning of the ambassadors. Would the tsar bind his Muscovite realm to Poland just as Lithuania and Poland were joined, perpetually and inseparably? Would he embrace the Roman faith? Would he obey the Pope? Did he agree to be crowned in Cracow, in the Latin church, by the archbishop of Gniezno? Did he plan to receive the Eucharist as unleavened bread and unite the Greek and the Roman faiths? Would he enter Warsaw within ten weeks after his election? Would the kingdom of Poland rank above the tsardom of Muscovy in his title?

The boyars answered that the kingdom of Poland and the grand principality of Lithuania would be linked with Muscovy eternally, that they might stand as one against any opponent. Their inhabitants might pass freely from country to country and might live, court and marry with the tsar's consent. Fedor would retain his Orthodox faith. He would hold his coronation either in Moscow or in Smolensk. He would esteem the Pope and not obstruct his control of the Polish clergy, but would brook no meddling in the affairs of the Greek church. The Polish crown would be below the tsar's cap of Monomakh,[67] the title being "tsar and grand prince of all the Russias, Vladimir, Moscow, king of Poland and grand prince of Lithuania." "Even if," said the ambassadors, "both the old and the new Rome, the imperial city of Byzantium, were to swear fealty to our sovereign, how could he subordinate his Muscovite realm to any other?" As to the time of his appearance in Poland, the ambassadors asserted "God and the tsar will determine that. He will arrive when he so wishes. We cannot guess this and the tsar gave us no command concerning this matter."

The lords declared that Fedor was unacceptable under these terms. In particular they insisted that he disburse money as soon as possible to sustain his faction in the Sejm and hire soldiers because his election would bring enemies down on Poland from all quarters. They cited the exemplary generosity of the emperor and the king of Spain. "Our sovereign," answered the ambassadors, "will provide suitably from his treasury for mercenaries. You say that the emperor and the king of Spain will bestow large sums upon you for their election, and over many years. Our sovereign would be king of Poland and grand prince of Lithuania not for the sake of his own profit and glory, rather solely for Christian peace, for the deliverance and expansion of these realms. He calls to mind that Muscovy, the Polish crown and the grand principality of Lithuania have long been at odds, and that Christian blood has flowed on all sides. His governance will staunch this outpouring and put Christians at peace. Yet you ignore our sovereign's zeal for peace, you point to the treasuries of the emperor and of the king of Spain. As you please, prefer money over a Christian peace. Why should our sovereign purchase your realm? With God's aid, he rules his own domain. Our tsar will have harmony prevail among all Christians and would see them stand united against the Muslims. When you argue that our sovereign must contribute his treasury and ordain warfare against those who did not choose him, it means that he must sow even more bloodshed amongst Christians, and not strive for the common Christian peace."

"Your sovereign," answered the lords, "cannot come to rule us on the basis of these articles which we have discussed." Then the Russian diplomats, honoring their instructions, declared that if the tsar could not be elected, he endorsed the candidacy of Archduke Maximilian. "It behooves neither you nor your tsar to designate our king," retorted the lords. "You know that we decide nothing by decree. We select whomever God shows us, in keeping with our liberties."

At the second session the lords reintroduced the matter of subsidies, asking "Will Fedor give us two hundred thousand rubles for immediate defense? Failing that, his election does not even merit discussion." The Muscovites reiterated that the tsar did not purchase realms but vouched that upon his election they, the ambassadors, having taken loans, would provide up to sixty thousand Polish zlotys. When the lords found this sum insufficient, the ambassadors increased the offer to a hundred thousand, which even this the lords declined. "The tsar pledges to grant the gentry land along the Don and the Donets," they said, "how will they prosper in such uninhabited places? Indeed the very journey there is long. We too hold much of such land beyond Kiev. Does it not shame you to write of such places in the articles! Will the tsar bestow upon our men property in the Muscovite realm, in Smolensk and the towns of Severia ?" "Whosoever comes to our sovereign's service," replied the ambassadors, "upon him the sovereign will confer patrimonial estates." "Will the sovereign," the lords asked, "honor the arrears owed the army by Kings Stefan and Sigismund Augustus?" The ambassadors replied that the tsar would recognize Stefan's obligations, but not those of Sigismund Augustus. "What sort of liberty is it," asked the lords, "which lets our people travel to you at will yet permits your men to come here only with dispensation from the throne? Should your tsar suffer no one to leave, would not departures cease?" The lords pressed for mutual freedom of movement, for which the ambassadors categorically rebuffed them. "The inhabitants of your domains," they said, "have the liberty to travel to any country but we do not live under such a custom in Muscovy, nor will it ever be appropriate for us to travel as we please, without the tsar's permission. We must speak with you no more about it."

Meanwhile arguments raged among the secular and the ecclesiastical lords, the partisans of Maximilian, Sigismund and Fedor. "The election of the Muscovite tsar," Cardinal Radziwiłł[68] observed, "would be most advantageous for the Commonwealth, except that religion creates an insurmountable impediment. Besides, this is our nation's hereditary foe. It would be unworthy of us to accept an enemy as ruler. His crown estates[69] would burden us. If we felt the late king's few hundred haiduks[70] to be onerous, the crown estates would oppress us even more. Most of all, the Muscovite cannot govern because he lacks the mental capacity." Krzysztof Zborowski also referred to Fedor's incapacity and expressed doubt that he would honor his promises. "I find it impossible to conceive," he said, "that this haughty Muscovite people, which places importance even on the removal of caps, will consent that their realm unite with the crown. They

will sooner hope to bind Poland to Muscovy, like a sleeve to a caftan."
Fedor's supporters objected that despite various rumors about his feeble-
mindedness his actions did not prove irrationality. He had curtailed domestic discontent, a much harder task than winning foreign wars, for an
internal heals less readily than an external wound. He liberated his captives
without ransom. All this demonstrated his wisdom and kind-heartedness.
Fedor's adherents particularly lauded his having released his captives
without payment.

ELECTION OF SIGISMUND VASA

These debates and negotiations with the Muscovite envoys, which could
lead nowhere, dragged on. Simultaneously the Austrian faction, that of
Górka and the Zborowskis, lost ground daily. People disliked the Habsburgs
as Germans and disapproved of the obvious propensity of their party's
leaders towards violence, towards breaking the deadlock swiftly by civil
strife. Archbishop Primate Karnkowski dealt the Austrian faction a sharp
blow when he defected openly to Zamoyski. The papal nuncio and others
of the Habsburg party, observing their declining fortunes, repeatedly
attempted to reconcile the Zborowskis with Zamoyski. To entice Zamoyski
from Sigismund they suggested a compromise guaranteeing that Maximilian
of Austria, once king of Poland, would marry Anna of Sweden, Sigismund's
sister. Zamoyski vacillated because of his own awkward situation. Despite
the fact that a strong majority of the aristocracy and the lesser nobility sided
with him, his monetary resources were dwindling. Victuals were extremely costly around Warsaw, which forced away from the Sejm those
lords and gentry who lacked sufficient personal resources. Thus Zamoyski's
material forces waned while the Zborowskis retained their mercenaries
with Austrian funds.

One night a perturbed Zamoyski brooded over his situation. He had no
cash to maintain his partisans. A degrading and desolate future would
follow the Austrian's election and the triumph of the Zborowskis, who
inevitably would continue to occupy the first place under Maximilian.
Suddenly Archbishop Primate Karnkowski burst in and announced that
they could delay no longer. He was ready to have Sigismund declared king.
Zamoyski concurred, and on August 19 (New Style) his followers elected
Sigismund. The party of the Zborowskis, unwilling to yield to its opponents, proclaimed Archduke Maximilian as king on August 22. Lithuania
participated in neither election. Contemporary observers remarked that
more than a few Poles judged both elections illegal.

Such disunity inspired the lords to send new deputations to the Muscovite ambassadors, announcing that Zamoyski and his comrades had elected Sigismund. Lithuania and a substantial part of Poland preferred the Muscovite tsar but could not proclaim him because the terms of his election remained unclear. Therefore the Muscovites must reply unequivocally. Would the tsar embrace the Roman faith? Could he arrive within ten weeks? How would he formulate his title, for the Polish crown must not be subordinate to the so-called tsar's cap? Would he furnish promptly one hundred thousand rubles for immediate defense? The Muscovite ambassadors replied that they had already given their final response to all these questions.

This exchange ended the affair in Poland but not in Lithuania, where the lords of the council advised the ambassadors "Zamoyski chose the Swedish prince, Górka and the Zborowskis have elected the emperor's brother but we, Lithuania and most of Poland, want your sovereign. The questions of the tsar's religion and delayed arrival hinder his cause. Were we certain that he would come speedily we, having elected him, instantly would appear before Cracow in our full array and bestow the crown on neither the Swede nor the emperor's brother, nor will we ever desire them. Now we are uncertain of your sovereign's arrival. Because of this and indeed because of religion we cannot elect him, still we have not elected the Swede or the emperor's brother. We have broken with this electoral diet and wish to nominate a new one. We cannot now draft a permanent peace with you because time grows short and we lords of the council are few, many having already departed. Let us arrange a truce."

The ambassadors agreed. A truce of fifteen years was concluded, each state remaining separate. After the pact was ratified Governors Krzysztof Radziwiłł of Wilno[71] and Jan Hlebowicz of Troki called upon the Muscovite ambassadors at their inn and addressed them confidentially, after dismissing their servants. "Within five weeks," they declared, "we Lithuanians will assemble in a general conference at Wilno, and those Poles who selected neither the Swede nor the emperor's brother will do likewise. We all wish to have your tsar as our sovereign. Should he not come to rule us, it shall only be because of his reluctance. Speed a courier to him now with word that if he desires to be our lord he must rush a messenger to Wilno with letters to the Lithuanian nobility and the whole Lithuanian land. Bid him laud them in these documents, thanking them for desiring him as sovereign and proposing his election, and asking that they continue to do so in the future. As to religion, he should write 'You should choose me as sovereign and must not waver over religion. I cannot forsake the

Greek faith for the Roman, and as soon as I am elected I will dispatch my ambassador to beg the Pope not to compel me to do so.' Have the sovereign write that he will arrive three months or somewhat later after they proclaim him. He must donate one hundred thousand rubles for our prompt defense. We will elect him simultaneously in both assemblies.

"Your sovereign must not advise us about the emperor's brother. Should he write about this, everyone will abandon him. We incline more toward the Swede. Among us no one even mentions the emperor's brother, for he is not a wealthy sovereign and indeed is encumbered with debt. His brother the emperor is also indebted, and renders tribute to the Turkish sultan. Once the emperor's brother was among us as king he will want to grow rich quickly and discharge his obligations, and we would have to pay dearly. He will have us carry arms against the Turk and squeeze us with taxes. He cannot supply his own military needs. Offering little enough to gain election, in reality he has nothing.

"There are other reasons we do not want the emperor's brother. The emperor has violated every law of those realms subject to him. He imposes a tribute upon them which cannot be collected. Among us it has been written that the German race harbors no good intentions toward the Slavic, how then can we accept a German monarch? Should the tsar not desire to rule us, let him suggest in the letters that we take a sovereign from our own nation, and that our Piasts[72] enjoy high regard. This will please our people greatly. We Lithuanians are also consulting among ourselves. If the Poles do not agree with us in the election of your sovereign, then we, Lithuania, Kiev, Volhynia, Podolia, Podliasie and Mazovia will want to secede from Poland. Will the tsar then take us in, rule Lithuania alone without Poland, and shield us with his might?"

RZHEVSKY'S SECOND MISSION

The nobleman Rzhevsky carried back to Lithuania the response to this vital question, along with luxurious gifts for each noble, worth twenty thousand of our current[73] rubles. "We wish to rule you," the tsar's statement advised the lords, "but we cannot come to you now because you have not chosen a single sovereign, and because many would have us do that which cannot be done, namely that we abjure our true Orthodox Christianity to accept the Roman creed. Reflect briefly yourselves how this could be. Later, if God permits and the moment is appropriate, we will come to you."

Rzhevsky had secret instructions to tell the lords. "Take our tsar as your sovereign and come under his mighty hand, and you shall rule the Polish crown and the grand principality of Lithuania by your own laws and liberties. Then when our tsar looks upon you and beholds your affection for him, and when you observe his benevolence towards you, he will come to you and be crowned at his pleasure and when it shall please him. He will assume the crown by the Greek rite. He cannot even consider conversion to the Roman faith. Now you will need money for your immediate defense. When you have approved our tsar he will provide up to seventy thousand Russian rubles and up to two hundred and thirty thousand Polish zlotys."

The Lithuanian lords reiterated that Fedor could not become king without embracing Roman Catholicism. "It was your sovereign," they told Rzhevsky, "who broke off this negotiation with the content of his letters. We have never crowned a king by the Greek rite. Even if we, the lords of the council, sanctioned this, the archbishops and bishops surely will disapprove, and you can see that they weigh heavily in our council. They believe staunchly that their king must adhere to the Roman creed, and no one can gainsay them. Your sovereign did not need to write that he must be crowned by the Greek rite."

Rzhevsky reported that the nobles accepted Fedor's gifts most gratefully, many making obeisance and vowing to serve him as their lord. Only Mikołaj Krzysztof Radziwiłł declined the sables, having declared that he had sworn not to accept presents from any monarch. Even after the Lithuanian lords dismissed Rzhevsky with an emphatic rejection of his proposals they quietly let him tarry in expectation of news from Poland. He was allowed to depart without delay only after they learned Sigismund was crowned.

SIGISMUND VASA AS KING OF POLAND

Lithuania's lords rightly procrastinated and awaited word from Poland because neither of the rivals, Sigismund or Maximilian, would submit without bloodshed. Maximilian approached Cracow but was compelled to withdraw after a futile attempt to seize it. Sigismund, unhindered, then entered the city for his coronation. Zamoyski pursued the retreating Maximilian and captured him after a costly battle near Byczyna in Silesia.[74]

Thus it seemed that Zamoyski's schemes, so fraught with misfortune for Moscow, had borne fruit, but he would experience the same destiny as Bathory, whose ambitions ran counter to the entire history of the nation he was summoned to govern. Zamoyski's aspirations contravened a great movement then sweeping Europe, and of course the fortunes of the celebrated chancellor and hetman soon were turned against him. Zamoyski hoped for the combination of two powerful realms, Poland and Sweden. "Even if Sigismund does not annex all Muscovy," he said, "at least he will seize Pskov and Smolensk, and Swedish warships will blockade the maritime route to the White Sea, thus inflicting grievous harm upon the Muscovite realm." The religious question, however, then ranked uppermost in Europe. Poland's new king, Sweden's heir apparent, seemingly destined to unite both kingdoms under one rule, resembled the Austrian Ferdinand II[75] in that he was fully a man of his times, an individual obsessed by the predominant interest of his era. Sigismund, an ardent Catholic, thirsted to have his religion prevail everywhere and at any price. All his actions stemmed naturally and necessarily from that stance which he, loyal to his convictions, took towards the paramount question of the times. As a fervent Catholic, he became a major figure in the Counter-Reformation. As such, he profoundly sympathized with that institution which sought the triumph of Catholicism over all other Christian confessions. He strongly supported the Jesuit order, and fell under its influence.

Being so like Ferdinand II and so unlike Henri IV of France,[76] Sigismund was uncompromising about religion. Having become king of Sweden, he would not have Protestantism triumph there. This cost him his paternal throne and, instead of unity, produced an intense struggle between Poland and Sweden. In the very same fashion, later he could not countenance his son Władysław's conversion to Russian Orthodoxy, thus compelling the inhabitants of the Muscovite realm to rise as one against the Poles.[77] He could not look indifferently upon dissidence in his Polish and Lithuanian territories, and his endorsement of the Uniate movement[78] paved the way for the secession of Little Russia. In his relations with his Western neighbors he was bound to regard favorably the Catholic aspirations of the Habsburgs, and therefore immediately made friends and allies of his former rivals. Thus all Zamoyski's hopes were dashed cruelly.

Moscow was quick to discern the collapse of Zamoyski's schemes and to cast aside that fear which the election of a Swedish prince to the Polish throne at first inspired. The clerk Andrei Ivanov,[79] dispatched to Lithuania for information, wrote that Sigismund was ill regarded because he lacked talent. He was considered unreasonable, and was unloved because the nation at large gained nothing from him, while the aristocrats dominated everything. It was essential to flatter these lords, especially the Lithuanians, as shown by Godunov's letter to the strongest, Governor Krzysztof Radziwiłł of Wilno. "You know, our esteemed brother," he wrote, "that I, when sitting in the privy council of our great sovereign, am always solicitous and with my brothers, the boyars, I act with wisdom and guide the tsar so that love may prevail between him and your sovereign. I have sent you a gift as a token of my affection, fine thin linen, a Persian product. Shah Abbas of Persia[80] sent me this from his own shoulders." Godunov then wrote that on Radziwiłł's behalf he had petitioned the tsar that Lithuanian merchants might trade without duties, and that thanks to him they would suffer no punishment[81] for having scuffled with crown officials.

RELATIONS WITH SWEDEN

It was vital for Moscow that Poland and Lithuania not cooperate with Sweden, against whom war was considered inevitable. The status of Livonia, ceded to Bathory under Ivan, was disputable, whereas the Swedes held towns that long were Russian. The honor of the realm demanded their recovery. Early in Fedor's reign, while Bathory still lived and a breach with Lithuania seemed imminent, war with Sweden was unthinkable. When the lord lieutenant of Estonia, the famous [Pontus] de la Gardie,[82] learned of the death of Ivan the Terrible he asked the governor of Novgorod, Prince Skopin-Shuisky, whether Moscow would respect the Truce of Pliussen concluded under the late tsar, and whether Muscovite diplomats would travel to Stockholm and seek a permanent peace.[83] De la Gardie also provided safe conducts for these ambassadors. The Muscovite administration resented the notion that its ambassadors travel to Stockholm as a great insult inasmuch as it was unaccustomed to practicing even equality of relations with Sweden. Moreover De la Gardie's correspondence misstated Fedor's title, and referred to King John as grand prince of the Izhora land and Shelon districts of Russia.[84]

After a long wait for a reply De la Gardie relayed a second message, again calling Muscovite representatives to Sweden. The deputy governor of Novgorod, Prince Lobanov-Rostovsky,[85] answered this letter. "You, a newcomer to the Swedish land," he wrote, "are unwitting of royal usages, of how your lord's father corresponded with the vicegerents of Novgorod. Our sovereign needs no safe conducts for ambassadors. This is unbecoming business, and I am returning the safe conduct with your courier. You wrote the tsar's title in an improper fashion because you have not lived under the sovereigns, and you do not know our ruler's title, by which to address him."

De la Gardie took offense at this response, resenting the fact that the deputy governor and not the senior governor of Novgorod answered him. "I have always been your equal," he wrote to Skopin-Shuisky, "if not your better." To Lobanov-Rostovsky he wrote "You are puffed up with your Great Russian mindless ignorance and pride. You would be well advised to desist, for you derive little benefit. Know that I have long resided in this most praiseworthy Swedish realm. I am not a foreigner, nor am I so called. You write that I was absent from my king's court for some time. This is true. I think that you, your sovereign, and his other subjects know this because I came upon your land with a Swedish army and made war upon it. Know that under no circumstances will my king send ambassadors to your sovereign until all things are resolved and confirmed at the border."

King John, in a letter to the tsar, personally demanded negotiations at the border. Even this royal document contained an insult for Fedor because the king could not forbear venting his hatred for Fedor's father. "Your father," he wrote, "ruled his land and his subjects mercilessly, with blood-shed. He was an evil and troubled neighbor." "We," responded Fedor, "ought not have granted leave to your messenger. Everywhere couriers bearing such censorious words are punished. We are a Christian sovereign, therefore at the pleas of our boyars and in our Christian clemency we did your courier no harm. We did not allow him into our presence because he came with a document in which was inscribed an unheard-of reproach to our father. You say that we should send our diplomats for a conference. The old traditions and the words brought by your courier make us loth to do so. Yet out of our customary benevolence and at the petition of our boyars, we have ordered our envoys to attend."

In October 1585 the boyar Prince Fedor Shestunov[86] and the conciliar noble Ignaty Tatishchev[87] met the Swedish dignitaries Claus Thott[88] and De la Gardie at the mouth of the Pliusa, near Narva. With no possibility of engaging in war, the Muscovite officials directed their representatives to avoid breaking the peace under any circumstances. They first were to demand the uncompensated return of the Russian towns and, failing that, offer fifteen thousand rubles to redeem Ivangorod, Yama, Koporie and Korela. Should the Swedes insist that the tsar write addressing the king as his brother they might concede even this only as a last resort. If the Swedes would not surrender Ivangorod the Muscovites could sign a peace without it, paying up to six thousand rubles for the other three towns.

The Swedes scorned the demand that they surrender the towns without compensation. "Who has ever heard of giving up towns for nothing? One parts with apples and pears, but not towns. Were we to let the towns go, we should sooner give them to the Lithuanian. He most humbly begged them from our king and will pay well for them. He wants to ratify eternal peace with us and stand as one against your sovereign. What is more, he is our king's relative by marriage." The Swedes asked four hundred thousand rubles for Yama and Koporie alone! They also were willing to trade lands, ceding Yama and Koporie, claiming in exchange either Oreshek or the land beyond the Neva and the trading settlement at Suma. They even offered money for a permanent peace agreement whereby Fedor acknowledged John as his brother as long as they retained the contested towns. This proposal caused the Muscovite envoys to reply "We are instructed to speak of the towns of Ivangorod, Yama, Koporie, and Korela, our sovereign's hereditary estates, which your sovereign wants to surrender to him. Our Christian sovereign wants to restore the monasteries and churches to their former condition to glorify God's name, for all these places now are ruined. Our ruler has established twelve towns in his patrimony, far away in the steppe, along the Don and beyond the Tikhaia Sosna, where he has erected monasteries and churches. These places were desolate for three or four centuries. Nor does our sovereign have need of your king's money. He has vast treasures even without your sovereign's money."

While the negotiations continued De la Gardie drowned while crossing the Narova river. When Shestunov and Tatishchev relayed the news to Moscow they received this response in the tsar's name. "You wrote us that Pontus de la Gardie has drowned. This is the work of the divine mercy and of the great and merciful Nicholas the Miracle Worker." Notwithstanding the death of the formidable De la Gardie, the envoys were allowed to offer up to fifteen thousand rubles for Ivangorod, Yama, and Koporie and, if pressed, to sign a treaty even without the towns. Under no circumstances were they to terminate the negotiations without a truce. Constrained to accept the final measure because they saw that the talks were inconclusive, in December 1585 the ambassadors signed a truce of four years with no concessions.

An abusive message renewed relations during the summer of 1589. King John complained to Fedor that Russians were encroaching upon Swedish territory, burning, robbing, beating and tormenting young and old. The tsar's subjects having thus violated the armistice the king had deployed his army in Livonia. If the tsar sought peace he must send his august ambassadors before St. Lawrence's Day [August 10]. Should Fedor not so desire, he was warned, the king could not keep his armies inactive before the truce expired. "Your message," replied the tsar, "reached us the eve of St. Lawrence, August 9. We heard your letter and marveled at your boundless vehemence. We ought not have communicated with you after your arrogant assertions but we are a great Christian sovereign and clemency is our wont, and we shall address you." After denying the accusation of Russian aggression and countercharging the Swedes with attacking Muscovite domains, the tsar continued "You have written that you will not await the expiry of the truce. Such haughty declarations ill become you. With us, with great rulers, with the most devout Russian tsars, it has always been that wherever our emissaries and envoys seal a pact by kissing the cross, or even where they merely utter a word, it is observed without fail. Should you make war before the term of the truce the blood will be on your head, and our armies stand vigilant against you. After your fervor and proud letters we ought not to correspond with you concerning your proposal about ambassadors. Yet we are a Christian sovereign, and at the entreaty of our boyars, and in order to prevent an outpouring of Christian blood, we have sent high ambassadors to confer at the Narova river, near to the confluence with the Pliusa."

These ambassadors were the lord-in-waiting Prince Khvorostinin and the treasurer Cheremisinov.[89] Their original instructions were to demand Narva, Ivangorod, Yama, Koporie and Korela in exchange for up to twenty thousand rubles and a treaty recognizing the king's status as *brother*. Without Narva they could pay only up to fifteen thousand. They might sign a permanent peace addressing the king as brother in return for only three of the towns, Yama, Koporie and Korela. If the Swedes offered only two towns, nothing could be settled without referring the proposal to the tsar. The ambassadors departed and even were engaged in preliminary conversations with the Swedes, trying to fix an opening date for the conference, when new orders arrived from Moscow. "Treat with the ambassadors in broad and lofty terms, but ultimately demand Narva, Ivangorod, Yama, Koporie and Korela without concession, without paying a penny. If they do not assent to these stipulations, take no initiative without consultation with the tsar. Should they agree, sign a permanent peace without recognizing the king as brother." Of course negotiations failed. The Swedish delegates declared that they would not yield even an inch of territory, let alone towns. "Why should our sovereign make peace with yours," the Russians retorted, "when he has not yet sought his patrimony, the towns of Livonia and the land of Novgorod. Your sovereign needs to surrender all the cities to us now, and be quick to pay what our sovereign asks."

This dramatic change in tone stemmed from the fact that Bathory had died. Although the son of the king of Sweden sat on the Polish throne relations with his subjects promised no tight bond between them and the Swedes. Moscow realized that Sigismund held his domains precariously. Lithuania at least might submit readily to Fedor. In his message to King John, Fedor threatened to form an alliance with Emperor Rudolph and the Persian shah, and candidly declared that the Lithuanians wished to become his subjects. "Your letter," John responded, "written in poor taste and with insolence, has reached us. We care not to reply further, and trust in divine providence. You write that you are expecting help from the emperor and other sovereigns. We rejoice that you are powerless and must seek the aid of others. Let us see what assistance they will afford you! You write that Lithuania wishes to come under your sway. An utter lie! We are sure that Lithuania will not deviate from its oath. Know that we both, I and my dear son, can pacify those of our subjects who betray us and take vengeance upon you for your swollen pride. Your father in his conceit refused to yield, and his lands passed into foreign hands. You covet our lands and towns. Try and seize them by force of arms, for you shall not take them with vanity and supercilious messages."

WAR WITH SWEDEN AND ITS AFTERMATH

Moscow resolved not to let pass an opportunity to reconquer the tsar's lost patrimony. In January 1590 a mighty Russian host advanced toward the Swedish borders. Fedor himself accompanied them. Prince Fedor Mstislavsky, the ranking boyar since his father's exile, commanded the Great Regiment.[90] Prince Dmitry Khvorostinin, considered to be the most talented officer,[91] led the vanguard. With the tsar rode Boris Godunov and Fedor Nikitich Romanov,[92] who bore the title of household or privy commanders. Yama was taken. Near Narva Khvorostinin routed an army of twenty thousand Swedes under Gustav Banér.[93] Despite an abortive and costly Russian assault on Narva the Swedes calculated that they could not continue the war fruitfully, and on February 25 signed a one-year truce. They relinquished Yama, Ivangorod and Koporie, while promising further concessions at a diplomatic conference.

This meeting proved inconclusive. The Swedes ceded the Korela region, but the Russians would accept no permanent peace without Narva. Although a new round of fighting terminated with an ineffectual Swedish

THE TSAR-CANNON, MOSCOW KREMLIN

Cast by Andrei Chokhov, 1586

siege of Ivangorod, Moscow elected not to launch a third campaign. The storming of Narva had illustrated that the investment of major fortresses promised no sure success. The temperament of the regent Godunov was such that he was not easily moved toward any venture which did not guarantee certain gain. Moreover despite Lithuania's profound reluctance to assist Sweden and renounce the truce with Moscow, it could not be assumed that Sigismund of Poland would long remain a tranquil spectator to Russian victories over his father. No danger was posed by Sweden, from which it was relatively easy to obtain what was wanted. Indeed not much was required, for the Muscovites already had secured what they must have wanted most, a victorious campaign. Sweden and Poland, and most significantly Lithuania, saw that Moscow was not decrepit, not hesitant to challenge the conquerors of Ivan the Terrible. The tsar, once called incompetent, led his own regiments. Hitherto Fedor's supporters in Poland and Lithuania could cite only the achievements of his domestic regime, now they could point to his military feats.

Given the confused state of Sigismund III's realm it was vital to strengthen Fedor's faction in Lithuania. Moscow learned that the Crimeans were raiding Lithuania and that Sigismund visited his father without returning to Poland. They decided to communicate with the Lithuanian lords in order to reintroduce the question of unification, and at the same time to gather information. Messages went from Prince Mstislavsky to Cardinal Radziwiłł, from Boris Godunov to Governor Radziwiłł of Wilno, and from Fedor Nikitich Romanov to Governor Jan Hlebowicz of Troki. The boyars warned the lords that the khan again wished to plunder Lithuania. He invited the tsar to follow his lead, which the tsar declined. Lithuania and Moscow, they argued, must unite against the infidel. This initiative led nowhere. The lords thanked Fedor for his benevolence toward them, and added that their intelligence from the Crimea blamed the tsar himself for inciting the khan against Lithuania.

Simultaneously the Muscovite administration had to deploy troops toward Czerniakow and seek satisfaction for an insult although the offense was given without the knowledge of the Polish-Lithuanian government. Even the stern Bathory was compelled to complain bitterly of the impertinence of the Dnieper Cossacks,[94] whom he called brigands. In 1585 they threw in the water his emissary Glebowicki, sent to dissuade them from bothering the Crimean khan and from violating existing agreements. Not surprisingly, the cossacks' insolence grew irrepressible after Bathory's death. Coming together from Kanev, Cherkassk and Pereiaslav, they appeared before Voronezh and proclaimed to the local commander that they were gathered to join the Don Cossacks against the Tatars. The commander trusted them, issued them supplies and posted them at a blockhouse near the settlement. Then that night the cossacks burned the town and killed many. Prince Ostrozski, governor of Kiev, responded to Moscow's subsequent complaint. "The lords of the council," he said, "ordered Prince Alexander Wiśniowiecki to arrest the Dnieper ataman Potrebatsky and his comrades who put the torch to Voronezh. The lords threatened Wiśniowiecki that should he not apprehend the cossacks he would pay with his head because they were causing the truce with the Muscovite sovereign to be broken. Wiśniowiecki caught Potrebatsky and seventy cossacks with him."

In the fall of 1590 Moscow heard that ambassadors from Sigismund, Stanisław Radomiński and Gabriel Wojna,[95] were on their way. Then from Smolensk came news of the ambassadors' odd conduct. They had lingered briefly in the city, and then turned back. Governor Trakhaniotov of Smolensk assigned the junior boyar *Andrei Dedevshin*[96] to tell them that such conduct was unprecedented. Envoys never left before reaching the tsar. Why did they?

The envoys explained their behavior thus. "Ambassadors from earlier kings of Lithuania have journeyed often to your sovereign, but no such indignity ever befell them. We were starved, given no provisions, and were quartered with the musketeers. We became prisoners, not ambassadors. The bailiffs dishonor us. We are going back. We want to cross swords with you over such an insult. We will fight our way out, and no man will reproach us. You will fight us, and in all lands it will be said that the Muscovites have mistreated ambassadors."

The governor did not permit them to return and forbade his junior boyars to combat them. The ambassadors broke the heads of two junior boyars with maces and when musketeers and cossacks rode up Radomiński and Wojna, observing their numbers, retreated. They did not go to the Bogdanov quarter outside the town, where lodgings were reserved for them, instead camped in tents on the meadow. They accepted no supplies from the official escorts, then sent their servants to commandeer around the villages. These men set fire to hedges and smashed mills. At Mozhaisk the local magistrates and the town chancellery official collected provisions for them.

Godunov, never missing a chance to strike a profitable pose and to curry favor with foreigners, shipped his private stores to Viazma, to his village of Nikolskoe. "You were forced to stay here at Viazma," he instructed a bailiff tell the ambassadors, "where the villages are off the road and the manor houses are shabby. The boyars' villages are not suitable for dignitaries. I have received a decree from the boyar and master of the horse bidding us to remain with you in his settlement at Viazma. He does this in hope of witnessing brotherly love between the two great sovereigns and to render honor to you, most exalted ambassadors."

Moscow's worst fears were materializing. The ambassadors maintained that the tsar had broken the truce when he seized Swedish cities, and must return them. The boyars responded that Fedor would not even listen to such immoderate speeches. They explained that the tsar, at the request of the Lithuanian lords, ordered his armies into the towns of Severia to aid the Poles against the Turks. The ambassadors rebutted that neither they nor the king knew anything about this. For about two months both sides discussed terms for a permanent peace. Sigismund's envoys first claimed Smolensk, and later requested at least some concession. "If your sovereign cedes a single village to us, would he not gain eventually?" "A village is a simple matter," replied the boyars. "We can hand over to our brothers village after village, out of love, but great sovereigns do not hold villages dear, rather they prize fame and honor. How can our lord let cities depart from his love and his union? He cannot concede either cities or villages."

Grave difficulties blocked agreement regarding permanent peace. Thereupon questions were addressed about Russia's relations with Sweden in order to find grounds for a truce. The Muscovite government wanted Narva from Sweden. Poland, having predicated Sigismund's election on the annexation of Estonia to Poland, absolutely precluded this. On January 1, 1591 Fedor convoked an assembly of the clergy, boyars, conciliar nobles and secretaries. He explained that Poland's ambassadors would confirm no truce without keeping Narva, and that Sweden had made no amends to the tsar. To invade Sweden now, lacking a treaty with Lithuania, would bring the Lithuanians to the aid of the Swedes. This would benefit neither the tsar nor the interest of the realm. The tsar and the assembly decreed that Narva must not appear in either truce document, neither the tsar's nor the king's. The boyars and the ambassadors were to draft articles prohibiting both sides from warring over the city or from having access to it until the tsar's ambassadors came to Sigismund and negotiated.

A truce with Poland for twelve years was concluded. The Polish ambassadors demanded further that the tsar refrain from hostilities with Sweden.

He consented to avoid war for one year. The tsar also agreed to leave undisturbed for the full twelve-year period those Livonian cities now in Swedish hands which the Swedes were transferring to the Polish crown, except Narva.

Finally the boyars told the ambassadors "It has been stated in the charters of the truce to deliver according to customary law the thief, the runaway, the serf, the slave and the debtor. Such has been written since time immemorial yet it is not observed. Neither party ever hands over runaways. Should this pledge now even be written in the charters?" "This is an old admonition that ought not be set aside," objected the ambassadors. "These, you know, are not fugitives who flee from sovereign to sovereign. These runaways who frequent the borderlands, dwelling along the frontier, are common brigands who have run away from both Polish and Russian gentry. Once across the line, they lurk nearby. Such men, when apprehended, are to be handed over."

Sigismund's diplomats stipulated that the tsar not war with the king of Sweden for a full year. Yet hardly were they out of Muscovite territory when John, anticipating an alliance with the Crimean khan, had his soldiers renew military operations. In the winter the Swedes burned villages near Yama and Koporie. In the summer an army marched against them. Peter Nikitich Sheremetev[97] led the main army group and Prince Vladimir Timofeevich Dolgoruky the vanguard.[98] The vanguard was defeated, and Dolgoruky taken prisoner. For their part the Swedes attacked the White Sea coast, but here they failed.

Meanwhile Saltykov[99] and Tatishchev,[100] the Muscovite high ambassadors, traveled to Lithuania to receive Sigismund's confirmation of the truce. Muscovy dreaded above all the prospect of simultaneous hostilities with Sweden and Poland, and instructed its envoys accordingly. They were to speak plainly and not to bicker with the escorting bailiffs about provisions. They were to point out that despite the misconduct of the Polish ambassadors at Smolensk Fedor listened to their complaints. For Sigismund's sake he imprisoned the bailiffs and dismissed and punished the governor on the basis of the accusations of the Polish envoys. The instructions specified that the diplomats must observe carefully how the king kissed the cross. He must kiss it above both copies of the treaty, resting his lips squarely upon the cross and not at its base, not passing the cross with his lips, and not kissing it with his nose. "Should they press to have Narva ascribed to the king," a secret directive advised, "pay up to twenty or thirty thousand for Narva if you must. Most grudgingly give for Narva up to fifty thousand in Hungarian gold, so long as you confirm the truce and acquire Narva for the tsar. If absolutely compelled, concede that the tsar will not wage war for Narva during the entire twelve years of the truce."

The ambassadors carried two extra safe conducts in the event any prominent individuals wished to desert Poland or Lithuania for the tsar. "When you are ours," said these documents, "we shall favor you with our generous bounty. We shall set aside for you a patrimony, a military service estate, and a suitable salary entitlement." Another safe conduct was reserved for a physician willing to come to treat the sovereign. It included the same promise, but also guaranteed freedom to return at will. Finally, the ambassadors had orders to complain about the Little Russian cossacks (Cherkassians)[101] who beat and abducted Muscovite residents of cossack settlements and captains of patrols in the steppe, hampering them from keeping watch for Crimean raiders.

Saltykov and Tatishchev encountered an inauspicious reception. They were detained on the road. Hoping to learn the cause of the delay they plied with drink a Polish noble, Prince Lukomski. He revealed why they were being delayed. The king was staying in Cracow, among the bellicose Poles. Lithuania's aristocracy and lesser nobility, eager for peace, desired the ambassadors to call upon the king in Lithuania, not Poland. From Warsaw the ambassadors reported to the tsar that the king sought some cause to abrogate the truce with Moscow for the sake of his father, the Swedish king. Under most heavy pressure they were forced to accept reluctantly an article in the truce banning Muscovite operations against Narva for the entire twelve years of the truce. Saltykov and Tatishchev insisted that the king first ratify the truce and afterwards consider the other matters left unresolved in Moscow. The lords of the council refused. "We know why you want this," they protested. "You would deceive us, as you trick foolish little birds. Having snared one, you then will trap them all. We are telling you that unless we resolve every controversy left unsettled our sovereign will not sign the truce or kiss the cross." The lords would consent to address Fedor as tsar only after he surrendered Smolensk and the towns of Severia. They spurned a monetary settlement for Narva. "These are not wares. Rulers do not sell great cities. Look, your sovereign holds Pskov and Smolensk. If only you would sell them we would collect a great sum from our realm, and pay it for Pskov and Smolensk."

PEACE WITH SWEDEN

Muscovy's government was obligated not to act against Narva. This did not stop it from taking revenge on the Swedes by devastating Finland around Vyborg and Åbo in the winter of 1592. King John died in November of that year. Sigismund began to wear the Swedish crown, although not for long. During his brief sojourn in Sweden for the coronation he angered the entire nation by his frank animosity toward Protestantism and flagrant disregard for the concessions the estates imposed upon him before the coronation. When Sigismund returned to Poland he left as ruler of Sweden his uncle Karl,[102] who gained the affection of the people by conduct contrary to Sigismund's. The king cooled to the interests of Protestant Sweden, so openly antagonistic to him. The ruler grew occupied with domestic affairs preparatory to a breach with his nephew. This of course drove both men to seek a most expeditious peace with Muscovy. As early as January 1593 a two-year truce was concluded. Each country was to retain what it then held.

Muscovite envoys sent to Lithuania assured the tsar that Sigismund inspired no fear despite the fact that he was nominal king of Sweden. Ambassador Riazanov, who visited the Polish court in 1592, reported that Sigismund was disliked for marrying an Austrian archduchess[103] and for being unlucky. The moment his reign began there was widespread famine and plague. He might have been dethroned and replaced by the tsar had the lords not feared that Fedor would reclaim the royal cities from them. Moreover, the minor nobility, who now served them, might shift their allegiance when all of them came to serve the tsar. When the royal ambassador Chreptowicz demanded that the tsar return to Sigismund the towns taken from the Swedes, the boyars answered "You will create a river of blood through your extravagant and unbridled speeches. We will go to the tsar although there is no use for him to hear your words. You speak in vain. It was fruitless for you even to come here with this." Chreptowicz then announced that he was empowered to draft an agreement fixing a boundary with Sweden, valid for as long as the truce with Poland lasted. Fedor advised Sigismund, however, that he would honor the pact with Sweden only for the term specified in 1593, that is for two years.

Before this time expired, late in 1594, the Swedish ambassadors, Sten Banér,[104] Horn[105] and Boije[106] met the Muscovites, Princes Turenin[107] and Pushkin,[108] at Täysinä, near Ivangorod, on Russian soil. The meeting began with a written exchange of positions. The Swedes threatened with the fact that they and the Poles now shared a common monarch. "Although," replied Turenin, "the Polish crown and the Swedish kingdom unite, we are not afraid. You should not write about this with threats." The Swedish delegates again claimed the cities Fedor had conquered recently. The Russians admonished them to cease such improper speech, which could only cause much suffering, and seek within themselves the means for a good deed. At first the Russians wanted Narva and Korela, later they limited their requirements to Korela. When the Swedes referred to the very costly and extensive fortifications they had constructed in Korela, the Muscovites commented "Who made you take unjustly another's land, and then fortify it as well? How much of another's can one not hold, and even if building with gold then surrendering with blood, still profit?" The Swedes requested payment for Korela and demanded the razing of Ivangorod. "Many were the savage words about Korela uttered on both sides." Finally the Swedes abandoned the city without compensation.

The talks then turned to trade. "God created man absolute," argued the Muscovite diplomats, "and made him free to roam wherever he pleases, by land and by sea. You should not resist God's will. You are wrong to delay and to detain, by land and sea, wealthy merchants and other traders from the maritime and German states." "We will not let tradesmen carry their wares past Reval and Vyborg to Ivangorod and Narva," replied the Swedish envoys, "because it is our sea, and we have complete jurisdiction over it." Finally they compromised. Foreign merchants might use the moorings at Vyborg and Reval only. Only Swedish subjects might enter Narva, where the market would stand on the Narva and not the Ivangorod side. There was to be free trade between the inhabitants of both realms. Muscovite ambassadors were to enjoy unimpeded passage through Swedish territories to other countries, and the envoys of other states, to Moscow. The Swedes were to let pass without hindrance foreign merchants bringing to the tsar products of value to his treasury. Likewise they must give free passage to doctors and physicians, contract servitors and artisans traveling to the tsar. Both sides must liberate prisoners without exchange or ransom, save captives desiring to stay voluntarily. The Russians were allowed to send agents into Swedish territory to search out captured Russians. The king would gather tribute from the eastern side (East Bothnia) towards Varanger, while the tsar would take it from the Lapps who lived towards the Dvina and in Karelia towards the town of Kola. A permanent peace was concluded on these terms on May 18, 1595.

Relations with Sigismund as king of Poland were insignificant. The Muscovite government, cognizant of the profound dissatisfaction with him in Poland, judged it necessary to exacerbate this feeling by pointing out to the lords the humiliation the king inflicted upon their lands. Thus a Muscovite courier told them in 1594 "Our august lord and all the boyars marvel exceedingly at how King Sigismund institutes such improper practices, inscribing in his title beneath the kingdom of Sweden such illustrious domains as the Polish crown and the grand principality of Lithuania. Everyone knows how much greater than the Swedish realm are Poland and Lithuania which are from ancient times the peers of famed kingdoms, and the Swedish land insignificant. At first it gave allegiance to the Danish king and was under regents, not kings.[109] Although kings rule it of late earlier rulers corresponded merely with the boyars and vicegerents of Novgorod. The boyars hold that King Sigismund wrote his title in this way without the advice of the Polish lords of the council, at the instigation of his Swedish counselors. You personally have known the deceits of the Swedish foreigners. Their lies are manifest to the entire universe."

III

RELATIONS WITH OTHER FOREIGN POWERS

AUSTRIA

As previously, Polish issues formed the basis of relations between the Muscovite and the Austrian courts. Luka Novosiltsev, dispatched to Emperor Rudolph to announce Fedor's accession, reported that dignitaries at the court had sought him out and argued privately that their most honorable sovereigns should share what was in their hearts. When the truce with King Stefan expired the tsar should consult his brother Emperor Rudolph. They would join forces against Stefan because he did not reign over his native land[1] whereas they, Austria's emperor and Muscovy's tsar, ruled by hereditary right, and therefore enjoy the prerogative of partitioning his realm. After Bathory died, Rudolph's brother Archduke Maximilian sent a courier to Moscow requesting that Fedor either pursue the throne personally or endorse Maximilian's candidacy. He wrote to Godunov about this, addressing him as dearest and most beloved, first among the tsar's friends, chief privy councilor and regent. Maximilian likewise invoked the aid of the conciliar secretaries the Shchelkalovs, whom he called chosen and esteemed.

In January 1588 the tsar *with the boyars* decided to have a messenger ride to Rudolph and Maximilian with proposals concerning the situation in Lithuania. These documents observed that the Polish crown and the grand principality of Lithuania lacked a monarch, and urged collaboration to assure that these countries not slip through the hands of the great sovereigns into those of another. The courier was to cross Lithuania, concealing papers relevant to his central mission and carry openly others referring to Persian relations, tradesmen and contraband. The reports concerning Persia revealed that the shah had asked the tsar, Emperor Rudolph and the kings of Spain and France to ally with him against all enemies. They indicated that the tsar eagerly pursued a firm alliance with Persia. Regarding merchants and contraband, Fedor wrote "For many years, under our grandfather and our father, tradesmen from every German land frequented Pskov, Novgorod and Narva with sundry wares. They brought us products useful to our armies, such as copper, tin, lead, sulfur and saltpeter. They trafficked with our wholesale merchants in all goods, without exception, and both sides sought profit, but when upon my father's death I reminded you of this, you answered that your ancestors Charles V and Ferdinand [I], upon the petition and counsel of the electors and princes, banned the export from the Holy Roman empire of war materials, and that you could not alter this without the advice of the electors and princes. It amazed us mightily that in bygone years tradesmen exchanged all wares, sparing none, yet now, by your law, your tradesmen will not export to us products needed for warfare."

The courier reported from Smolensk that he encountered the tsar's emissary Rzhevsky, who informed him that the son of the Swedish king now occupied Cracow, where a few lords placed him on the throne. Sigismund had yet to consolidate his position throughout Poland, and the emperor's brother had invaded the country with a large army. The courier was ordered to continue his journey. Nevertheless, fear that he would be barred from crossing Lithuania led to the dispatch of a second secret letter to Rudolph by way of Riga with the foreigner Lukash Pavlusov,[2] a third with a Muscovite merchant Timokha Vykhodets, also through Riga or another suitable route, and a fourth with the courier Zagriazsky. The Russian messengers turned back from the Lithuanian frontier at the news that Sigismund had secured Poland and that Zamoyski had defeated and captured Maximilian. Timokha Vykhodets was intercepted and jailed at Riga, but the message carried by the foreigner Lukash got through.

WARKOTSCH'S FIRST MISSION

The emperor replied through his ambassador Nicholas Warkotsch.[3] His adventures on the road are recounted in a report to the tsar submitted by Lukash Pavlusov, who returned with him. "When we entered the town of Stettin in Pomerania we found a certain tradesman called Kron, with whom we made secret arrangements to conduct us across the German land (Livonia). We traveled separately so as not to be detected. In merchant's garb, with only his servant, me and Kron, the emperor's ambassador traversed the Prussian land. When we were near the Muscovite frontier at Livonian Novgorodok [Neuhausen] we heard of a warrant against us. Patrols blocked every road. A great fear beset us. We did not know where to turn. We dared not ride on or turn back. Resting our faith in God, heedless of our lives, we sallied forth to meet death. We took up muskets, matchlocks and cutlasses, and forced our way past the frontier post near Neuhausen. Behind us came a hot pursuit, a hue and cry, an extraordinary clamor, the tolling of the city bells. They hoped to overtake us, but by God's mercy we escaped. The prefect of Neuhausen pursued us with fifteen horsemen for three versts, as far as the Pechora, but God bore us to safety."

Warkotsch conveyed the gratitude of the emperor and the entire house of Austria for Fedor's diligent support of Maximilian at the electoral Sejm. He then asked what support the emperor might expect from Fedor in a war against Poland and Turkey. Warkotsch equivocated about contraband, saying that the emperor favored free trade. Merchants from the Holy Roman empire should journey unconstrained to the Russian lands, and Russian tradesmen travel to the German empire. The ambassador also relayed messages to Godunov, who received him like a tsar. Seated, Boris beckoned him to his hand, entertained him with wine and mead, and posted men at his inn with special provisions instead of the usual repast. In the emperor's name Warkotsch rendered homage to Godunov for his efforts at allying the tsar with Rudolph, and asked that Boris labor even harder for this goal. Boris, he declared, was held in great repute, honor and glory by both the emperor and the Spanish king on account of his worthy deeds. He would never lack their affection. Godunov reported all this and Fedor ruled *with the boyars* that the boyar and master of the horse Boris Fedorovich Godunov now and henceforth be empowered to write in person to the Holy Roman emperor and his brother Maximilian. It exalted the tsar's honor to have his master of the horse and privy boyar communicate with great sovereigns. Indeed, when any sovereign chose to correspond with Boris Godunov, the documents containing Boris's replies were drafted at the Chancellery for Foreign Affairs, along with other official papers.

Warkotsch's speeches were answered in the tsar's name. "The sovereign desires his dearest brother Emperor Rudolph, having conferred and allied with the Roman Pope, the king of Spain and all the Christian rulers of the maritime lands, to join fast with him against the Turk. The Persian shah also solicits the sovereign's fraternal affection, and would league with him against the Turk. When the shah's diplomats come here and all has been negotiated the tsar will convey the details to his imperial majesty. You have spoken of Maximilian, that we might aid him in his quest for the crown of Poland. That is why the sovereign's delegates have not signed a permanent agreement or a long armistice with Poland, to incline the lords to elect Maximilian."

"Sire, I have accepted your bounty," wrote Godunov to the emperor, "and have heeded your address with loving submission. I have praised you, great lord, before our sovereign, before many Tatar rulers and princelings, before rulers' sons of many lands under our tsar's sway, before boyars, princes and diverse servicemen, saying that you, lord, have favored me with your splendid benevolence and endearment, have sent me your letter. Hereafter I hope to sing your praises, mighty sovereign. In the past I have shown concern for your interests, now I am even more solicitous, and I will be even more industrious and zealous for you in the future." To Maximilian, who sent him a letter and the gift of a clock, Godunov replied "I have received your present humbly, with deep affection, and for it I prostrate myself before your highness. Henceforth, great lord, I shall extol you and shall render homage to your excellency. Take my small offering, forty sables."[4]

Warkotsch was sent back on the high seas, through the new town of Kholmogory (Archangel). The escorting bailiff had instructions to arrange his passage to Hamburg on ships of Ivan Beloborod[5] without fail, within three or four days, lest the English merchants traveling from Vologda discover the emperor's agents at Kholmogory. If English vessels arrived earlier than those of Ivan Beloborod, Warkotsch was to hide at Beloborod's establishment. When his ships arrived, Warkotsch must depart secretly, at night or early in the morning.

In the summer of 1590 Maximilian informed Fedor that he was freed from captivity on condition that he renounce the Polish crown. To add to the insult, the emperor and Sigismund arranged his liberation against his wishes. Now he sought vengeance in war against the Poles. Because this war required large sums of money, he asked the tsar for a subsidy. Maximilian sought funds for his war with Poland and in 1591 Warkotsch also invoked the tsar's largesse because he was giving his daughter in marriage. In addition Warkotsch asked the tsar to take into his service Count Shkot, a member of a renowned Italian family who was uniquely accomplished in all the principal arts. "You bother me with such trifles," responded Godunov, "but fail to mention the crucial matter initiated between our ruler and yours. Our sovereign, relying upon alliance with Emperor Rudolph, heeded your words, shunned relations with the Turkish sultan and the Crimean khan and refused to find a permanent peace with the king of Lithuania. Now rumors reach us that Emperor Rudolph is bargaining with the Turkish sultan over a truce, and with the Lithuanian king about a permanent peace and a marriage alliance. I am greatly astounded how such a noble cause, beneficial to all Christianity,[6] was undertaken and forsaken. As to your words concerning Shkot, this knightly and outstanding man deserves to be in attendance on our sovereign, but it is inopportune for him to come now. When it is time I will write to you. I am shipping to you in love forty sables for your daughter's wedding. I am presenting the same to Count Shkot. Please give them to him."

WARKOTSCH'S SECOND MISSION

The *noble cause of benefit to all Christianity* existed merely in words and on paper. Austria turned to the Muscovite court only when in need of assistance, when Maximilian required help in gaining the Polish throne, when Rudolph sought aid against the Turk.[7] In the fall of 1593 Moscow learned of the dispatch of yet another embassy[8] headed by the same Warkotsch. The Muscovite government felt sharp anxiety about foreign affairs at this time because of the death of King John of Sweden, the Polish king's subsequent inheritance of the Swedish throne, Sigismund's family ties with the Habsburgs, and Turkish affairs. The bailiff assigned to meet the ambassador had orders to seek answers to several questions. To what extent were Rudolph and his brother Maximilian favorably disposed towards Sigismund? Why did the emperor marry his niece to Sigismund? What rumors were heard about Sigismund? Would he return to Poland or reside in his Swedish kingdom? Should he no longer remain in Poland, who would be chosen as king of Poland? How were the emperor's current dealings with the Turks? Did he ship them large presents[9] as in the past?

Warkotsch declared that the emperor anticipated heartfelt love and cooperation from his dearest brother the sovereign tsar. They were now strong monarchs, potent, the hope of all Christendom, and the whole world observed them. The infidel Turks and Tatars, filled with nefarious designs to trample all Christendom, opposed them, the great sovereigns. Now all Christian rulers must extend their arms in fraternal love and close ranks against the oppressors of Christians. The emperor was striving for peace between the tsar and Sigismund, king of Poland and Sweden. He entreated his majesty the tsar to let his most illustrious excellency offer brotherly aid, reach out his arm to defend his imperial majesty and all Christendom. Let him express his notion of how to proceed against Islam.

Meeting in confidence with Godunov, Warkotsch asked Fedor to ward off the Crimean Tatars, preventing them from riding with the Turks into Hungary, and also to convince the Persian shah not to make peace with the Turks. Sigismund, he maintained, wished to rule Sweden, not Poland, because the Polish and the Lithuanian lords of the council were headstrong men. They did as they pleased, ignored the king, failed to support him, and left him no freedom. He was kept like a prisoner, not like a monarch. Chancellor Jan Zamoyski was plotting to transfer the throne to Bathory's brother whom he would summon to Cracow the moment he heard of Sigismund's abdication. The ambassador also noted that the downstream (Zaporozhian) cossacks had sworn fealty to the emperor. They wanted to ride into Hungary and fight there against the Turks.[10] Rudolph instructed Warkotsch ask Godunov if these cossacks obeyed Fedor loyally and faithfully, and lived peaceably along the frontier. If they did not anger the tsar in any way, served honestly and did not quarrel with the tsar's men, the emperor intended to enlist them and employ them against the Turk. Godunov promised to implore Fedor to join Rudolph against the enemies of the Christian faith and offer him every assistance.

Warkotsch then asked permission to confer with the Persian ambassador Azi-Khozrev, who happened to be in Moscow. The tsar allowed the imperial ambassador and the Persian to circulate among the nobles, urging them to elicit discussions about an alliance against the Turks. Warkotsch

sent a nobleman to inform Azi-Khozrev of Rudolph's eagerness to ally
with the shah, whose emissaries could reach the emperor through the tsar's
domains. "Shah Abbas sent me here," replied Azi-Khozrev, "with a special prayer that the great sovereign tsar receive him with love, and that they
stand together against his own and the shah's foes. The shah places his
entire hopes upon the tsar's brother-in-law Boris Fedorovich Godunov, for
he is most wise and just. He works for any worthy cause among rulers. His
name and his glory shine in all the Eastern and Southern lands. Should I
reach his majesty the shah in good health I will relate to our sovereign
everything, and our sovereign will rejoice greatly. If three mighty monarchs unite and stand against the Turk, the Turk will not last out the hour."

After these conversations Warkotsch was advised that the tsar was
prepared to ally with the emperor. First, however, Fedor must know when
Emperor Rudolph meant to strike against the Turks, and who would be his
other allies. Would the Pope, the king of Spain, the king of Denmark, the
doge of Venice and the other maritime sovereigns cooperate with the
emperor? Had Rudolph corresponded with the king of Lithuania concerning an alliance? Fedor, for the sake of his brother Rudolph and at the behest
of his brother-in-law Boris Godunov, had couriers hastening to warn the
Crimean khan not to participate in a Turkish campaign in Hungary. He was
prevailing upon the Persian shah not to make peace with the Turks. As to
the ambassador's private conversations with Boris about King Sigismund,
Emperor Rudolph above all must strive to gain Poland for his brother
Maximilian. The tsar would assist this cause in every possible way.

Warkotsch replied that the emperor, the Pope and the king of Spain had
confirmed a mutual agreement against the Turk[11] and entrusted the matter
to Rudolph, who had yet to communicate with the other monarchs. The
Danish king was young. His advisers recommended that he remain at
peace. Rudolph did not write to Sigismund because the Polish lords
constantly disagreed with their king and ignored him completely.

"You were here before," the boyars commented, "and the tsar gave you
leave with the message that the emperor, having taken counsel with other
rulers, dispatch illustrious emissaries here for a binding agreement, and
that the Spanish and papal ambassadors accompany the emperor's representatives. Did you report this to the emperor?" "I did," Warkotsch replied,
"but the dispatch of ambassadors was delayed because war started between
Spain, England and the king of Navarre (Henri IV).[12] The English queen
kept sharp watch on the sea routes, that none might sail from the emperor
to the tsar."

The tsar would do well, Warkotsch went on, to return ambassadors with him to the emperor for final conferences and negotiations with Spanish and papal diplomats in attendance. For the boyars, this was out of the question. "Such a policy cannot be accepted," they declared. "The great sovereign cannot send his envoys to the emperor in advance." "As the tsar wishes," replied Warkotsch. "I merely suggested this and will say no more."

Finally Warkotsch divulged the essential purpose of his embassy. "You told me," he said to the boyars, "that the great sovereign wishes to be in brotherly love with Emperor Rudolph and aid him against any foe. Our emperor now asks your sovereign that should the Turkish sultan, that oppressor of Christians, violate the armistice and attack our sovereign, will the tsar see fit to sustain Emperor Rudolph from his treasury with sables, martens and other pelts? Our sovereign will use them to hire soldiers and will vie with the Turk while other Christian rulers unite." The boyars answered that Fedor would support Rudolph with his treasury, and not leave him defenseless against the Turks.

Austria's situation was so difficult that it felt constrained to seek the Muscovite sovereign's subsidy for a war against the Turks. Yet it could not forsake ambitious projects, and attempted to guarantee beforehand quite unjustifiable annexations. "Emperor Rudolph," Warkotsch told the boyars, "charged me to tell your sovereign in secret that he wants to annex Liffland, to take it under his imperial sway, wresting it from Lithuania and Sweden. Our sovereign wishes to ask whether it will please your sovereign that the emperor bring Liffland under his rule?" The boyars replied that the tsar would concede Liffland, except Dorpat and Narva with their respective environs, out of brotherly love for Rudolph.

The Austrian court, seeking relief from every quarter against the Turks, turned its attention to the cossacks and asked the Muscovite boyars about them. Moscow lacked interest in the Ukrainian Cherkassians of the Dnieper,[13] but felt obliged to characterize them for Warkotsch in its sincere desire for Rudolph's victory over the menacing Turks. The cossacks, according to this appraisal, excelled at pillage, the devastation of hostile lands and quick raids. Offsetting this, they were an indomitable, cruel and fickle people. Although they could bear hunger better than other troops, they could not be entrusted with fortresses. It would be better to turn them loose to forage for themselves on enemy soil.

The Polish nobleman Stanisław Chłopicki[14] undertook recruiting an eight or ten thousand-man detachment of cossacks for imperial service. He appeared in Moscow in 1594 with a charter from Rudolph addressed simultaneously to Fedor, to Hospodar Aaron of Wallachia, Prince Zbarażski, governor of Bracław,[15] and to all the most gallant and daring knights living in the Dnieper Cossack host. The emperor requested that Chłopicki and his force receive favorable treatment and free passage. The cossacks, in the document's words, must lie in ambush for the Crimeans along every road, and thereby prevent them from aiding the Turks. They were also to ride against the Ottoman realm and ravage it. These instructions illustrated how well the Austrians benefited from Moscow's commentary on the cossack temperament. Chłopicki personally observed that he came to Moscow because the Dnieper Cossacks long served the tsar and dared not take the field without his knowledge. He proposed that Fedor, having added his own men to the cossack force, send forth the entire army under his banner and subsidize it from his treasury. The enemies of the cross of Christ would lose heart once they heard of such a legion led by his majesty the tsar. Besides seeking money from the tsar, this petition could have concealed a ruse aimed at embroiling Moscow in a war with Turkey, and thus diverting Turkish forces from Austria.

Fedor ruled that Chłopicki did not merit an audience because his document simultaneously invoked both the tsar and Prince Zbarażski. It was improper to address both the tsar and a Lithuanian "slave" in the same letter. Chłopicki deserved severe punishment yet for Rudolph's sake the tsar spared him and discharged him to the emperor. As for Rudolph's instructions pertaining to the Dnieper Cossacks, Chłopicki was assured that their hetman Bogdan Mikoshinsky was charged to assist the emperor.

WARKOTSCH'S THIRD MISSION

Late in 1594 Warkotsch reached Moscow a third time, coming to remind Fedor of his vow to assist the emperor. "If you want to help," he said, "help now, for the Turk is upon us with all his might." "The emperor," Warkotsch told Godunov, "has bestowed upon you the tokens of fondness which he presents to his brothers and to the electors: two golden chains, one with the imperial person (a portrait) and a gilded clock showing the planets. His imperial majesty, my sovereign, implores your illustrious excellency to display pity, to lament the shedding of Christian blood, and to petition his majesty the tsar. Let him pour out his treasury, with which the Lord God has endowed him so abundantly. Have him transport it with haste, for now is the time. God will bless you and your children with many pleasures and joys in this world and with eternal reward in the next. You shall enjoy great and lasting fame among all monarchs and all Christian people."

The boyars had Warkotsch told that Fedor sorrowed for Christianity, and was heeding the request and petition of his brother-in-law Boris Godunov. Out of love for Emperor Rudolph he was shipping soft goods, sables and other furs from his treasury for use against the Turkish sultan, the foe of all Christians. He would dispatch emissaries to accompany this treasure. Having heard this, Warkotsch bowed deeply and said "This will overjoy our sovereign, all Christian rulers, and all Christendom. The emperor personally, with his lands and possessions, will serve and will render gratitude for this. This came to pass by the intercession, zeal and labors of the tsar's brother-in-law Boris Godunov. His imperial majesty will repay his most illustrious excellency with every example of love, sparing naught."

We do not know to what extent Godunov's ambition influenced the decision to aid the emperor from the treasury. Boris was enticed by the blandishments of the emperor and his ambassadors, by the prospect of winning the gratitude of the paramount ruler of Christian Europe. Very possibly Godunov's aspirations played a vital role in this affair, yet it must be noted how easily Boris could justify his conduct in his own eyes and in those of others. Upon Bathory's death and thereafter, as it became obvious that Sigismund's election in Poland lacked those consequences feared earlier, Moscow came to dread Turkish power above all. To provide the Austrian house with indirect support against the Turk might have been judged a wise policy.

Warkotsch assured Godunov of the emperor's gratitude and of his willingness to stop at nothing in demonstrating it. In this sense the bailiff assigned to the ambassador was ordered to chat casually with him. "The tsar's brother-in-law Boris Fedorovich," he was to say, "owns horses befitting his illustrious ancestry and bravery from many kingdoms, yet he lacks the full-bodied ones from the imperial domain which should prove useful under his saddle. Should the emperor see fit to ship fine horses to Boris Fedorovich, he will find much pleasure in them."

In April 1595 the conciliar noble Veliaminov[16] and the crown secretary Vlasiev[17] delivered Moscow's subsidy for Austria's use against the Turk. They transported the pelts of sables, martens, foxes, squirrels, beavers, and wolves, as well as chamois leather, valued at 44,720 rubles. When they reached Prague, where Rudolph was residing, Veliaminov and Vlasiev required a place to exhibit the furs. They were allotted twenty rooms in the imperial palace where they displayed pelts of sable, marten, fox, beaver and wolf, leaving the squirrel skins in boxes. When all was ready the emperor and his privy councilors came to inspect the shipment. Rudolph was delighted at the tsar's generosity and wondered how such an impressive treasure was collected. He commented that previous emperors and their advisers never beheld so lavish a stock of furs, such precious sables and foxes, and he asked the envoys what country such beasts inhabited. They answered that these animals roamed the tsar's domains, Konda and Pechora, Ugra and the Siberian kingdom, near the mighty Ob river, over five thousand versts from Moscow. The following day the imperial advisers requested that Fedor's expert sable handlers fix a market price for the furs. "We were sent to his imperial majesty on a mission of love and friendship," replied the ambassadors, "with the tsar's subsidy, and not in order to evaluate the sovereign's treasure. We lack experience or knowledge at such appraisals. The sable handlers accompanied us as skilled porters and do not trade in such rich goods." The ambassadors were told later that Rudolph had merchants from Prague evaluate the shipment. They estimated its value at four hundred thousand rubles, and could not fix a price for the three superior grades of sable, because of their outstanding and rare quality.

ABRAHAM VON DONAU'S MISSION

In the spring of 1597 the distinguished imperial ambassador Burgrave Abraham von Donau rode to Moscow with presents for the tsar: relics of St. Nicholas the Miracle Worker[18] in a gold and silver jeweled reliquary; two enclosed sleighs with fittings, each with six sledge horses, six gray and six bay; a clock divided into quarter hours, with men bearing trumpets, Jews' harps, kettledrums and tambourines which, when the quarter hour struck, played as though they were alive; another clock divided by quarter hours which chimed various tones when it struck the quarter hour; two crystal drinking vessels decorated with gold.

Having thanked Fedor for the shipment of furs, Abraham declared that they rested in the imperial storehouse, as yet to be exchanged for money, and requested that in the future the tsar provide silver and gold. He asked how much more Fedor would send, and when. "Our sovereign," he told Godunov, "bade you to beg that your great sovereign shield him from the Crimean Tatar khan, lest he fall upon the Hungarian land." "The great sovereign," Godunov replied artfully, "has many soldiers. He can safeguard Emperor Rudolph from enemies only when the king of Poland allows our host to cross Lithuanian and Polish territories along the Dnieper river. Then the sovereign would launch his coastal forces against the Crimean and unleash his cavalry from the Severian land. Where might the Crimean flee from such a host? The khan would not last out the hour." Rudolph presented gifts to Godunov: a twin-bowled silver goblet, gilded and set with pearls; an upright striking clock with astrological signs; two stallions with velvet horse blankets; two parrots. Boris's son Fedor received an upright striking clock with a bear, four parrots, and two monkeys attached to it.

The keeper of the seal and crown secretary of the Chancellery for Foreign Affairs, Vasily Yakovlevich Shchelkalov, was charged to deal with the ambassador. Shchelkalov opened the talks by recalling that the emperor more than once proposed an alliance with the tsar, and pledged to appoint high ambassadors to conclude it. "Now the emperor has dispatched you," continued Shchelkalov, "a man of highest rank. Speak, then, how did the emperor instruct you about sealing an alliance?"

Abraham responded that the king of Spain was waging war against the queen of England, the king of France, and the Netherlands,[19] and therefore repeatedly failed to send envoys to the emperor to draw up an alliance. Hence the emperor did not direct the ambassador to draft a treaty with the tsar, for Rudolph lacked a firm agreement with the Pope and the king of Spain. "Why then," objected Shchelkalov, "did the previous ambassador Warkotsch assert here earlier that the emperor had concluded an alliance with the Pope and the Spanish king?" "This Warkotsch spoiled everything," replied Abraham. "He disregarded his instructions when he spoke here. Having returned to the emperor, he misrepresented what happened here."

"Our major task," continued Shchelkalov, "is to consolidate the bond of brotherly love and unity between our sovereign and Emperor Rudolph from which all else will follow. The emperor shall join the Spaniard, and we shall unite with the Persian. Now that you are here, an eminent diplomat, and an ambassador of the Roman Pope is also present,[20] let us secure this most worthy cause, for the general welfare of Christendom."

"I personally," the ambassador answered, "know this to be a most fitting venture between great monarchs, still what may I do if I bear no charge from my emperor? Had I wings, I would fly, obtain the emperor's mandate and accomplish my mission here." "If such a vital project benefits all Christianity," retorted Shchelkalov, "and you desire it, then tarry here, and our tsar's servitor shall ride to your sovereign for the instructions."

"This is not a sufficiently weighty matter," Abraham replied, "and besides I dare not so far exceed my lord's bidding."

Negotiations ended thus. The Austrian court demonstrated plainly what it expected from the Muscovite tsar, who was considered extremely wealthy.[21] One nobleman in the ambassadorial suite did insist on speaking to Shchelkalov on behalf of Archduke Maximilian. The archduke, he asserted, was pursuing the Polish throne by every means, and hoped fervently that Fedor would assist him.

"As you know," replied Shchelkalov, "the great sovereign was concerned, and took great pains toward this end, but if it was not the will of God what could be done? Indeed you know that even now the tsar would have Maximilian ruling over the Polish kingdom, but judge for yourself whether the kingdom can be mastered by force. The leading men, and what is more the entire land, must want you and elect you king. Should the country at large not acquiesce, the kingdom will be unruly. Tell me, does Maximilian communicate with those lords of the council who crave him as king? Do many lords desire him?"

"Maximilian does correspond secretly with the lords of the council," the nobleman answered. "Prince Ostrozski, governor of Poznań, the Zborowskis, and other lords, and much of the knighthood, upwards of seven thousand men, favor him. If only his majesty the tsar provides aid, Maximilian can gain Poland." "What help," Shchelkalov asked, "does Maximilian want? "

"Your tsar," replied the nobleman, "cannot help now with troops because five years remain in your truce with Lithuania. He should deign to open his coffers, agree to convey this assistance to Lübeck, first having dispatched his envoys to Lübeck. Maximilian will send emissaries there for acknowledgment." "This is too trifling a matter," objected Shchelkalov, "for the tsar to send his emissaries to Lübeck, to such negligible trading men." Thus ended Fedor's relations with the Austrian dynasty.

POPE PROPOSES, TSAR DISPOSES

The Pope's name figured constantly in dealings with the Habsburgs and in discussions of a league of all Christian powers against the Turks. He lost no opportunity to make himself known to the Muscovite government, to acquaint it with his influence. Both Gregory XIII[22] and Sixtus V[23] approached the tsar with their desire to send Antonio Possevino[24] to Moscow once again. Sixtus observed that Stefan Bathory wanted to restore to Lithuania lands taken by Moscow during previous reigns, and thus fulfill an oath he swore on assuming the Polish throne. That being the case, Sixtus would charge Possevino to avert a war. Bathory's death rendered such intervention unnecessary.

Twice, in 1595 and in 1597, Clement VII's ambassador the Illyrian priest Komulius[25] came to Moscow. A Slav was selected precisely because the Russians could understand him without recourse to a translator. Komulius had orders to induce the tsar to war against the Turks, persuading him by inspiring fear of Turkish power and by stressing the benefits the Russians might reap by annexing fruitful southern lands in cooperation with militarily talented peoples. He was to recall the ancestral claim of the Muscovite tsars to Byzantium, and to point out that the Turks were oppressing nations akin to the Russians in language and religion. Komulius also was to solicit the reunification of the churches. He was to suggest that only the Pope could invest monarchs with their royal dignity, and that the true church rested in Rome, not Constantinople, where the sultan enslaved the patriarchs. The course of the negotiations and their outcome remain unknown.

ENGLAND

We have that before Ivan the Terrible died he ordered talks held with the English ambassador Bowes,[26] who aggravated the tsar by refusing to share his vision of an alliance pitting Muscovy and England against Poland and Sweden. We have also seen[27] that Bowes considered his main adversaries to be Nikita Romanovich, Bogdan Belsky and the crown secretary Andrei Shchelkalov who, upon the ambassador's complaint, was removed from dealing with him and, if Bowes's account is reliable,[28] was even beaten by the tsar. Upon Ivan's death Bowes (by his own version) succumbed to his enemies, Nikita Romanovich and Andrei Shchelkalov. For nine weeks they held him under house arrest, watched him closely and treated him badly. Every day he feared even worse. After the uprising against Belsky ended the ambassador was summoned to the palace. His sword was taken from him when he entered. "Had I not girded myself with patience, I would have fallen," wrote Bowes. "Boris Fedorovich Godunov did me great service and would have done even more, but before the tsar's coronation he did not yet have the authority. Despite that, he often called for me and presented me with precious gifts."[29]

Bowes was sent home with a letter in which Fedor assured Queen Elizabeth that English merchants would enjoy the same privileges extended by his father's most recent charter. Fedor expected the queen to reciprocate, enabling Muscovite merchants to trade in England and, through England, in other states. He also desired her to let foreign merchants ship assorted goods to Russia through England: armor, copper, tin, oil, lead, saltpeter and various weapons. Fedor besought Elizabeth to authorize passage to Russia for military experts, skilled artisans, stonemasons, builders of fortifications, casters of cannon, and bell founders, then an embittered Bowes threw away the tsar's letter and gifts at Kholmogory. The Livonian Beckmann,[30] an interpreter, then was sent to England *as a special emissary on an urgent mission.*[31]

Thanks to Bowes's complaints the queen did not receive Beckmann for a long time. When at last she did, she challenged him. "Why does this tsar," she asked, "not care for me as did his father? He bids everyone from other realms to trade in Russia, but why does he not invite my subjects?" Beckmann denied that any such exclusion existed. Bowes then was summoned to the queen, who asked why he informed her that Fedor denied Englishmen the right to trade in his land. Bowes disclaimed having said that, asserting that a tariff was not levied upon other foreigners, rather was collected from Englishmen. "This is false," retorted Beckmann. "The English pay one half of the duty, while others are charged the full sum. Had Bowes not discarded the tsar's documents at Kholmogory your majesty would have learned in truth how the present tsar desires to hold you in still greater affection than before." Beckmann departed with a charter by which Elizabeth agreed to allow Russian merchants to trade in England provided the tsar award the Anglo-Russian Company[32] a monopoly over commerce in his own territories.

Nevertheless Beckmann was denied a last audience with Elizabeth before embarking. Moscow took offense. The tsar *with the boyars* resolved to confront the queen frankly, denouncing her ambassador and her merchants, and protesting that her secretary of state, although not she personally, violated tradition when he dismissed Beckmann. This was to be argued in detail in a written message delivered by an Englishman. "It is improper to tell us in our realm," it stated "to trade with one but not another. Your leading merchants do not petition you honestly about business. They seek solely their own profit, and wish to permit none to others. By the grace of God our domain contains enough of every product, even without your merchants. Ours is a broad and populous realm with every kind of ware."

JEROME HORSEY

The Englishman entrusted with carrying this rebuke to Elizabeth was Jerome Horsey.[33] He must have clarified in London the state of affairs at the Muscovite court and must have specified whose influence to cultivate. Elizabeth sent Horsey back with a letter for Tsaritsa Irina, in which she wrote that she had heard often of her honor and her wisdom, and that praise of her sagacity resounded in many countries. She dispatched to her Dr. Robert Jacob,[34] a gynecologist. More important, Elizabeth addressed a letter to Godunov, flattering him as her "most dear and loving cousin,"[35] as it was translated in Moscow. Elizabeth's message to Fedor justified Bowes's conduct by citing his rage when forced to remove his sword for the audience with the tsar. "Such distrust saddened us deeply," wrote Elizabeth. "In our lands it is a great dishonor when a sword is ordered removed. This affront brought heartfelt anguish to our ambassador, and whatever he did, he acted out of rancor. Now Horsey has advised us that it is your custom to take an ambassador's sword, that it is always done so in your tsardom. Having learned this, we lost our sadness, and we hope that unending amity will prevail between us."

Horsey advised Elizabeth that Moscow was unhappy that she received Beckmann in a garden which he described as a cabbage patch. "The place where Beckmann came," the queen explained to the tsar, "is one of honor, near our palace, where only outstanding and esteemed servants are permitted entry. Neither onions nor garlic grow in this 'cabbage patch.' Beckmann spoke falsely. Not only should you punish the courier Beckmann, you should beat him for his knavish provocations."

Godunov lived up to the expectations of his "dear and loving cousin." In 1587 the English merchants were granted free trade. All commercial taxes on their goods were rescinded, whether customs, city taxes, storage fees, transit duties, ship taxes, poll taxes, tolls on bridges, or ferries and fords. They were prohibited only from importing foreign [other than English] wares, employing Russians as middlemen, holding the property of Russians as security, and circulating jobbers around the towns. They were to engage in wholesale trade and barter at their establishments, and not to trade or exchange in small quantities. Cloth must be sold by the bale and as whole cloth, damask and velvet by the piece, and wine by the keg. When the English merchants wished to journey to other countries or return home they must carry with them stocks from the tsar's warehouses.[36]

These were to be sold and exchanged for commodities Muscovy needed, and transferred to the tsar's treasury. English merchants leaving Moscow must first appear before Conciliar Secretary Andrei Shchelkalov at the Chancellery for Foreign Affairs. Should an English ship be wrecked and stranded on the Russian coast the tsar pledged to order an honest and thorough search for the cargo, and have it returned to the English. Merchants were to dwell as always at their residence next to St. Maxim's church, behind the market, where they might retain a Russian doorkeeper or their own foreigner, and hire no other Russians. They could maintain also places of business at Yaroslavl, Vologda and on the naval wharf at Kholmogory. The Chancellery for Foreign Affairs would furnish them with travel permits for their people leaving Muscovy. The conciliar secretary for foreign affairs and the tsar's treasurer were to judge any litigation involving an Englishman. Whatever normal investigation left undetermined would be decided by lots. He whose lot was chosen would be exonerated.[37]

Godunov assured Elizabeth in his letter that Fedor "for you, his sister, upon our entreaty has favored your subjects more than ever. I will continue to petition him on their behalf, and will sustain them. Before the tsar and the tsaritsa I will extol your kindness and affection toward me." Thanks to Elizabeth's profound and cousinly regard for Godunov, English merchants gained relief from payments ranging in excess of £2,000 annually. Even so, other foreign merchants accused the English of barring their ships from Muscovy. Such denunciations caused Fedor to write to Elizabeth, "Many foreigners from diverse lands appeal to us. Englishmen (not with the Company), French, Netherlanders and others accuse your leading merchants of trying to block their vessels from our realm. We surely do not wish to believe this. If it is true, is it just that your leading merchants drive away foreigners while at the same time having advantage of our great charter? By what right may God's road, the high seas, be intercepted, restricted and closed?"

For their part Elizabeth's ministers relayed to Godunov and Shchelkalov a document detailing the English merchants' accusations against Muscovite civil officials. Shchelkalov alone answered. "Having put faith in rogues and bandits," he wrote, "you write many unseemly words to such an august man (Godunov). You fill your letter with reproach for such an honorable and distinguished person, the tsar's brother-in-law, as if your tradesmen cannot survive because they live in great terror of the tsar's officials. You write that they want to stop trading, and that if commerce came to a halt this would bring disgrace to our sovereign and his officials. The boyar Godunov has no desire to write a personal answer to such words. Your words amazed him greatly, and he delegated me to answer you."

Relations were renewed with controversy over the Englishman Anthony Marsh,[38] who accumulated cash loans from Godunov, boyars, servicemen, merchants and monks. He asserted that this money was for [the Company's] common expenses, for common merchandise, but his partners repudiated the debts, maintaining that he borrowed the money independently and without their knowledge. Godunov charged Beckmann to escort Marsh to England in 1588. The queen was slow to summon Beckmann. "For a long time I kept you from my presence," she told him, "because I was sick with grief at the death of my majordomo (the earl of Leicester).[39] Moreover I was sorely angry with you about what you told your sovereign, likening our pleasure garden to a cabbage patch where onions and garlic are planted. You deserved retribution for such misconduct, yet we forbore vengeance upon you."

"I beg your majesty," pleaded Beckmann, "let me speak openly." Elizabeth consented. "As God is my witness," Beckman commenced, "I did not think this and I have not said it. If it was so written in the tsar's message or if an accuser comes forward, I beg no clemency from your majesty, I wish only to suffer for my wrongdoing. An evil man who seeks the destruction of my good name visited this upon me, and I hope that a rock will fall upon his head." Elizabeth saw fit to forget the affair.

When Marsh was summoned for questioning he testified that he had repaid the money borrowed from the tsar's treasury. He admitted to some private loans, disclaimed others, while complaining that fifteen thousand rubles of his personal funds were sequestered in Moscow. When the lord high treasurer told Beckmann of this testimony he argued that the tsar's document must be believed, not Marsh's groundless statements. "That is true," conceded the treasurer, "but why was Marsh given such sums? He was a petty wholesale merchant, rather a mere servant of the wealthy merchants, and no substantial businessmen underwrote the notes."

"Marsh," answered Beckmann, "frequented the merchants' hall, bought and sold, borrowed money and loaned it. He was not like a servant, rather like a respected merchant who could be relied upon. Above all, he knows how to read and write Russian, and your prominent merchants gave us no warning of his untrustworthiness."

GILES FLETCHER

Even before Beckmann's return, in the fall of 1588, Elizabeth's envoy
Fletcher[40] reached Moscow. He declared to Fedor that many sovereigns
enjoyed kinship, amity, and affection with Queen Elizabeth but she cher-
ished none with such friendship and regard as she did the tsar. "If some
Englishmen," continued Fletcher, "have behaved poorly here, his majesty
ought not to blame others, the innocent, for the sake of a guilty few. He
ought not upbraid and scold an entire country for the sins of one man, for
there is no nation or commerce that does not have some evildoers. Although the scoundrels were the queen's subjects they would not have acted
so badly had the tsar's people not been their accomplices. The queen hopes
that the sovereign will follow his father's example and continue heartfelt
friendship towards her. Even better than following his father's example, he
serves as his own model, for he has graced the queen's subjects with his
kindness."

Fletcher submitted a long list of articles encompassing Elizabeth's
requests of Fedor. She asked him to confirm for her merchants the latest
charter of immunities, with the addition of some new clauses from Ivan the
Terrible's earlier charter. The English merchants, she said, must cease
trading with Russia should they feel they could rely upon the tsar's charter
no longer, or must worry that the tsar might rescind the charter over such
a trifle as the Marsh affair. "The English merchants," Fletcher was told,
"put no value on the tsar's charter. That is not cause to threaten to cease
coming for trade in our realm. Many wealthy merchants, not just the
English, come to us for trade." The queen requested that chancellery
officials stop forcibly seizing goods from English ships, as happened
recently. Neither treasurers nor crown secretaries, stated the reply, committed any violence against the English, who were the most attended of all
merchants. Should anyone confiscate the cargo of an English merchant
without compensation, or offend him, the malefactor need only be identified and the tsar would have him punished.

The queen wanted the English merchants absolved of responsibility for
Marsh's debts because he contracted them as a free agent, and not as a
member of the Company. The tsar's chancellery officials had granted him
a special charter for trade to all points overseas. Neither the English
merchants nor their agents were aware of this document. When these
merchants and their agents warned those Russians now demanding payment from Marsh not to trust him or deal with him, the Russians replied that
they were doing neither. Elizabeth also learned that some of Marsh's funds

remained sequestered in Moscow and were not being disbursed to his creditors. Lest such tiresome questions bother the tsar ever again, the queen petitioned that the chancellery officials recognize as members of the Company only those Englishmen registered as such by the Company clerk. In reply the Muscovites noted that a close investigation revealed that when Marsh borrowed the money the English merchants were living together in the same residence and trading jointly. They did agree to acknowledge as members of the Company only those Englishmen formally named by its agent.

The queen sought the right for English merchants to buy all products without exception. The Russians replied that this already was the case, excluding wax, which is exchanged only for saltpeter, gunpowder or sulfur. Elizabeth requested that no Englishman accused of any crime be tortured. Moscow replied that Englishmen were never seized or detained. Torture was never considered, nor would it ever be. The queen desired Godunov to hear cases involving her subjects. The response explained that it was inappropriate for Boris Fedorovich, a man entrusted with administering the most vital functions of the realm, to consider mercantile matters. Chancellery officials would judge English merchants and adjudicate their cases, and inform Godunov. Elizabeth asked the tsar to permit English merchants to cross his lands to Bukhara, Shemakha, Kazbin and Persia, and prohibit all other merchants from going there, except for his own emissaries. This request evoked a sharp response. Fedor would admit English merchants into these countries without duty, but must grant the same concession to Muscovites. How could the sovereign's subjects not be permitted to go there? The tsar's great charter to English merchants let them pass to such distant realms, whereas other foreigners might not venture a verst beyond Moscow. Elizabeth requested that Englishmen be permitted to construct an establishment on the Vychegda to discover and refine iron. They wanted the forests for seven or eight versts around those places for construction of offices and foundries. In return they would pay a tariff of one Moscow denga.[41] The tsar granted this request.

Queen Elizabeth requested that English merchants be allowed to hire and retain jobbers and forestallers, paying them wages under contract. The Russians refused. Such jobbers and hired men, they argued, caused widespread turmoil and thievery. Certain English merchants, Richard Richardson[42] and his partners, once came to grief through such middlemen. They had in their employ a tradesman, Vakhrush Semeonov of Yaroslavl. Whenever the English sent their agents through Lithuania, secretly and without safe conducts, Vakhrush arranged passage. He hired thieves posing as teamsters who absconded with documents in which Richard wrote unseemly things about Muscovy.

Elizabeth wanted mint masters throughout Russia to recast efimoks into dengas for the English merchants without fee, charging only for the coal used and their labor. This was granted, although a general tax was retained. Once more the queen sought a monopoly for the Company, asking Fedor to ban English interlopers and all foreign traders from his realm. As earlier, the Muscovites refused adamantly. This was, they avowed, improper and unheard of anywhere. Should Queen Elizabeth press the tsar over this, she would display her dislike of him and flaunt her desire to inflict losses upon the realm by barring the way to it. Elizabeth moved that English merchants, their agents and servants might worship freely. The tsar, the Russians answered, took no interest in their religion. Men of various faiths inhabited his realm, and he would make no man renounce his beliefs. Each might live by his own creed. Finally Elizabeth asked whether English merchants sent to find the land of China might seek guides, ship's crews, ships, provisions for their crews and other supplies in Russia. This was rejected. The tsar found it unseemly for people to cross his lands in search of other countries.

Along with these answers Fletcher was presented a bill for more than twenty-three thousand rubles owed by English merchants on account of Marsh's promissory notes. Then the ambassador was advised that Fedor, in affection for his sister Queen Elizabeth, ordered the recovery of only half this amount. Meanwhile Anthony Marsh testified to Queen Elizabeth's ministers that he incurred his debts in the Company's name at the suggestion of the conciliar secretary Andrei Shchelkalov, who also had him fabricate a seal identical to that which Marsh owned while employed by prominent merchants. Shchelkalov pledged to clear Marsh in all this and to aid him in meeting the debts. Marsh dared not disobey Shchelkalov, a chancellor and one of Fedor's highest officials. Besides, Marsh had no other friends. Elizabeth transmitted this testimony to Moscow, giving it full credence, and also sent back Marsh but Fletcher, who presented this plea to the tsar, was told in reply that Marsh, a known thief, lied about Shchelkalov. The Russians found it astounding that honest men, the queen's councilors, did not manage to see through such a notorious criminal in his own homeland and did not inquire among his companions about his thievery.

Elizabeth continued to flatter Godunov in her letters. He repeated to her that his sovereign had extended various kindnesses to her English merchants "loving you, his beloved sister, and thanks to my petition and obeisance." The queen shipped presents to Boris. Once again he refused them with this apology. "You, your majesty, have sent me your favor, your bounty, but I did not accept your bounty because your ambassador graced our tsar with gold pieces from you, half rubles, quarter-rubles and gold dengas.[43] Never did you, illustrious sovereigns, exchange such gifts. Our sovereign decreed that these presents not be accepted, hence I dared not take your bounty, but I thank you profusely for it, august queen. Henceforth I come before my lord and pray him to kindle between you a brotherly love secure forever and greater than before. I shall keep your future offerings to me, and shall watch over your merchants with all prudence."

Elizabeth's famous minister Cecil[44] (whom the Russian documents exalt with the title Most Honorable William Cecil of the rank of Knight of the Garter) wrote to Godunov "Because of many insults our merchants contemplated trading no more in your realm, now they yearn to trade in many diverse wares. Should you, Boris Fedorovich, be their protector, never shall they seek any other patron." Cecil requested both remission of Marsh's remaining sureties and free trade. "Only half duty is now levied on the English merchants," answered Boris. "I will have the other half rescinded, that they shall suffer no loss. I shall shield them from all ills, from any loss under any decree. Their trade shall be free as in the past, and the sovereign will command that no tax be taken from their offices." Cecil nevertheless continued to protest about insults. "When English merchants visit your land they cannot deal in all wares, and they are made to buy the tsar's goods at a fixed price out of all relation to their true value. Should they not desire to purchase these things at so high a price they are detained for a long time at the mouth of the Dvina. There they live in great anxiety at returning through frost and storm. You know how unseemly is violence against tradesmen. If they continue to be mistreated, burdened with unwanted goods and overcharged for necessities, it will not be free trade, but coercion." Boris replied that complaints about compulsion were groundless, and again promised that trade would be freer than ever.

IV

TATAR RELATIONS

Relations with Denmark during Fedor's reign were unimportant, involving demarcation of the frontier with Norway. The Muscovite government had to turn far more serious attention southward. There it anticipated that the Crimeans might invade at any moment, nor did the Turks cease threatening to retrieve the conquests made by Ivan the Terrible.

ISLAM-GIREY OF THE CRIMEA

The Crimeans did sweep into the Ukraine several times between 1584 and 1588. Fortunately for Moscow, just when a clash with Bathory seemed imminent civil war erupted in the Crimea. Khan Muhammad-Girey[1] was killed by his brother Islam-Girey.[2] Muhammad's sons Saadet and Murad, having been driven off by their uncle, set out to dethrone him. The nephews managed to ravage the entire Crimea, plunder the khan's treasury and abduct his Russian and Lithuanian wives and children, but the uncle Islam ultimately crushed them. They then sought the protection of the Muscovite tsar. Saadet was permitted to wander as a nomad with the Nogay[3] near Astrakhan, while Murad took up residence in the city itself.

Islam, fearing the nephews, who were popular in the Crimea, came to depend upon the Turks, whom he permitted all sorts of cruelties. This further embittered the Crimeans against him. "We, the entire Crimean land," they declared, "want the junior prince Saadet as khan, for no one loves Islam-Girey.[4] The Turks have despoiled the Crimea. Their janissaries have committed terrible outrages and murders." The distress which this civil war brought to the Crimea can be seen in the words of Islam's heir Prince Alp to a Muscovite courier "Your sovereign has sent me few gifts,"[5] he said, "but we did not expect that he would even care to communicate with us at such a time."

"Should you truly wish to befriend us," Islam wrote to Fedor, "you must not keep our foes Saadet and Murad, even though they have fallen into your hands. Send them where they can neither be seen nor heard. Do not favor them with money or treasure. If you befriend us, without fail we shall ride against the faithless Lithuanian." Moscow's ambassador had to reassure the khan that Saadet and Murad would not raid the Crimea, provided the khan in turn avoid the Muscovite borderland, restrain the princes, dissuade the sultan from campaigning against Astrakhan, and advise Moscow of Turkish plans.

The Zaporozhian Cossacks rendered considerable service to Moscow. They gave the Turks and the Tatars no peace, and by irritating the sultan and the khan against Lithuania diverted their attention from Moscow. Now the cossacks descended upon the Crimean nomads' encampments, now they offered to enlist in the khan's service, and then they raided the Crimea. Thus in 1585 cossacks under Yan Yaryshevsky twice rode into the Crimea, carrying off more than forty thousand horses and cattle and taking many captives. Then four cossacks, representing this same Yaryshevsky and all the other atamans, came to tell the khan "The cossack atamans of the Dnieper sent us so that you, sire, might favor them, make peace with them and shower your bounty upon them. The chiefs and all their Cherkassians would do your will. They will ride wherever you send them against your foe, except against the king of Lithuania." "It pleases me," the khan replied, "to favor the atamans and all the cossacks. When I have need of them, I shall reward them with my bounty. Let them make ready." Instead of serving the khan, the cossacks seized Ochakov. In 1588 about fifteen hundred cossacks landed their boats at Tuptarakhan in the Crimea, between Kozelov and Perekop. They captured seventeen villages. The sultan warned Islam-Girey that should this persist, he would oust him from the Crimea.

KHAN GHAZI-GIREY

Islam died in 1588. His successor Ghazi-Girey[6] had to fulfill the sultan's edict and punish Lithuania for the cossacks' depredations. Therefore he dealt most amicably with Moscow. "In the past," Fedor reciprocated, "when Islam-Girey ruled in the Crimean land, we sent our great host under many commanders to the Don and Volga. They joined Prince Murad-Girey against Prince Islam-Girey because of his many crimes. Indeed we had Captains Likharev[7] and Khrushchov[8] descend the Dnieper beyond the rapids to Prince Kirik and Prince Mikhail Ruzhinsky,[9] to the atamans and Ukrainian Cherkassians, to ride with all the cossacks against the Crimea. When we learned that you had assumed the throne we put aside the campaign and dispatched to you an informant, a Tatar whom the officers

Likharev, Khrushchov and the Ruzhinsky princes sent us from the Dnieper."
Moscow felt obliged to render some service to the khan, at least on paper,
with a favor in the Tatar fashion. Ghazi-Girey wrote Fedor that he should
put to death the Tatar Atalyk-Musly, who was captured by the Russians.
The khan considered him a scoundrel. Fedor replied that the khan's request
was honored in that Atalyk had been executed.

All this notwithstanding, both the tone of the tsar's messages and the
paucity of his presents illustrated that Moscow did not fear the khan
greatly. The tsar greeted him only with a bow, not with an obeisance, yet
the khan saluted Godunov effusively. "To the great vizier and worthy
dignitary of our brother," he wrote, "to the leader of the boyars of the
sovereign of much of Christendom, to the most honored among his peers
in the Christian law of his country, to our friend Boris, many, many bows."
Boris shipped no extravagant presents to the Crimea neither did he maintain or reward that multitude of Tatars which usually accompanied messengers in order to share in the tsar's bounty. When the Russian courier
Mishurin departed for the Crimea, he was instructed to admonish the khan,
the princes and the khan's privy councilors to dispatch small ambassadorial suites not exceeding thirty men. Should the Crimeans send envoys with
a large entourage it would harm their relations with the tsar. Ghazi-Girey's
messenger had just arrived with eighty companions, an unprecedented
retinue. Should such large embassies come in the future, they would
receive neither supplies nor presents.

COSSACKS AND TATARS

Fedor's letter to the khan alluded to his relationship with the Zaporozhian
Cossacks, who were to have joined his forces for an invasion of the Crimea
in Islam-Girey's time. The nature of the Muscovite government's contact
with the cossacks is evident in the orders handed to the courier Peter
Zinoviev, bound for the Crimea. After Peter left Livny he was to await
news that the cossacks, Matvey Fedorov and his comrades, had reached the
Donets from the Dnieper, from Zaporozhia. When Peter determined that
the cossacks were friendly and had set no traps for the tsar's delegation, he
was to dispatch an advance party to the Zaporozhian Cossack settlement.
It would arrange his rendezvous with Matvey Fedorov's band and announce that Peter was bringing messages and a speech from the tsar for all
the cossacks. They were to command their brethren along the length of the
Donets not to harm Peter, the Crimean couriers, or their guides. Peter, they

should say, was hurrying to the Crimea with Crimean couriers on a minor mission, and carried no presents with him. When the atamans and their lads gathered Peter was to bow to them in the tsar's name and present the tsar's documents. He must again warn them not to interfere[10] with him or the Crimean messengers, and was to promise that a junior boyar would soon deliver the tsar's grant to them. The sovereign, who deeply valued their efforts, would give them abundant rewards.

The Zaporozhians could point to continued services like those which appeared in the report of the courier Mishurin in 1589. The cossacks, he stated, seized a Turkish ship at sea near Kozlev. Then they informed Ghazi-Girey that Lithuanian mercenaries, led by the Ukrainian ataman Kulaga with nearly eight hundred followers, landed small craft by night in the outskirts of Kozlev. Ghazi-Girey rushed there in full force, whereupon the marauders vacated the city, having looted the shops thoroughly, singling out the best. They were butchering some Turks and Jews and taking others prisoner when Crown Prince Feth-Girey attacked them. A battle raged through the town's business quarter. The Tatars caught over thirty cossacks. Kulaga perished and the rest fled. Besides this, the cossacks burned all the settlements around Belgorod (Akkerman) and fought in the environs of Azov. They dragged away three hundred hostages and assaulted merchants from Bukhara. The sultan later dispatched three galleys, each bearing five hundred janissaries with firearms and four culverins, with five more galleys of janissaries to follow. Having posted them at the estuary of the Dnieper where they could bar the cossacks from the sea, the sultan commanded the khan to raid Lithuania.

The Don and the Terek cossacks also harassed the Tatars and the Turks, although less relentlessly than did the Zaporozhians. "Your cossacks of the Don plague the city of Azov," the khan wrote to Godunov. "They come stealthily from the Don and from Samara to the Ovechi waters, to our encampments, and they steal livestock. The sultan wrote to me that he expended his treasury to conquer the city of Derbent, but now his subjects cannot journey from Azov to Derbent. Russian cossacks dwelling along the Terek ambush them at fords and in the marshes. The sultan cannot abide this. He wants to make war on Moscow and take the forts [on the Terek] with a mighty host and cannon.

Having been directed by the sultan to keep watch on Lithuania, Ghazi-Girey sought Fedor's subsidy for his labors. "We want to pass this winter along the Dnieper and patrol there," he wrote to the tsar, "and we ask you to furnish us with money." On one hand, Ghazi-Girey wanted the tsar to turn over to him Murad-Girey, who continued to live in Astrakhan. On the other hand he wanted to wheedle some money, so he wrote most affectionately "Russian cossacks swept down on our herds and led off over seven hundred horses. Both our people and the Azov cossacks chased them. We had our men overtake these raiders, intercept them, and punish them. One junior boyar was just being taken captive when we saved him from them and released him to you, our brother." Such courtesies failed to move Moscow, which delivered neither Murad-Girey nor money. Quite understandably the khan felt vexed, especially over the money.

GHAZI-GIREY'S MARCH ON MOSCOW

Murad-Girey died in Astrakhan. Moscow maintained that agents from the Crimea poisoned him. The Crimeans in turn asserted that the assassins were Russians. This rekindled old enmities and inspired thoughts of revenge. The sultan, angry with Moscow over the depredations of the Don and the Terek cossacks, also stirred up the khan's hostility. Finally King John of Sweden incited Ghazi-Girey to strike at Moscow. He promised him rich presents if he would crush the Muscovite tsar, and led him to understand that the Tatars would face no resistance because the tsar's army would be in the North, on the Swedish frontier. Ghazi-Girey resolved to gaze upon the banks of the Oka and if possible to ride well beyond them.[11]

The Russian ambassador Bibikov[12] reached the Crimea late in 1590. First he greeted the khan with a bow and carried out his embassy from the tsar. Then he rendered homage on behalf of the boyar Boris Fedorovich and handed over documents and presents. The khan did not rise for the sovereign's bow and salutation. On January 11, 1591 Akhmad-Aga rode into the Jewish town of Kyrkor where Bibikov was staying, summoned him and delivered the khan's message. "The khan," he declared, "dispatched a message to you to ask for the fifty squirrel skin coats and fifty marten skin coats that have not been delivered to the mullahs, as well as the lists, the instructions and the registers. Neither did you heed the khan's word, thus the khan has commanded that all your property be seized." The bailiffs robbed Bibikov and the interpreters. They confiscated everything from them: fur coats, hats, clothing, money, supplies and wine. That spring the horde gathered for war. On May 5 the khan let Bibikov be assured that he would ride against the Lithuanian king, and not the tsar's Ukraine.

Moscow knew by June that the opposite was the case. Consequently, on June 26 orders went out to the commanders of all regiments ordinarily deployed on the banks of the Oka, and to the governors of the borderland garrison towns, to gather and confer with the boyar Prince Fedor Ivanovich Mstislavsky at Serpukhov. When more detailed intelligence revealed that the khan personally was leading his main force directly at Moscow the boyars and commanders had to rush their regiments to the capital in order to forestall him. These forces reached the city around vespers on July 1 and were drawn up before Kolomenskoe. On July 2 they were ordered to occupy the leaguer[13] erected opposite the Danilov monastery. The tsar personally reviewed them the same day. He gave awards to the boyars, commanders, gentry officers and junior boyars, asked about their health and inspected the regiments. On July 3 the officer Koltovskoy arrived in Moscow from the Oka frontier, where he was posted on guard, and reported that the khan had forded the Oka close by Teshilov, passed the night in Lopasnia, and was riding straight for Moscow. After this news two hundred and fifty junior boyars from Smolensk, Aleksin and Tula, commanded by Prince Bakhteiarov-Rostovsky,[14] advanced to the Pakhra river. They were to take their stand at the river line and harass the Crimeans' advance guard. The Tatar vanguard brushed them aside from the Pakhra, injured the commander, and killed or captured many rank-and-file.

In Moscow the army now received orders to fight from within the leaguer. Prince Fedor Ivanovich Mstislavksy commanded the Great Regiment, Prince Nikita Romanovich Trubetskoy[15] the right wing, Prince Timofey Romanovich Trubetskoy[16] the vanguard, and Prince Vasily Cherkassky the left wing. A Godunov was attached to each of the first three commanders.[17] Boris was with Mstislavsky, Stefan Vasilievich with Nikita Trubetskoy, and Ivan Vasilievich with Timofey Trubetskoy.[18] Mstislavsky and Boris Godunov had a staff composed of the court carver Alexander Nikitich Romanov, the lord-in-waiting Andrei Kleshnin, the treasurer Cheremisinov, the armorer Bogdan Yakovlevich Belsky and the conciliar noble Pivov.[19]

On July 4, Sunday morning, Ghazi-Girey appeared before Moscow, personally arrayed his forces in front of Kolomenskoe, and unleashed the lesser Tatar princes against the Muscovite leaders defending the leaguer. These commanders counterattacked with every unit at their disposal. They flung at the Tatars Russian captains leading cossack hundreds, cavalry captains leading Lithuanian and foreign troops. They were ordered to *give chase* to the Crimeans, in the then current parlance. This mêlée continued until nightfall with no clear outcome. The Tatars disliked such encounters. They had no stomach for inconclusive pitched battles with the Russians

HORSEMAN'S WEAPONS AND ACCOUTREMENTS, SIXTEENTH CENTURY

Sigismund von Herberstein, *Notes upon Russia...,* 1549
Herberstein visited Muscovy in 1517 and 1526.

and they were even less eager to charge the leaguer with its concentration of Russian soldiers and cannon. Moreover their prisoners claimed that a new army was approaching Moscow from Novgorod and other regions, and that the Russian commanders planned a night attack with these reinforcements. Ghazi-Girey did not await the dawn and fled, abandoning his baggage train.

Swift regiments rode in pursuit of the khan on July 5, but failed to catch him because he fled without stopping at any town. His rearguard detachments were overtaken and shattered near Tula, and its remnants were annihilated in the steppe. The tsar's main force also abandoned the protection of the leaguer, following as far as Serpukhov. Prince Kozlovsky arrived there from Moscow on July 10 to announce that Mstislavsky had fallen into disfavor because his dispatches to the tsar mentioned only his own name, failing to allude to the boyar and master of the horse Boris Godunov. Then the table attendant Ivan Nikitich Romanov[20] came on the same day to hail the boyars and commanders in the tsar's name, and to ask the entire army about its health. He awarded Prince Mstislavsky and Boris Godunov with Portuguese gold ducats, and the other boyars with two English or French gold pieces, while others received only one, and some were given Hungarian gold coins.

The junior commanders remained at the Oka river defense line while the senior officers returned to Moscow. Here Godunov received from the tsar's shoulders a fur coat worth a thousand rubles, as well as a golden chain, also from the tsar a golden vessel called Mamay because it was plundered from Mamay's baggage train after the battle of Kulikovo,[21] and three towns in the Vaga region. Godunov now bore the title *Servant* which, as Moscow's ambassadors in Lithuania had to explain, was more exalted than that of boyar. Prince Mstislavsky got a fur coat from the tsar's shoulders, a goblet with a golden cup, and the bytown of Kashin with its district. Other commanders and conciliar nobles acquired fur coats, drinking vessels, patrimonial holdings, military service estates, money, Chinese silk fabric, velvets, satins, furs and broadcloth. For several days the tsar feasted at the Palace of Facets. The Donskoy monastery was built in thanks to God.

The Crimean crown prince returned from the campaign late in July. He was asked about the khan's whereabouts, but knew nothing, having retreated hastily. Only about a third of the army returned, on foot and with few captives. The khan, wounded and in a cart, entered Bakhchisaray at night on August 2. It was noticed later that his left arm was in a sling.

Late in August Ghazi-Girey summoned Bibikov. He ordered him to sit, and then spoke. "I visited Moscow," he said, "and they did not regale me. It did not please them to receive guests." "Willful prince!" Bibikov retorted, "You have robbed our sovereign and ridden into his land against your word. Indeed you did visit our land and did linger briefly at Moscow. Had you tarried a while longer, our sovereign might have entertained you."

The khan made no reply. He invited Bibikov to dine, and after dinner had a golden cloak placed on his shoulders. Bibikov made inquiries to learn why the khan attacked Muscovy. It was explained that Ghazi-Girey hoped to prove himself, because when he assumed the throne he never had raided the Muscovite borderlands. His people considered this a dishonor, hence the khan planned the attack for some time. Bibikov was also told why the khan fled Moscow. Prisoners asserted that units were arriving from Novgorod and Pskov, and that the tsar wanted to order his chief commanders against the khan. "Who," asked Ghazi-Girey, "is the supreme commander?" The captives answered that it was Boris Godunov. Then the princes and the murzas said "If Boris has been sent he must have with him many troops." Then the khan fled. One of the Crimean princes said to Bibikov "Why does your tsar found numerous towns in the borderlands, along the Terek and the Volga, around the Crimea?" "In the sovereign's land," Bibikov explained, "the population has multiplied. The people are hemmed in. The sovereign is strong and so he builds towns." "Your tsar," the prince retorted, "wishes to act as Ivan the Terrible did at Kazan. First he constructed a town[22] nearby, and then he took Kazan, but the Crimea is not Kazan. The Crimea has many hands and eyes. Your sovereign will need to go beyond the cities, into the Crimean heartland."

AFTER THE INVASION

It was the khan who reopened relations with the tsar. Within two months of returning from the field he assigned couriers to Moscow. When the boyars asked why they visited, they replied "The khan seeks neither Kazan nor Astrakhan from your sovereign merely, as he says in his letters, wishes that your sovereign send gifts."[23] The boyars let them be advised "Should the khan confess to his faithlessness, he must show deep submission. Gifts are sent out of friendship and, seeing the prince's perfidy and hostility, it is a waste to send them." "Had our prince not acknowledged his falsehoods," the couriers replied, "he would not have dispatched us. Your tsar should pardon Khan Ghazi-Girey for his attack upon Moscow. Indeed, our prince making war caused your sovereign no great trouble. He departed by the very same road by which he entered."

Such impudent contrition proved to be cunning. The khan needed the Muscovite authorities to lessen their caution, as they then put it. Moscow actually did err. It thought that after their unfortunate expedition the Crimeans were in no position to raid the borderlands soon. This was a cruel mistake. In May 1592 the crown prince Feth-Girey[24] burst into the border-lands without warning and marauded through the lands of Riazan, Kashira and Tula. The Tatars slaughtered droves of people, put the torch to many villages and hamlets, capturing numerous noblemen and junior boyars who, surprised by the attack, failed to seek refuge in the towns for their families. Prisoners were so numerous, say the chroniclers, that even the elderly could not recall such a war with the unbelievers.

Ghazi-Girey recovered his health and changed his tone. "I marvel most," he commented to a courier from the tsar who was dispatched before the heir apparent's raid, "that around Trinity Sunday you did not augment your forces at the river line or in the Ukraine. Those frontiersmen who did gather kept to the woods and did not challenge our troops in the open field. Only a few Lithuanians fought. The tsareviches and all the princes tell me that our warriors have never known such fighting. Neither saber nor arrow was drawn, and prisoners were herded up with whips." "You sent your messengers to the sovereign with amicable letters," the courier answered, "and thus no soldiers were assembled in the borderlands. If we made such a mistake this time, we shall not repeat it. Our tsar will not err again by giving credence to your word."

Ghazi-Girey, certain that he could alter his tone and again ask for gifts, no longer contemplated war with Muscovy. He now must participate in the sultan's expeditions to Moldavia, Wallachia and Hungary. He did renew his requests, with the usual assurances that the crown prince acted on his own initiative when he raided the Muscovite borderlands. "We are sending ambassadors to you with plentiful presents," Fedor sent word in reply. "We still wish to regard you as just. One of your ambassadors, Murza-Allaberdey, will stay here for essential business so that we will not lack a worthy negotiator and that our relations will not be interrupted. When our envoy Semeon Bezobrazov[25] and your couriers reach you in the Crimea, immediately send to us a swift courier. Write which trusted diplomat and which prominent official will accompany your messengers. They will meet with our respected delegates at Livny and speak about a permanent peace. Specify when they should wait at Livny to receive our ambassador and your ambassador, Allaberdey, along with abundant presents and extraordinary gifts (bribes). At this time we will dispatch our ambassador Prince Merkury Shcherbatov[26] and our worthy intermediary, who will discuss matters and exchange our ambassadors with your great privy advisers, as always has been done. Our envoy Prince Shcherbatov and your envoy Allaberdey will come to you, and your new emissary and our former emissary Bezobrazov will come to us."

Bezobrazov's orders outlined his mission. "He bears with him a thousand gold pieces. He must conceal them on his person. Once amidst the Crimean clans he is to learn whether the khan is hostile as in the past, and if a campaign against the Muscovite borderlands is to be expected. He must discover whether the khan expects treachery from the Turks, if some other ill has befallen him, or if he will campaign in Lithuania at the Turk's behest. Bezobrazov must give no one the gold, concealing it on his person so that no one knows, not even the Russian interpreters. Should he find the khan healthy, in readiness and at the tsar's borders, he is to distribute the gold: seven hundred to the khan, two hundred to the crown prince, one hundred to the lesser prince Nuradin."[27]

Bezobrazov also had orders to ransom prisoners. The usual rates ranged widely, from between fifty and a hundred rubles for a junior boyar, fifty for a captain of musketeers, twenty-five for a priest's wife, and fifty for a prince's daughter. Several notable individuals were taken in the most recent raid. Bezobrazov was ordered to liberate without fail Nikifor Yelchaninov, paying two hundred rubles for him, Tutolmin's wife, for whom he would give two hundred rubles in crown funds as well as an additional two hundred rubles provided personally by her husband, and the mother of the Shchepotievs, for whom he was allowed to provide up to seventy rubles, to which her children added forty more.

Before Shcherbatov and the intermediary could leave to discuss a permanent peace Ghazi-Girey's courier brought new demands in the name of both the khan and the sultan. The Terek and the Don cossacks must be resettled. Fedor must subsidize the khan with thirty thousand rubles to construct a town on the Dnieper at the Koshkin ford, which the Russians call "the crossing at Dobry above the rapids." He must have the wife of the deceased Murad-Girey released to the Crimea. Crown Secretary Andrei Shchelkalov answered this courier, "This cannot be," he argued. "Our sovereign cannot heed the Crimean and the Turk in this. The Turk writes all sorts of things! He once wrote thus of Kazan and of Astrakhan, and was he then heeded? How did that turn out?[28] This latest episode is equally unacceptable. Our sovereign will not demolish Tarki. He built Tarki in his patrimony of Kabarda for just cause. The cossacks of Kabarda have been his *slaves* for many years. They fled the Riazan borderlands for the mountains, where they served our sovereign's father and now serve him. They entreated him to construct a town on the Terek for their protection. How could our sovereign now relinquish it from his patrimony?"[29]

"The khan secretly instructed me," the courier insisted, "that the tsar need not level the town or eject the cossacks from Tarki, he should mislead. He should write the khan that Tarki will be evacuated, which the khan can report to the sultan. The Turk will be pacified and will not demand a campaign against the tsar. Meanwhile the khan will build a town at Koshkin ford on the Dnieper, resettle all the Crimeans along the Dnieper and destroy Perekop. The sovereign is to send thirty thousand rubles to the khan to help defray his expenses." "Is this not incredible?" replied Shchelkalov. "When did the khan renounce allegiance to the Turk? Can he stand up to the Turk? In what fashion will he establish and fortify the town? Does the khan have artillery? Does the Turk know about the town?" The courier responded that Ghazi-Girey would offer hostages as guarantees, his own son and a representative from each of the eminent clans.

The same proposals were placed before Godunov, who reacted similarly and added "Judge for yourself. If anyone creates a tiny village, even if not on his own land, but nevertheless builds it, he will not relinquish it without a fight, indeed without bloodshed." Boris also commented on the khan's secret instructions and his request for thirty thousand rubles. "How," he asked, "can such an extraordinary request be honored? It is impossible even to gather such a sum. It must be asked whether this really can be done? Can the khan be believed? The khan has not stated directly that his word be given to our sovereign." After these deliberations the boyar council decided to assign Prince Shcherbatov to the Crimea and supply with him gifts equaling those sent previously, worth forty thousand rubles or more, and with ten thousand rubles for the khan. Murad-Girey's wife would be freed.

SHCHERBATOV AND AKHMAD-PASHA

Prince Shcherbatov went to Livny in November 1593 to negotiate a permanent peace with Ghazi-Girey's plenipotentiary Akhmad-Pasha. The boyar Prince Fedor Yakovlevich Khvorostinin[30] and the armorer Bogdan

Belsky accompanied him. When they reached Livny, Khvorostinin requested that Akhmad-Pasha cross the Sosna river for the talks. Akhmad
found it beneath his dignity to comply. His older brother Prince Murad
once traveled to Putivl for a similar exchange of ambassadors with Andrei
Nagoy, who crossed the Seim river to Murad's tent. He, Akhmad-Pasha,
could not lower his ruler's prestige by ignoring this precedent. Khvorostinin
objected that Andrei Nagoy was an ordinary crown servitor on a mission
of no great importance whereas now high-ranking officials were to negotiate vital transactions. Akhmad responded that indeed he was an eminent
representative of his sovereign and that, moreover, his service to Tsar
Fedor Ivanovich was well known. The khan enjoined him from crossing
the Sosna. When Khvorostinin reported this impasse to the tsar he received
a directive. "You know," it read, "that both the near and the far banks of
the Sosna are ours. Inform Akhmad-Pasha that for such a worthy undertaking you will exceed our mandate and raise the conference tent on their
side, as long as he comes to meet you in your tent."

Khvorostinin reached a different arrangement with Akhmad-Pasha, to
confer at the middle of a bridge spanning the river. Akhmad in the name of
the khan and the tsareviches swore sincere amity and brotherhood with the
tsar. "If the khan, the heir apparent and all the princes are true," promised
Khvorostinin, "if they do not pillage Moscow's borderlands in the summer
of 1594, that summer the sovereign will dispatch his emissaries with the other
half of what the khan requested (Shcherbatov brought the first half), and
henceforth he will make presents yearly. Our sovereign will honor his vow."
"I trust your word," replied Akhmad.

Akhmad again argued that the tsar must evict the cossacks from the
Don and thereby secure a clear road from Derbent to Shemakha. "On the
Don dwell cossack brigands, runaways," replied Khvorostinin. "Living
along the Don, they band together with the Ukrainian cossacks of the
Dnieper and hem in Azov without the sovereign's consent. They disregard
his envoys. Once our sovereign unites with yours, our sovereign can send
forth his host to the Don, have the thievish Don Cossacks caught and
hanged, and expel the others from the Don. Henceforth no man will inhabit
the Don. The tsar also strictly will enjoin his commander at Tarki not to
hamper or molest the Turks anywhere."

Despite Khvorostinin's understanding with Akhmad-Pasha matters
were not resolved easily for Shcherbatov when he arrived in the Crimea
with presents. The princes, murzas and uhlans congregated at the

ambassador's temporary quarters to receive the tsar's grants. Some accepted the presents, others complained "Your lord the tsar wrote to our sovereign that he awarded us a bountiful grant, mere couriers have brought us more than this. Whoever once got cloth in tens now receives it in fives or sixes, and the caps are of poor quality." The ambassador observed that Ghazi-Girey received ten thousand rubles and that the heir apparent, princes, murzas and uhlans were given seventeen thousand dengas and clothing. "The khan's share is of no concern to us," retorted the Tatar princes. "That money serves solely to erect fortifications. Do not confuse our cloth and money with the special funds requested by the khan." The heir apparent was infuriated that he was sent so little. If they paid the khan ten thousand, he said, he should at least have five thousand. He railed against the khan, saying "You have taken much money, kept it all for yourself, and now you go against Hungary. I shall remain in the Crimea and plunder the Muscovite borderlands."

Ghazi-Girey also refused to swear to the peace, demanding that the tsar send him ten thousand rubles yearly. Thereupon Akhmad-Pasha warned him "Should you now not swear an oath of eternal peace before Moscow's ambassador and then march in the sultan's service against Hungary, the tsar will make peace with the Lithuanian king, and you will get nothing more from him." The khan hesitated, fell silent and finally took the oath. He consented to inscribe the tsar's full title in the sworn text of the treaty and to affix his seal beneath the document, something that he usually did only for the Turkish sultan. "Tell my brother," he advised Shcherbatov, "that I have not refrained from showing him a lofty honor such as never was rendered by previous khans." Shcherbatov insisted that both sides free their prisoners without payment of ransom. "I cannot," replied the khan, "seize captives held by the Tatar princes. I hold not a single prisoner, if I did I would not shirk from this for my brother. It has never been known in the Crimea for the khan to seize captives belonging to the princes, who live thereby. Let those Tatars whose brothers and kin are held by the tsar ransom or exchange for them. It is not my concern."

Shcherbatov's account sheds interesting light on how he acquired needed information. "We have," he wrote, "former prisoners whom we have bribed into the tsar's service." For example Shcherbatov learned of the crown prince's quarrel with the khan from Senka Ivanov, a Russian prisoner long in captivity who had lived with a certain murza's millers. Shcherbatov also recounted how Ghazi-Girey and the crown prince wined and dined at his expense. Once the crown prince rode out from the khan's palace, passed the ambassadorial lodgings and dispatched a Tatar to Shcherbatov. The emissary demanded the ambassador provide wine, mead and food to the crown prince, who was in the field. Shcherbatov sent wine, mead, cakes and pastilles. Likewise he entertained the khan himself.

Talks with the Crimean ambassador in Moscow also encountered obstacles. He demanded the return of Pashay-Murza, who rode with Murad-Girey in poverty, *like a cossack*, as the ambassador put it. When Murad-Girey died, Pashay enlisted in Muscovite service. Fedor granted him the choice of returning to the Crimea or staying in Moscow. The ambassador sought an audience with Pashay, where he urged him to come back to the Crimea, to the khan and to his father. Pashay declared that he would not renounce the tsar's bounty for the sake of the Crimea. Fedor endowed him with a lavish grant, with extensive patrimonial holdings and military service estates, with villages and with money. His entire family in the Crimea never experienced such generosity from the khan. The tsar even bestowed a princess upon him, a daughter of Kaibula.[31] The Crimean envoys and couriers then protested heatedly, characterizing Pashay as a driveling fool whose statements were unwise. They notified Conciliar Secretary Andrei Shchelkalov that they would transport Pashay forcibly in chains to the khan in the Crimea if only the tsar would release him. "Should he not wish to leave," asserted Shchelkalov, "the sovereign will not surrender him against his will. It is unseemly that you grow vexed and utter abuse about that." "If the sovereign does not release Pashay-Murza," one Crimean courier warned, "all of this worthwhile negotiation will come to naught." Shchelkalov was not threatened. "Such inappropriate speeches and contentious words," he said, "do not further worthy business. No one, even the khan, frightens our mighty tsar. Let the khan broaden negotiation to include such trivialities, and our sovereign will forego his friendship. The khan must strive to secure the love and affection of our tsar." The ambassador closed the matter. "Such words came from the heart," he first observed. "The khan will not part with the sovereign over such a petty dispute, and will hold brotherhood and love for eternity."

Moscow understood clearly why the Tatars needed peace. War with Austria diverted them from the Muscovite borderlands. Similarly it hindered the sultan from turning much attention to Muscovy, although he did not cease regarding it with hostility, given the complaints of Nogay chieftains against Muscovite oppression and specifically against the cossacks' activity. A Nogay ambassador to Islam-Girey recounted their grievances to Muscovite interpreters in the Crimea. "Your sovereign the grand prince," he asserted, "started the war with us. He had brought dishonor upon the emissaries of Prince Urus and gave them leave from Moscow without bestowing a grant upon them. The Volga Cossacks sorely offend us. Long have they raided many of our encampments and planted numerous forts along the Yaik and beyond, hemming us in tightly. Prince Urus dispatched me to beg the Turkish prince to hurl his forces against Astrakhan, and we will ride with them." The interpreters countered that the Nogay, having forgotten Tsar Ivan's generosity toward them, instigated the robbery and dishonor of Muscovite ambassadors and made yearly incursions into the Muscovite borderlands.

Despite this tension the Turks did not mount a campaign against Astrakhan. The Nogay were compelled to submit to Moscow. The Nogay candidly and guilelessly explained the causes of their submission. "Prince Urus," his emissary told the Muscovite ambassador to the Crimea, "sent me to the Turkish sultan that he would not reproach Urus and his murzas for succumbing to the will of the Muscovite tsar. He who holds Astrakhan, the Volga and the Yaik must dominate the entire Nogay horde." "The Nogay murzas and all their best men," the Muscovite ambassador then reported to the tsar, "have been forced to ride to the Crimea. Filled with grief at having abandoned fathers, mothers, wives, children and property, they say 'Prince Murad-Girey and the Muscovite commanders of Astrakhan requested as hostages our most respected men, our brothers and children, yet our fathers, grandfathers and great-grandfathers lived their lives without giving hostages. Although they often swore fealty to the Muscovite sovereign, never did they know such bondage as Murad-Girey now imposes upon us.'" The murzas and the aristocracy therefore petitioned the sultan to accept them as his subjects. Naturally the sultan could not hear these laments with indifference, nor could he remain impassive at reports that the Don Cossacks incessantly attacked Azov, pirated ships and galleys and murdered Turkish subjects.

BLAGOV'S MISSION TO TURKEY

Ambassador Blagov[32] journeyed to Constantinople in July 1584 to announce Fedor's accession to the throne to Sultan Murad.[33] He announced that the new tsar intended to abolish tariffs and tolls for Turkish merchants and recalled that the late tsar, for the sake of Sultan Selim,[34] withdrew his garrison from the Tarki fortress, which the Volga Cossacks now occupied without Fedor's knowledge. There were, he claimed, no constraints on the Muslim faith in Russia, for the Muslim Mustafa-Ali had mosques in Kasimov.[35] On the Don and near Azov lived cossacks, all fugitives. Other cossacks had long resided there. Quarrels arose because the men of Azov, along with the Crimeans and the Nogay, invaded the sovereign's border-lands, abducting many Russians and spiriting them away to Azov. The cossacks, whose families and kin inhabited these borderlands, could not stand for this and raided in reprisal.

Blagov insisted that the sultan's envoy escort him home. Moscow deemed this necessary in order to impress on other monarchs the friend-ship between the tsar and the dread and haughty sultan. The pashas with-held their consent for a long time, saying "The sultan is a great ruler. His ambassadors travel to such great monarchs as the emperor, the French, Spanish and English kings, because they send him treasures. With you we have only commercial ties." "It is true," Blagov admitted, "that our sov-ereign has never yielded treasure to the Turk, but in brotherly love your sovereign should have his emissary, a worthy chiaus,[36] return with me. Should the emissary not accompany but follow me, our sovereign will feel that he is not sent with affection, and will not allow the sultan's emissary into his presence." "It will be fourteen years since your envoy came from your sovereign's father," said the pashas. "Then he bore lavish gifts, now your gifts are mean. Why must our sovereign now dispatch his emissary?" Blagov explained by asking "Did that envoy not exceed the sovereign's mandate and add his personal gifts? For this reason our sovereign punished him. I have brought that with which I was sent."

When the bailiffs visited Blagov and asserted that the pashas wanted payment from him for his passage across the Black Sea, he inquired "Where is it not customary to furnish envoys with a cart or a ship?" "The pashas told us," replied the bailiffs, "that the sultan has directed that money be taken from you, for you came with so few presents." "I have brought what was allotted to me," Blagov objected. "Sultan Murad must write to our sovereign about this. When the sultan confiscates money from me for the ship, my sovereign will see that I suffer no personal loss, but brotherly love and amicability between sovereigns will vanish over such a trivial issue, and future communication between them will be impossible."

Blagov won his point. Sultan Murad sent his emissary Ibrahim back with him to Moscow. This delegate, like his predecessors, refused to discuss with the boyars an alliance between the sultan and the tsar, then demanded that Moscow give up Tsarevich Murad-Girey and recall Ataman Kishkin of the Don, who was raiding Azov. Ibrahim was dismissed with the response that more Lithuanian than Muscovite cossacks were marauding along the Don, that Kishkin had been recalled to Moscow, the remaining cossacks were forbidden to attack Azov, and that a new ambassador from Fedor would advise the sultan about Murad-Girey.[37]

While in Constantinople Blagov invariably reiterated his view of the Terek and Don cossacks. "You yourselves," he said, "know that brigands and runaways roam the Terek and the Don without the tsar's knowledge. They heed no one. What business of mine are these cossacks?" Besides repeating this official position Blagov could draw on his own experience to offer a similar opinion of the cossacks. When he descended the Don the cossacks fell upon him, dishonored him, seized his boats, and looted many supplies. When Moscow learned of this and heard that Blagov was returning with the sultan's emissary, it sent Vasily Birkin to meet him.[38] Upon reaching the Don this Birkin was to join Ataman Kishkin and other cossack chiefs and warriors loyal to Fedor. They were to track down and apprehend the outlaws, convey three or four of their ringleaders to Fedor and while on the Don use the knout to punish the others for robbery. If this could not be accomplished openly Birkin was to deceive and cajole them, then arrest them that seeing this the others would learn not to steal. Moscow also learned that the cossack leader Yushka Nesvitaev and his gang had crossed from the Volga to the Don to attack and rob Blagov. Birkin and Kishkin were directed to catch him and bring him to Moscow. If Yushka reformed and began to serve honestly he might be left alone.

Birkin reported that the cossacks had seized Circassian fishermen at sea. He tried to convince them to free their prisoners lest Blagov, then in Constantinople, suffer for their actions. Not only did the cossacks refuse to release the captives for Blagov's sake, they threatened to tear out their hair. Loyal cossacks warned Birkin that others planned to murder Blagov and the Turkish envoy, leaving no survivors to tell the tale in Moscow. Azov too knew of the cossacks' plot to kill Blagov and the emissary because a Muslim, Muhammad, who once was a Don Cossack, alerted the officials there. As a result the Turkish emissary refused to leave Azov, and Blagov was detained there at length because the Turks insisted the Don Cossacks solemnly pledge not to raid the delegation. Blagov finally had to exchange his crown scribe and an interpreter for the Circassian hostages.

NASHCHOKIN AND THE COSSACKS

A second Muscovite representative, the nobleman Nashchokin,[39] was dispatched to Constantinople some time before April 1592. The boyar council concluded that relations with Turkey might be broken were an ambassador not sent soon. He was instructed to recall the earlier discussions, explain the delay in assigning a new envoy, and announce that the Persian shah had approached Fedor about an alliance and joint military expedition, for which the tsar gave him no troops and dismissed his ambassadors with empty hands.[40] Likewise, he must state verbally that the emperor and his allies, the Pope and the kings of Spain and Poland, were prevailing upon the tsar to make war against Turkey, but Fedor was not listening to them. The ambassador must ascertain whether the sultan meant to continue friendly relations and gather other information.

Nashchokin was to explain to the sultan that Fedor delayed so long to dispatch an envoy because the king of Poland prohibited the tsar's emissaries to cross Lithuania. Moreover Lithuanian cossacks along the Don joined the treasonous Don Cossacks, nominally loyal to Moscow, in blocking free passage of the embassy. Finally there was a rush of complex affairs such as the campaign against Sweden.

Besides this, Nashchokin was given a special memorandum. Metropolitan Dionisy of Trnovo, when visiting the tsar, told the chancellery officials that his relative John the Greek was the Turkish sultan's privy councilor. Dionisy vowed to serve the tsar and make use of this situation in every possible way. What he learned would be transmitted to the tsar's envoy, who would bring the tsar's grant for John the Greek. When Nashchokin reached Constantinople he must meet in secret with Dionisy and Patriarch Jeremiah.[41] He must arrange for them to serve the tsar by swaying the sultan's privy councilors, who in turn were to dispose the sultan towards favorable policies, towards heartfelt friendship and amity between the rulers. The sultan then would dismiss Nashchokin under good auspices and return with him a Turkish diplomat, an eminent dignitary with authority to negotiate. Should the patriarch and metropolitan agree to serve the tsar they might need copies of the documents which Nashchokin carried to the sultan to comprehend fully the matters of state which they were to influence. Nashchokin was to provide them secretly with the copies along with the tsar's grant to John the Greek, which also was to be transmitted confidentially.

The tsar also sent a writ to the Don Cossacks, "the atamans and cossacks along the upper Don and those downstream near Azov," urging them to keep the peace with the inhabitants of Azov while Nashchokin was there. Fedor further wrote that they leave unmolested the residents of Azov who customarily came upriver for fishing and firewood, and release their Turkish and Circassian hostages, for whom the tsar would compensate them handsomely. The cossacks also were notified that while Nashchokin was in Turkey the junior boyar Peter Khrushchov[42] would stay on the Don. With their cooperation he was to keep Muscovy's borderlands free of brigands.

Nashchokin proclaimed the tsar's decree to the cossacks. "We stand ready to escort you, ambassador," they replied, "and to serve the tsar, but we cannot surrender prisoners taken with our own blood. These Circassians chased us and sought our heads, although we did not go against them. The men of Azov carry off our brothers, atamans and cossacks, and enslave them in the galleys. Not only do they refuse to release them, they will not accept ransom. In peacetime they kidnapped about twenty-four cossacks for the galleys. This winter they and the Circassians abducted more than a hundred men from the settlements and sold them into hard labor. It is a sign of the tsar's disfavor that he takes our prisoners, gained with our blood."

This said, the cossacks walked away from Nashchokin, formed a circle, and studied the tsar's charters. As they read them the atamans and cossacks grumbled noisily that they would not part with prisoners. Several of them then again approached Nashchokin and rebuked him. "Once the tsar showed us his favor," they protested. "He used to address us in documents, 'to the downriver atamans,' mentioning the more significant by name, and then wrote 'and to all the atamans of the lower and the upper reaches.' Now he writes first to the upstream atamans and cossacks, and only afterwards to us on the lower reaches, neither does he mention anyone by name. Yet the cossacks of the upper Don render him no service. If he has sent a ransom with you now we will liberate the captives, we cannot yield them without recompense. Were we to release them now without payment we would not see the ransom, not even in ten years. Nor will we ride to Moscow for the ransom. If the tsar has ordered you to take the captives by force, you may manage to seize them from us after bloodshed. We will cut them loose and vanish, flying wherever the winds bear us."

"It is not proper that you threaten to flee the tsar," Nashchokin admonished the cossacks, "you who are his *slaves* and dwell in his ancestral lands." "How," they complained, "can we live on the Don without the tsar's favor? Will any prisoners be ransomed from us ever again? We will capture someone and the sultan will write to the sovereign, who will wrest them from us without payment and restore them to the Turk. How then can we remain on the Don?"

When Nashchokin asked them to remain at peace with Azov while he was conferring at Constantinople, they procrastinated. "Our ancient customs," they declared, "render it unfitting for us to deliberate now over war and peace. Our comrades, Vasily Zhegulin and his three hundred men, are at sea. How can we make peace before they return?" The envoy brought the cossacks the tsar's grant of cloth. He wanted to distribute it according to his instructions, reserving the best for the atamans and leaving the worst for the rank and file, but the cossacks asserted that they had no dignitaries, all being equal, and that they would divide the cloth by lot. When finally Nashchokin proposed that they cooperate with Peter Khrushchov, they refused. "We served the tsar in the past, and had no captains," they said, "now we are pleased to serve the tsar under our own captains, not with Khrushchov."

This all ended with more than mere words. When the cossack leader Zhegulin came back from his voyage six hundred cossacks carrying sabers and muskets advanced on the ambassadorial tent and shouted for Nashchokin to show them his instruction from the tsar. The ambassador replied that his orders referred to many matters, that he was unable to show the document. If they came to plunder the tsar's treasury, he and his men would die defending it. The cossacks became uproarious and seized by force the tsar's saltpeter and provisions. They grabbed Ataman Vasiliev of the Don, who accompanied Nashchokin from Moscow, beat him with clubs and threw him in the water in front of the ambassador's tent. This Vasiliev tried to persuade them to conceal their treachery, not to insult the tsar, and to release the captives.

After many trials Nashchokin finally reached Constantinople and carried out his mission. The sultan immediately granted him leave and decided to send a Turkish ambassador with him to Moscow. Suddenly news came that the Don Cossacks had abducted a hundred and thirty people from Azov, and that the tsar had erected four new forts along the Don and the Terek. The grand vizier assailed Nashchokin. "Is this your sovereign's love for us?" he asked. "You know that this calls for the saber, for war, not friendship! If your tsar chases the cossacks from the Don our sovereign will pacify the Crimean khan, the men of Azov and Belgorod. You say that the cossacks of the Don are headstrong men who rob without your sovereign's knowledge. The Crimeans and the men of Azov are equally willful. If your tsar does not remove the cossacks from the Don I swear by God we will call the Crimeans and the Nogay to ride. We too will come with an enormous army by land and by sea, with cannon and with fortresses. Even though it causes trouble for us, rest assured that we will march, and then there will be no peace."

"May God grant," Nashchokin responded, "that the brotherly love between our rulers deepen henceforth. Should the Crimean khan now invade the tsar's borderlands that is God's will. Our sovereign's host stands ready to meet him, and no one can guess whom God will favor. Better is it to calm the Crimeans lest fraternal love between our sovereigns vanish."

"True," the vizier commented, "when misunderstandings divide people both sides suffer. Now it is too late for this to be undone. We are deeply offended by what your cossacks have done. Ambassadors often suffer punishment for such things, but our sovereign has ruled that we make no reprisals against you, for such is not our custom. Honoring our traditions, he will release you to your sovereign and have his ambassador accompany you."

When Nashchokin related this to Moscow, the tsar's decree went out along to the Don. "Should you start any quarrel with the men of Azov," it read, "and thereby cause conflict between us and the Turk, our disfavor will fall upon you, and never again will we receive you in Moscow. We will dispatch a mighty host to the lower Don, to Razdory, where we will place a fort, and we will cast you out from the Don. Where then will you take refuge from us and from the Turkish sultan? Render us service by selecting your best leaders and brave young horsemen and sending them to the Kalmius river, to Aroslanov's settlement. Let them destroy his settlement, take informants, and bid your comrades escort these prisoners to us, that we may learn of the khan's schemes and of his campaign. If the khan or his tsareviches cross our border before the ambassador and the Turkish envoy reach Azov, and the men of Azov join them, ride against them at the ford, on the road, and on the Northern Donets, giving them battle on our behalf. Wherever along the Donets you encounter our men from Putivl and the Zaporozhian Cherkassians who came to the Donets against the khan at our behest, aid them and with our gentry who act in concert with them. For the Zaporozhian Cherkassians, Hetman Khristof Kositsky and the other cossack atamans and warriors have been ordered to patrol the roads to the Donets and to pursue the khan on our borderlands."

The cossacks not only refused to render the services Fedor demanded, they did not even provide guides to his ambassadors. Prince Volkonsky,[43] assigned to meet the Turkish envoy near Azov, reported to the tsar "The atamans and cossacks of the Don refuse us guides. They say they cannot compel guides to direct us, though they will not stop those who volunteer. Only about thirty volunteers will accompany us. Many atamans and warriors desired to guide us, then the cossack Nekhoroshko Kvartavy, who deserted your majesty's service at Serpukhov, came down river from the Ukraine to the cossack host. He told the cossacks that their comrades in Moscow were in great want, that they receive from the tsar no provisions or salary, nor were they granted leave to return to the Don. They serve on their own mounts, for which they receive no fodder. Some have entered slavery. When they heard this many cossacks and atamans changed their minds about escorting us. Some guides rode with us, but we do not trust them, since about forty fled from the Don Cossacks. We think that they rode to the Cherkassians."

As soon as Rizvan the Turkish ambassador reached Moscow he recapitulated the demands the vizier made of Nashchokin in Constantinople to expel the cossacks from the Don and raze the fortresses there and along the Terek. "Dismiss the Turkish ambassador," the tsar and the boyars decreed, "and return with him our ambassador to Sultan Murad lest relations be interrupted. Reply in writing to the sultan that the tsar is opening the road across the land of Kabarda for Turks wishing to travel to Derbent and Shemakha. Write as before about the cossacks that brigands and fugitives dwell along the Don and join with Lithuanian Cherkassians. They encircle Turkish cities without the sovereign's knowledge. The tsar has no forts on the Don."

Moscow's newly appointed ambassador the noble Isleniev set out in July 1594. He was to deliver a rescript and a grant to the metropolitan of Trnovo and to tell him "When Nashchokin was ambassador you served the sovereign, and he knows of your labors. Serve him now." Isleniev also brought a youth for instruction in the Greek language. The details of this mission are not known. Correspondence with the Austrian court suggests that Isleniev was detained at Constantinople by the new sultan, Muhammad III.[44]

RELATIONS WITH THE CAUCASUS AND PERSIA

All of these negotiations demonstrate that the sultan, besides pressing for the resettlement of the cossacks from the Don, continually insisted upon dismantling Muscovy's fort on the Terek. We have noted that after conquering Astrakhan in 1556 the Muscovite state perforce entered into relations with the peoples of the Caucasus who, fighting one another and fearing the Turks and the Crimeans, needed Moscow's patronage and besought the tsar's protection. Ivan IV established family ties with the Circassian rulers.[45] He also constructed a fort on the Terek, which he abandoned later at the sultan's demand. Under Fedor, in 1586, envoys from Alexander of Kakhetia[46] appeared in Moscow. Threatened by the Turks on one side and by the Persians on the other, Alexander requested in the name of his nation that the sole Orthodox sovereign take them as his subjects and save their bodies and souls. The tsar accepted Alexander as his subject. Teachers, monks, priests and iconographers were dispatched to Kakhetia to restore the purity of Christian learning and worship among a people surrounded by unbelievers. Material aid too was provided, in the form of firearms. The fortress of Tarki was renovated and garrisoned with musketeers. Moscow asked Alexander to furnish the fort with sufficient supplies for twenty-five hundred men, but he was unwilling. "Because of the great distance," he pleaded, "because of the high mountains, it is indeed impossible even to collect so many stores." Muscovite units easily protected Alexander from the ruler of Tarki (the shevkal) whom they hemmed in tightly and deprived of the Koisu river, so that he too was forced to give homage to the tsar.[47]

It was a wholly different task to support Alexander in an open confrontation with the terrifying Turks. They demanded from him supplies and passage through his lands to Derbent and Baku. Alexander boldly defied them. "I will not permit you to cross my land with supplies," he said, "nor will I give you any of my own stores. I am a slave of the Russian tsar, and have no fear of the Turk." Moscow, however, advised him to coexist with the Turks, flattering them while spinning plots against them. Alexander discerned that subjection to Moscow brought him no closer to his main goal. He could not rely on a swift and powerful defense. He perceived that Moscow counseled him to act as earlier, as the weaker party practicing cunning to the stronger, deceiving him. Thus his enthusiasm waned. He implored Fedor to dispatch a large army against the shevkal, to occupy Tarki and place as their agent there the krym-shevkal,[48] who was the father of Alexander's daughter-in-law. Moscow did consent to send an army, requiring that Alexander for his part provide his personal forces under his son and the krym-shevkal. The Muscovite commander Prince Khvorostinin[49] actually penetrated the shevkal's territory and seized Tarki, then waited in vain for the Kakhetian regiments. Instead hostile people, various mountain tribes, appeared, compelling Khvorostinin to raze and evacuate Tarki. Few soldiers returned with him to the Terek, for the mountaineers

massacred three thousand. Clearly, in the late sixteenth century the Muscovite realm could not sustain such remote holdings, even though Fedor
did assume the titles of sovereign of Iberia, tsar of Georgia and Kabardia,
of the Circassians and of the mountain princes.

Even while Godunov conducted negotiations with the German emperor concerning the union of all Christian sovereigns against the Turk his
representatives in Constantinople assured the sultan that the tsar out of
friendship was declining the proposals of emperor, king and Pope. In like
fashion Godunov engaged in talks with Persia about the very same alliance, and had his ambassadors at Constantinople vouch that the tsar was
not listening to the shah's suggestions. Shah Khudabanda's unsuccessful
war with Turkey in 1586 forced Persia to solicit an alliance with Muscovy
against the sultan. The shah spared no promises. He offered to deliver to
the Russians Baku and Derbent, even if he personally conquered them
from the Turks. His son Abbas the Great continued to direct relations
towards this same goal. As well as Derbent and Baku, he ceded to the tsar
Kakhetia, the domain of Russia's vassal Alexander. Striving to incline
Godunov towards the alliance, the shah's envoy asserted that two such
great monarchs as the tsar and the shah not only could defy the Turk, they
could even drive him from his lands.

The Muscovite administration had nothing to learn in the way of
political morality from this new ally. Abbas sent word to Godunov that his
truce with the sultan was merely a ruse, and that consigning his six-year-
old nephew to the Turk as a hostage meant nothing. "As far as I am
concerned," he said, "my nephew is already dead." "The Turks do have one
of the shah's nephews," Persia's ambassador explained to Godunov, "the
two who remain with him have been exiled and blinded. Our rulers have
no love for their brothers and nephews." Negotiations with Persia towards
an alliance against the Turk, like those with Austria, proved fruitless.

ONGOING CONQUEST OF SIBERIA

Local circumstances and resistance from still powerful Muslim states
impeded the extension of Moscow's authority towards the Southeast and
the Caucasus. All the more could it spread unchecked in its traditional
direction, towards the Northeast. The Cheremiss of the former khanate of
Kazan rebelled against Fedor as they did against his father, and again were
subdued. The principal means of pacification remained the construction of
towns inhabited by Russians: Tsyvilsk, Urzhum, Tsarev-gorod on the

Kokshaga, Sanchursk and others. Russian settlers managed to gain a foothold in the Urals, where Yermak and his cossacks paved the way under Ivan IV. We have seen that Ivan, once he recognized Yermak's achievements, sent his officers Princes Bolkhovsky and Glukhov to Siberia. These commanders joined Yermak in the fall of 1583. He received them with great honor. The cossacks presented them with precious furs but failed to provide what was most essential, victuals to tide their guests through the winter. In the resultant famine many cossacks and Muscovite military servitors perished, among them the commander Prince Bolkhovsky.

Starvation ended with the spring of 1584 only to be followed by a different kind of misfortune. Karacha,[50] who had left Kuchum[51] after the capture of Muhammad-Kul,[52] camped with his followers on the Tura river. From there he asked Yermak's aid against the Nogay horde. On the assurance of an oath alone and without having obtained hostages, Yermak sent him Ivan Koltso[53] with forty cossacks. All were treacherously slaughtered by Karacha. Another cossack leader, Yakov Mikhailov, who rode up to Karacha's encampment as a scout, also was killed. Karacha then besieged the few remaining cossacks in the fort at Isker, where he stayed until the middle of June, hoping to starve out the Russians. One night, while Karacha's followers slept, Ataman Meshcheriak made a sortie from the fort and attacked the unsuspecting enemy. Karacha fled the camp, having lost two sons. At dawn the Siberians gathered their forces and gave the cossacks battle, hoping to overwhelm them with numbers. Meshcheriak, firmly ensconced in Karacha's camp, repelled them until midday and forced them to withdraw. Karacha lost hope of defeating the cossacks and rode off beyond the Ishim.

The cossacks' triumph was short lived. Merchants from Bukhara sent a complaint to Yermak that Kuchum would not allow them into the town of Sibir. Yermak assembled a small force (fifty men) and sought to meet them along the Irtysh. Unable to find them, on the night of August 5 he camped on the riverbank. Yermak's cossacks, exhausted from their ride, slept soundly, but on the other bank Kuchum was awake. In the dead of night during a driving rain he forded the river, fell on the slumbering cossacks and exterminated them. Yermak, according to rumor, drowned in the Irtysh while trying to reach his boat.

The famine and three defeats left so few cossacks in Siberia that Ataman Meshcheriak considered it impossible to remain, and set forth on the road for Russia. Kuchum retook Sibir and in turn soon was ousted by

YERMAK'S CAMPAIGN TO SIBERIA

his rival Seidiak, but these princelings could not continue for long to expel one another at leisure. Muscovy's new administration assigned commander after commander to Siberia. Commander Mansurov came in the fall of 1585 and erected a small fortification on the Ob, near the mouth of the Irtysh. The Ostiaks came to besiege it, bringing with them a widely adored and famous idol, which a cannonball fired from the fort soon shattered. Having lost faith in their deity, the Ostiaks no longer bothered the Russians. Luguy, prince of two major towns and four fortified smaller towns on the Ob, traveled to Moscow to beg that the Russian forces posted at the mouth of the Irtysh stop warring with his people. He offered to give tribute to the chancellery officials in the Vym country. Because Luguy's petition preceded all others, the sovereign consented, and ordained that Luguy, his brothers or his nephew bring seven times forty of the finest sables. Commanders Sukin and Miasnoy founded the city of Tiumen on the banks of the Tura, and Commander Chulkov established Tobolsk in 1587. Seidiak took it into his head to assault this city, but he was defeated and captured.

Seidiak's rival Kuchum held out in the Barabinsk steppe, raiding Muscovite possessions. Commander Prince Koltsov-Mosalsky routed him near Chili-kul lake, capturing two of his wives and a son, Abdul-Khair. After this Kuchum turned to Fedor with a request that he grant him an encampment, free his nephew Muhammad-Kul, and that he himself be taken under the tsar's wing. For three years Moscow made no response and in the fourth year Kuchum apparently again proved dangerous, since in 1597 the tsar sent him a letter enumerating all his insolence under Tsar Ivan and afterwards.

"We have constructed fortified towns in our patrimony, the Siberian land," wrote Fedor, "we have outfitted them with siege garrisons and cannon. We have yet to order our mighty host against you, for we have awaited your salutation. Had we sent our mighty host to Siberia they would have found you, wherever you were, and taken vengeance for your false-hoods. We, a mighty sovereign, wished to bless you, to establish you as tsar of the Siberian land. We settled your nephew Muhammad-Kul in our realm, graced him with towns and districts fitting his station, and he now he serves his majesty the tsar. We know that you roam the wild steppe like a cossack, with but few followers. The Nogay warriors who used to wander with you, and upon whom you placed great hope, have deserted you.

Murza-Chin deserted you for his majesty the tsar. The remainder of your men departed with the two tsareviches, others fled to Bukhara, to the Nogay, to the cossack horde. You have few men with you, this we know as a certainty. Even had you many warriors, how could one as unjust as you hope to stand against our host? You know in person how great were the Muslim realms of Kazan and Astrakhan, and that our father, marching forth *personally* as tsar, conquered them. How could you, dwelling in the steppe and living as a cossack, escape our host and the roar of its cannon? We would be justified if now we ordered our host and the fire of its cannon leveled against you in retribution for your past insolence and lies, and thus crush you completely. Yet we, a truly Christian and merciful sovereign, following the benevolence customary to tsars, give life to the dead and clemency to the guilty. Witnessing your deep misfortune, we proclaim to you our grace and leniency, that you may approach his majesty the tsar without any hesitation. You must agree to dwell in Muscovy, under our hand, and we shall provide you with towns, districts and monetary grants befitting your worth. If after some time with us you wish to return to your Siberian homeland, we will anoint you prince and maintain you there with kindness."

Kuchum replied with a demand for the Irtysh shore. "Until this time I have stood against you," he wrote to the commander at Tara. "I did not surrender Siberia, you seized it. Now let us try to find peace. Will it not be better in the end? I am united with the Nogay, and if we become tied to both parties my princely treasury will be drained. I want a just peace and will make many gestures to this end." Nothing is known of subsequent relations. In all probability they ended as a result of Kuchum's unwillingness to go to Moscow.

Other princes also were slow to submit. In July 1592 the tsar instructed the Stroganovs to recruit a hundred soldiers from their towns, pay them a monthly wage and supply them for the fall and the winter. Fifty of them, infantry, were to escort the commander Trakhaniotov to Siberia, and the other fifty, cavalry, were assigned to fight against the prince of the inhabitants of Pelym. Even so, the most certain means of consolidation in Siberia remained the construction of fortresses which, along with their surrounding districts, were settled by Russians. Pelym, Berezov, Surgut, Tara, Narym and Fort Ketsk were erected during Fedor's reign.

V

DOMESTIC AFFAIRS

Ivan the Terrible's reign oppressed not only those social classes[1] which his anger singled out for special tribulation, and not just the places he sacked. The very existence of the separate crown estates[2] exhausted the rest of the country, which suffered as well from incessant warfare. Fedor's accession found the realm in the most pitiful condition. A council convened in July 1584 proposed to set aside the charters of tax immunity caused by military service or impoverishment "until the country is put in order and aid is rendered to all through the tsar's dispensation."

Fedor's thirteen-year reign allowed the nation to recuperate. There occurred no prolonged war. The regent Godunov delighted in proving his concern for the general welfare, his hostility toward abusive officials, and his charity as long as his personal income remained unaffected. Thus contemporaries rightly praised Fedor's happy and serene reign, when both the ruling elite and all Orthodox Christians found respite from their previous woes.

THE TSAR'S ADMINISTRATION

Godunov acted in the tsar's name. He drew strength from the authority flowing from the tsar, a power sufficient to provide him the means of mastering the great lords. He of course saw it in his interest to sustain the monarch's eminence at the height to which previous sovereigns elevated it. Special assemblies, extraordinary sessions of the boyar council where the clergy deliberated alongside the boyars and councilors, were convened to consider the most vital issues such as the temporary suspension of charters of ecclesiastical immunity, negotiations with Poland and other matters. [Giles] Fletcher[3] relates how the tsar summoned to these assemblies dignitaries from the council whom he personally favored, while the patriarch invited bishops, archimandrites and monks who enjoyed particular repute and esteem, as well as the metropolitans and the archbishops. The assemblies usually gathered on Fridays at the throne room, with Fedor presiding from the throne. Not far away, at a modest rectangular table which could accommodate about twelve, sat the patriarch with the clergy and certain principal members of the boyar council, alongside two crown secretaries who recorded all that transpired. Others present occupied benches against the walls. One crown secretary placed before the assembly a list of the business it was charged to consider. When asked their opinion the clergy commonly observed that the sovereign and his council were wise and experienced, much more competent than they to judge the interests of the realm. They as churchmen looked after serving God and matters of religion. Therefore they asked the tsar and his councilors to draft the necessary decrees. They themselves would assist with prayers instead of advice.

Chancelleries existed to administer both foreign and domestic affairs. Several bore the special title of taxation chancelleries.[4] First came the Chancellery of Foreign Affairs under the control of Conciliar Secretary Andrei Shchelkalov who received a hundred-ruble salary. Second was the Chancellery of Crown Service and Appointments under Vasily Shchelkalov but directed by Sapun Abramov.[5] Here too the salary was a hundred rubles. Third was the Chancellery of Military Tenures under Conciliar Secretary Yelizar Vyluzgin,[6] the recipient of a five-hundred-ruble salary. Fourth came the Chancellery for Kazan under Conciliar Secretary Druzhina Penteleev,[7] a man of outstanding intelligence and efficiency. He earned one hundred and fifty rubles a year.[8] The tsar's charters named the taxation chancelleries after the crown secretaries directing them. "The taxation chancellery of our crown secretary Vasily Shchelkalov." Boyars and lords-in-waiting headed the other chancelleries. Thus in 1577 the tsar appointed the boyar Prince Grigory Andreevich Kurakin[9] and the lord-in-waiting Prince Lobanov[10] jointly to head the Chancellery for Criminal Affairs.

As previously, crown secretaries and their assistants were attached to the regional authorities, or more precisely supervised them, since these crown secretaries directed all their activities. Regional administrators routinely were rotated annually, save a handful held in exceptionally high regard whose term of office might be extended a year or two. They made salaries of one hundred, fifty or thirty rubles. The populace, Fletcher contends, despised them for their venality, and a Russian chronicler observes that Godunov, for all his fine intentions, could not wipe out extortion. Regional officials sought bribes all the more readily because they had to share them with the officers of the taxation and other chancelleries.

Two eminent individuals, one of whom represented the tsar's personal coterie, served as rulers in each of the more important frontier cities such as Smolensk, Pskov, Novgorod, and Kazan. These men discharged broader duties than those in other cities, and they enjoyed executive authority in criminal matters. They too were replaced annually except in certain cases. Their salaries ranged between four and seven hundred rubles.

FINANCES

Fedor entrusted the Tsar's Household, or the Chancellery of the Tsar's Household, which administered the ruler's private estates, to Grigory Vasilievich Godunov,[11] a man renowned for his thrift. Under Ivan IV the chancellery's revenue from farming out surplus taxes paid in kind never exceeded sixty thousand rubles, but under Fedor the figure approached two hundred and thirty thousand. Ivan lived a more regal and luxurious style than his son. Considering all sources, the taxation chancelleries collected nearly four hundred thousand rubles annually from taxpayers in the rest of the land, distributed by region as follows: Pskov 18,000, Novgorod 35,000, Torzhok and Tver 8,000, Riazan 30,000, Murom 12,000, Kholmogory and the Dvina 8,000, Vologda 12,000, Kazan 18,000, Ustiug 30,000, Rostov 50,000, Moscow 40,000, Kostroma 12,000, Siberia 20,000. Duties on commerce, court costs, legal and other fees, and residual sums from the various departments subsumed under the Chancellery of Crown Revenues provided 800,000 rubles annually. The yearly revenue on duties for trade, broken down regionally, was Moscow 12,000, Smolensk 8,000, Pskov 12,000, Novgorod 6,000, Staraia Rusa (from the saltworks) 18,000, Torzhok 800, Tver 700, Yaroslavl 1,200, Kostroma 1800, Nizhny Novgorod 7,000, Kazan 11,000, Vologda 2,000. Thus the treasury receipts from all sources totaled 1,430,000 rubles.[12]

Commercial duties were collected by customs officials, to whom they were farmed out at a price. Charters distributed to crown franchise holders stated "Let him postpone the due date of the tax for two months, but should it be two months in arrears and then not delivered on the due date in future take double payment from the franchise holder and his sureties." Tax farming franchises lasted for one year. According to a charter given to a customs official on the Dvina in 1588 "Charge every boat a tonnage rate of two rubles and two grivnas for every thousand puds, and seven altyns and two dengas for every hundred puds, no matter what the circumstances. Should a boat dock, collect a docking fee of ten altyns and a head tax of one denga for each crew member. The fee for mooring boats is twenty-two altyns. Those who come in sledges, on horseback or on foot pay a registration fee."[13]

Unloading duties are also mentioned: fifty copecks on a thousand puds, two dengas for a cartload and so forth. It cost two dengas for weighing. An admonition to "lift the wares on both ends of the scales" was necessary because those with loads weighing less than a pud could avoid this toll. Weighers lifted the cargo of wealthy merchants for a hoisting fee and charged other buyers and sellers at the market one denga for raising a load, and one denga for lowering it.

Customs officials reported numerous evasions of these duties. Privileged English merchants[14] were exempt, as were the boats of the Trinity, St. Cyril and other monasteries. Fedor Kobelev's boats did not pay the duty for out-of-town merchants, only the local rate for traders on the Dvina river on the basis that Kobelev owned businesses and property all along the Dvina. Based on the same argument, neither Daniel Stroganov's nor Daniel Brenkov's boats paid duty. Fedor advised his agents to levy duties on every Russian without exemption, the Dvina rate for those from the Dvina and the rate for out-of-town merchants for those from other areas and for all foreigners save the English, who held a charter of immunity. In 1592 the boyar Dmitry Ivanovich Godunov gained the right to impose commercial duties in the villages of Charonda and Korotkoe.

In 1588 the elder and fishermen of a fishing settlement in the Pereiaslavl region submitted a petition. The office of administration of palace land, they wrote, took from them nearly fifty rubles through a combination of annual assessments and fees, duties on mash, levies on the fishery and on pike from the river, special fees for the majordomo, the crown secretary and the steward, postal taxes, hay money and court fees. Under these burdens fishermen were fleeing the settlement. The tsar and the tsaritsa consented to relieve them for two years of the taxes for postal service and the court fees. In 1590 inhabitants of Kolsk, Kereta and the Kovda districts were freed from trade duties and corvées because the Swedes had ravaged the area. In 1591 peasants of the Glotova settlement complained that the men of Vychegda, Vym and the Syslova regions compelled them to contribute to joint payment of all sorts of taxes, thereby reducing their own burden. The Glotova settlers claimed to be the poorest sort of people. They subsisted on wild game and neither sowed grain nor engaged in commerce whereas along the Vychegda and the Syslova lived men of substance, merchants and farmers who marketed various wares and cultivated their fields. Fedor heard their plea. He ordered that Glotova's peasants bring their taxes to Moscow personally, as before, and that the residents of the Vychegda, Vym and Syslova regions take no taxes from them.

TRADE

If Fletcher's account is reliable, revenue from commercial activity must have lessened during Fedor's reign because of a notable decline in the level of exports of almost all products. Furs valued at four or five hundred thousand rubles were shipped abroad. Exports of wax were less than ten thousand puds whereas such shipments once nearly totaled thirty thousand puds. Fletcher vaguely mentions rather large honey exports. Tallow exports dipped from a hundred thousand to thirty thousand puds. Once nearly a hundred ships loaded flax and hemp at the docks of Narva, but no more than five appeared in Fletcher's time.

Fletcher's work fails to explain satisfactorily the causes of this diminution of exports. He cites as the first cause the Russians' loss by conquest of the docks at Narva. Second comes the interruption of overland communication between Smolensk and Polotsk during the war with Poland. Third was the decline of foreign trade stemming from the recent imposition of unbearable taxes on merchants and peasants, and from insecurity about their property. The second cause is unacceptable, at least as Fletcher expressed it, because no war with Poland occurred during Fedor's reign. Assuming that Fletcher means that war with Poland had curtailed overland trade under Ivan, and that this situation remained uncorrected under Fedor, Fletcher's use of the word *once* must refer to the first half of the century. If that is the case, the expression "heavy and intolerable burdens that have *of late* been imposed"[15] must also apply to the reign of Ivan, not of Fedor, who is not known to have created any special fiscal hardships. It is known that the decline in the export of wax was because the Muscovite administration, knowing the great foreign demand for this product and aware that foreigners would not exchange military supplies for it, decreed that wax be traded only for niter, powder and sulfur.

Fedor's Muscovy traded with Poland. Muscovite merchants journeyed to Warsaw and to Poznań and as before[16] complained fiercely of oppression, fraud and brigandage. Rubtsev, a merchant from Toropets, rode to Vitebsk on business. His dealings finished, he returned to Velizh. There a cavalry captain Drobovsky beat him and robbed him of two loads of rye, each about thirty-five chetverts, which cost twenty altyn and one grivna for each chetvert, seven pounds of gold and silver, worth over six rubles a pound, about twenty-five liters of silk of various colors, which cost forty altyns a liter, fourteen rubles worth of azure broadcloth, two dugout canoes valued at five and a half rubles. Two merchants from Smolensk petitioned against two merchants from Orsha. They arranged a barter transaction whereby the Orsha merchants would give them forty puds of alum and two puds of frankincense. The Orsha merchants shipped two barrels to Smolensk, claiming that they contained alum When the Smolensk merchants broke open the barrels in the presence of the customs inspectors it turned out that although alum rested on top, beneath it they found only assorted stuff. Two other merchants from Smolensk complained after they traveled to Orsha with hops, having agreed with three Lithuanian merchants to exchange them for cloth. They appraised the cloth at thirty altyns less one grivna for each arshin, and the hops at thirty altyns for each pud, then the Lithuanians attempted to substitute an inferior half-English grade of cloth. Two tradesmen, residents of Moscow, protested after they rode to Warsaw and Poznań and delivered sables worth fifteen hundred rubles to Poznań merchants in exchange for a signed and sealed promissory note. Poznań then burned to the ground and the debtors denied having any means of honoring the note.

Merchants from Moscow, Novgorod, Pskov, Smolensk, Belsk, Toropets, Viazma and all cities presented a formal petition. When they traveled the Smolensk road to Lithuania the prefects and elders in every town and large village as far as Wilno extorted money from them such as head taxes, bridge tolls, registration and ferry tolls. Officials in every large town wanted bribes from them, regardless of whether they traded there. Elders, extortionists and tax collectors profited by holding them for one or two weeks in places where they did not wish to stay, and obliging them to pay bribes. At Wilno they were forbidden to deal with visiting merchants and not allowed to hire their own draymen. Lithuanians hired the draymen and doubled the cost for Muscovites. Conversely at Smolensk their own Muscovite officials levied only a customs duty on the Lithuanians and let pass without charge those wishing to travel to Moscow. Once at Moscow, the Lithuanians were charged only a low duty, no higher than four percent,[17] and they could trade freely with any incoming merchant, the men of Ustiug and the Dvina and those from Perm and Kholmogory. Merchants also complained of crime along the frontier, as runaway peasants crossed the border for robbery. A certain Mukhort was notorious for such banditry in the Rzheva district.

Merchants from Lübeck pleaded for the restoration of their trade in Novgorod, Ivangorod and Pskov, and in 1593 sought the tsar's consent to erect their establishments in these towns and pay only half of the duty Then the merchants of Reval insisted that Hanseatic vessels not be allowed past their city lest they be deprived of their livelihood.

Fletcher alludes to unbearable taxes imposed on merchants and peasants, yet the Muscovite ambassadors to Lithuania had to praise Godunov as follows. "This is the leading man of the realm, to whom the tsar has entrusted the entire land. There is such construction throughout the land as has never been. He has raised stone fortifications at Moscow and Astrakhan. There is no taxed holding in the realm. Every measure of taxpaying land enjoys immunities under tax exemption. No tribute is collected, neither the plowland tax, nor that on commerce. The treasury lets contracts for building, and more than a thousand carpenters have been organized."

PROTECTING THE FRONTIER

While it is an exaggeration to say that Fedor's government collected no taxes, his reign did see a great deal done in the construction of new and the strengthening of old towns. Expansion into the steppe was vital for the security of the nation. Constantly mobile patrols of cossacks could not suffice. Equally necessary were fixed outposts and fortified towns, beyond which the marauding Tatar bands could not ride with impunity. Creating towns in the steppe meant bringing the entire surrounding countryside under control, so that in a gradual fashion, unnoticed because it was unimpeded, the state broadened its already huge expanse. The fortified town and its garrison drew other kinds of settlers into the steppe where they could dwell in safety under its protection, and thus Russian colonization extended farther and farther. The Tatars were well aware of the danger this movement presented them.[18] The construction of fortified towns[19] also threatened the cossacks. The following towns were built in Fedor's reign: Kursk, Livny, Kromy, Voronezh, Belgorod, Oskol and Valuiki, in the steppe; Shanchurin (or Shanchursk), Saratov, Perevoloka and Tsaritsyn, on the meadow side of the Volga, among the Cheremiss, and finally the town on the distant Yaik. Archangel was founded with wooden walls in 1584. Stone fortresses were erected at Astrakhan in 1589 and Smolensk in 1596.[20] Early in the reign, in 1586, the White, or Tsar's Quarter was established in order to strengthen Moscow. Fedor Kon,[21] master mason of churches and palaces, built it.[22]

The methods used in such construction emerge from the instructions given to Prince Zvenigorodsky[23] and his associates. "When you have reached Smolensk, search the town and its surrounding district for sheds and kilns belonging to church hierarchs, monasteries or anyone, where bricks are cast and fired with lime. Requisition all these sheds and kilns in the sovereign's name and have them repaired and roofed. Also erect new sheds and kilns, prepare lumber and firewood and, if possible, have stone converted into lime and ashlar quarried. Money from the tsar's treasury is sent with you for this expense. Hire free workers, contract with them, but make the villages of the tsar's household cut the piles. Register each taxable assessment unit for a hundred piles, and direct the peasants of the same villages of the tsar's household to bring the piles to Smolensk in the winter. Obtain from the governor of Smolensk ten local sworn officials, better townsmen, and have them control all expenditures and inscribe them separately in detailed entries in their books. These local sworn officials must sign each entry in the books, attesting that no theft has occurred. For disbursements, seek about twenty junior boyars from the governor. See that the junior boyars, the local sworn officials and the apprentices accept no promises and make no profit from anything, and that Prince Zvenigorodsky and his associates accept no promises or gifts and make no profit. The tsar will execute whoever connives, whoever is careless about supplies or whoever takes bribes or indulges in profiteering."

THE ARMY

Ivan's war with Bathory, during which the prolonged defense of sturdy Pskov[24] assumed such significance, must have inspired the idea of buttressing Smolensk, especially since the field army was still unreliable, even against the Crimeans it fought from the leaguer before Moscow. According to Fletcher's account the army, besides an undefined number of soldiers mustered under extraordinary circumstances, consisted under Fedor of eighty thousand mounted noblemen and twelve thousand infantry including musketeers, five thousand of whom were quartered in Moscow, two thousand (selected) composed the tsar's household guard, and the remaining five thousand were stationed throughout the most important cities. High-ranking nobles received a salary of seventy to one hundred rubles annually, the ordinary noble was paid forty to sixty, and junior boyars earned twenty to thirty. Musketeers got seven rubles yearly with twelve measures of rye and as much oats. There is mention of mounted musketeers. Foreign mercenaries in Fletcher's time numbered four thousand three hundred, of whom four thousand were Cherkassians or Little Russian cossacks, a hundred and fifty Dutchmen and Scots, and a composite detachment of a hundred and fifty comprised of Greeks, Turks, Danes and Swedes. Besides these foreigners, crowds of Tatars, Cheremiss and Mordvinians continued to take the field for campaigns.

Regimental commanders led regiments. Under these leaders served officers directing units of one thousand, five hundred, and one hundred men. Sergeants commanded groups of fifty and corporals groups of ten. Lithuanian and German units served under their own cavalry captains. When the sovereign appeared on campaign he came accompanied by his retinue consisting of household commanders, armorers, officers acting as dispatch carriers, lords-in-waiting of the sovereign suite, noblemen with arquebuses, helmets or armor, nobles bearing standards. The tsar's household guards bore his personal weapons comprising the great archer's equipage, a reserve archer's arms,[25] a small lance, cold sidearms, another small archer's kit and a boar spear. The bodyguards had squires.

The army's primary mission was *standing watch at the shore*. Every spring regiments were deployed along the banks of the Oka to guard against the Crimean Tatars. This involved both riding patrol and manning fixed encampments. The commanders charged with constructing the towns of Livny and Voronezh were ordered "When news reaches Livny about the appearance of warriors in the sovereign's borderlands, pass the word from Livny to Voronezh, and from Voronezh to Livny. Ride along the closer and safer roads. Commanders are to schedule patrols, observing the most suitable places for them, and to establish outposts, also where most suitable." Thirteen patrols rode a circuit from Livny and twelve from Voronezh.

In 1591 the commander at Putivl reported that the Cherkass were raiding all along the defense line, having destroyed Putivl's major observation points and massacred all the patrols. The roads were cut from Putivl to the large encampments at the mouth of the Aidar and the lookouts patrolling the mouth of the Borova. "Assemble two select columns at Livny," ordered the boyars, "choosing cossack guides or anyone else suitable. Have one approach the Northern Donets along the main Muravsk road and the other ride towards the Northern Donets as far as the Izium burial ground, between the Donets and the Oskol."[26] Nine patrols from Elets were stationed along the Bystraia Sosna and beyond the Sosna, and seven units set out from Kromy. A decree in 1594 directed that officers of the forts at Putivl, Livny and Elets, the soldiers and their guides receive the tsar's grant for their service, for losses and for ransom. Each must be given four rubles for lost horses and three for geldings. Wives and children of soldiers and guides who died in action were awarded four rubles each for their service, their death and losses.

There has been occasion to comment on the conduct of the steppe cossacks during the period under consideration.[27] Just as the crown long dealt with the Tatars by enrolling them in its service and employing them against their hostile compatriots, so it employed loyal cossacks to track down their unruly or thieving comrades. In 1591 the Volga ataman Boldyr, together with forty comrades, petitioned the tsar. He asserted that earlier, in 1589, cossacks attacked him on the Volga, wounded him and held him prisoner for six weeks. He escaped and captured three of the cossack outlaws, whom he turned over to the commander at Perevolok. Then they ordered Boldyr to leave Tsaritsyn in pursuit of the criminal atamans and their followers, Andriusha Goloshchap's band. He apprehended Goloshchap. Assigned to scour the Medveditsa river valley for cossack highwaymen, Boldyr apprehended four outlaws. When he was dispatched from the new town at Saratov he captured the cossack bandit leader Shchegolev. Thus the sovereign should recognize his services, however God moved him. Boldyr received cloth and a ruble in cash. In 1591 the commander at Astrakhan was charged with enlisting a thousand Volga Cossacks and five hundred Yaik Cossacks for the campaign against the shevkal. He was to issue three bushels of meal for each man, six bushels of groats and oat flour for each unit, or even more, depending on the length of their stay at Astrakhan. Each man was to receive six bushels of oats for his mount. Should the cossacks need cash, they were to be provided fifty copecks each.

In exactly the same fashion the crown used its Little Russian cossacks or Cherkassians, enrolling them into service against former comrades. Concerning this, there is a most interesting report to the tsar from Commander Borisov at Putivl, dated 1589. "The Ukrainian cossack Vasily Andreev," it read, "accompanied by two Donets cossacks, rode into Putivl from the field, invoking your name, O tsar. At an interrogation he stated he was on the Donets with the Cherkassians, with the bandit Yevlashov. There they defeated the cossacks of the Donets, Vlas Yakovlev and Semeika Novgorodets, made them captive and brought them to the camp. Here Vlas persuaded Vasily Andreev to abandon his fellows. Vasily rode to Vlas's fellows, led them against his own ataman Yevlashov, defeated him, rescued Vlas and Semeika, and appeared with them at Putivl." The commander immediately assigned Vasily a task, sending him in the tsar's service with other Cherkassians recently arrived at Putivl, in pursuit of former compatriots. Twice Vasily and another ataman defeated the Cherkassians and recovered from them property and horses belonging to the hired warriors of Putivl.[28]

Of similar interest are the tsar's instructions to Afanasy Zinoviev.[29] In April 1589 Fedor wrote him to lead troops from Putivl and Chernigov and cossacks from Rylsk and Starodub into the open steppe along the Donets or Oskol. There he must take up strong positions and station outposts to gather information about the khan. "Couriers must ride to Ataman Matvey and his Zaporozhian Cossacks and ask if they are loyal to the tsar. How do the Zaporozhians intend to stand and serve the tsar? Are the pickets, the patrols, Putivl's cossacks and its proud servitors of the tsar poised along the Don, alert and ready? Are Crimean couriers being allowed to pass? Will the cossacks rob, riding alongside the cossack brigands Mishuk and his gang, or will they stand firm against them? If Zinoviev finds Ataman Matvey and his men to be trustworthy he is to join with them against the Crimeans. Should there be no news about the Tatars, Zinoviev must seek to capture and hang the cossack bandits Mishuk and his gang (even though Mishuk was a registered cossack from Putivl)."[30]

The tsar's decree empowered Zinoviev to gather a force of twenty junior boyars, fifty-seven freeholders and forty-five cossacks from Putivl, twenty junior boyars and about forty-seven cossacks from Rylsk, and approximately seventy junior boyars with ninety-three horses from Chernigov. The commanders at Putivl, Rylsk, and Starodub were to furnish an additional 277 cossack volunteers, paying each two rubles to bring two horses and two geldings as mounts. Nevertheless the authorities at Putivl and at Rylsk enlisted no one, and those at Starodub contributed only five men. Twenty-five of the best musketeers were to be selected from the hundred-man Putivl garrison, as well as twenty of the most able gunners and garrison soldiers. Because the musketeers declared they had no horses, and the gunners and the garrison soldiers protested that they lacked arquebuses, the tsar's decree remained unheeded. When Zinoviev reported this, the sovereign commanded that the musketeers, gunners and garrison soldiers must be refitted at once with horses and arquebuses. Cossack volunteers now were to have three rubles for the two horses and two geldings, if necessary two men might share three mounts. Zinoviev did find the Zaporozhian ataman Matvey encamped on the Donets, and he observed that the cossacks were serving the tsar faithfully. Because of their lament that famine along the Donets forced them to eat grass, Fedor shipped them supplies, meal and oat flour, and a hundred rubles to be divided among six hundred and twenty men. He sent gifts to the atamans.

THE CODE OF PRECEDENCE

Arguments about precedence[31] increasingly harmed the Muscovite army because of the ever more common disputes and the complex calculations needed to determine a family's rank and service. The keen attention with which the social classes involved in crown service observed the code of precedence, as well as the character of this practice, permeate the language of petitions. "Lord tsar, render your judgment upon me, have me honored in our native land, that I, your slave, will not end in utter ruin!" Or "Gracious sovereign tsar, cast your mercy upon your slave! Do not have my father and grandfather stripped from me, your slave, have the tribunal pass judgment." At a reception for the Turkish ambassador in 1589 Gavril Veliaminov was named as fourth honorary bodyguard. One of the other three honorary bodyguards complained against Veliaminov's grandfather, writing "If I, your slave, do not outweigh Gavrilov's grandfather, I will recompense the entire Veliaminov family for the dishonor."

In 1588 the sovereign ordered commanders Prince Timofey Romanovich Trubetskoy and Prince Dmitry Ivanovich Khvorostinin to lead the Great Regiment at Tula against the Crimeans. Simultaneously Prince Khilkov commanded at Orel, Prince Kashin at Novosil, and Krivoy-Saltykov at Belev. Customarily, once the commanders of frontier towns had word of the enemy they gathered for consultation with the commanders of the main army. Now, however, Khilkov, Kashin and Saltykov petitioned "If the dispatches are carried to one of the boyar commanders, Prince T.R. Trubetskoy and his colleagues, we are prepared to do the sovereign's service, if the papers come to both Prince Trubetskoy and to Prince Khvorostinin we cannot be less than Prince Khvorostinin."[32] The next year Khvorostinin and Trubetskoy again were assigned to command the Great Regiment at Tula, and Prince Andrei Golitsyn was given the vanguard. Golitsyn was unwilling to serve below Trubetskoy and feigned illness. "We are ready to serve the sovereign," Princes Nogtev and Odoevsky petitioned, "but it is not our place to be less than Prince Ivan Golitsyn." "I cannot serve below Prince Odoevsky," Prince Peter Buinosov asserted. Prince Turenin said "I cannot serve under Prince Buinosov." Prince Mikhail Odoevsky, having appeared for service, refused to accept the registers listing the servitors for Prince Ivan Golitsyn. Prince Turenin refused to accept the lists for Prince Buinosov, neither would Buinosov serve under Odoevsky.

Several renowned boyars were appointed to stand guard on the banks of the Oka in 1597. Mstislavsky, Boris Godunov, the Shuiskys, Trubetskoy and Golitsyn. The commander of the rearguard regiment, Prince Timofey Ivanovich Trubetskoy, lodged a complaint about precedence against the chief of the regiment forming the right wing, Prince Vasily Ivanovich

Shuisky. Ivan Golitsyn, who commanded the regiment forming the left wing, petitioned against Prince Nogotkov, Buinosov against Golitsyn, Sheremetev against Nogotkov and Buinosov, Kashin against Buinosov and Sheremetev.

When a complaint was unclear the government appointed a tribunal, usually composed of a boyar and a crown secretary. The crown service registers mention that the boyars sometimes betrayed bias in making their decision. For example a register for 1586 recording Fedor Kolychev's successful petition against Roman Alferiev notes "The boyar Prince Ivan Petrovich Shuisky rendered this judgment for the sake of Kriuk Kolychev." The highest ranking boyar Prince Fedor Mstislavsky sat on the tribunal judging the case of Prince Timofey Trubetskoy against Prince Andrei Golitsyn. When Trubetskoy submitted a written deposition Mstislavsky commented "Prince Timofey Trubetskoy wrote in his deposition that my grandfather Prince Fedor Mikhailovich served with Prince Mikulinsky, but my grandfather was never lower than Prince Mikulinsky, and Prince Trubetskoy does me a dishonor thereby." Indeed Mstislavsky became cross, rose from his place and stalked out. Prince Trubetskoy placated him. "Don't get angry, Prince Fedor Ivanovich! On the basis of your grandfather the status of your descent might be contended, but given your father, none should challenge you over precedence because the sovereign honored your father and deemed him great." The boyars likewise appeased Mstislavsky, who again sat as a judge.

Prince Trubetskoy referred to the wedding of King Magnus,[33] at which Prince Vasily Yurievich Golitsyn ranked below his brother Prince Fedor Trubetskoy. For verification the court called for a box containing documents ranking guests at weddings. In it they found only a brief list for the wedding of King Magnus, on which Trubetskoy's name did not appear. The list specified only Prince Sheidiakov, Prince Golitsyn and Crown Secretary Vasily Shchelkalov. The boyars asked Shchelkalov where he kept the books of records concerning King Magnus's wedding. Shchelkalov explained that although the tsar assigned him to the wedding, he became ill and his brother Andrei replaced him. Andrei professed that he could not recall having a book about the king's wedding. Prince Trubetskoy then charged that Andrei and Vasily Shchelkalov had stolen and altered the wedding records. Out of friendship for Golitsyn they did not list his brother, for the Golitsyns and the Shchelkalovs were family friends and related by marriage.

The Shchelkalov brothers sought justification with the argument that the short list was written in the hand of Undersecretary Yakovlev who, they averred, could not have changed it for to their benefit since he, like every other clerk in the Chancellery of Crown Service and Appointments, was their enemy. The next day Crown Secretary Sapun Abramov brought a rough draft of the king's wedding register to the boyars, saying that he had discovered it in Vasily Shchelkalov's box. On this list Vasily Shchelkalov enrolled himself alongside the boyars among the sponsors at the wedding, and corrections appeared in the hand of Vasily's brother Andrei. The boyars then asked Vasily Shchelkalov why he registered himself as a sponsor at the ceremony, when the previous day he vouched he was ill. "Indeed this could be written in my hand," replied Shchelkalov. "I fear that someone has forged my script." The boyars made him scrutinize it, and he had to acknowledge that it was his writing. Trubetskoy won his case.

Sometimes tribunals failed to reach a verdict because the disputed post already was occupied. When complaints were blatantly groundless the government had recourse to compulsion and punishment. In 1588 Prince Tiufiakin petitioned against Prince Khvorostinin. The tsar withheld the verdict and ordered Tiufiakin detained for four weeks in a prison for thieves. When Prince Andrei Golitsyn would not assume his duties because of a precedence dispute with Prince Trubetskoy, the tsar had him escorted to his post under guard. Even then Prince Andrei refused the service registers, whereupon Fedor had him incarcerated and made him contribute one altyn daily from his personal funds to support himself while in jail. After the tenacious Golitsyn sat it out in jail for two weeks the tsar released him and dismissed him from service.

Similar obstinacy characterized Peter Sheremetev, appointed as the third commander of the Great Regiment in 1596. He challenged Fedor Nikitich Romanov, the second commander of the regiment forming the right wing, spurned the tsar's commands and refused to go on duty. The sovereign put Sheremetev in chains, placed in a cart, and carried to his post. Once there, he balked twice at the service registers, then finally relented and took them. In 1589 Table Attendant Prince Gvozdev brought charges over precedence against another table attendant, Prince Odoevsky. Without even a hearing the tsar directed that Gvozdev be beaten with rods and then placed at Odoevsky's mercy. At Aleksin in the same year the commanders Princes Odoevsky and Turenin were imprisoned for not accepting the lists and not registering junior boyars as they arrived. In 1591 the commander Prince Boriatinsky was exiled to Siberia because he disputed precedence with Prince Dolgoruky. On occasion the government went beyond warnings of punishment, which scarcely intimidated some, and turned to the more awesome threat of substantially lowering an entire family's honor. Thus when in 1592 Prince Andrei Golitsyn, named chief of the vanguard, petitioned against Prince Ivan Mikhailovich Glinsky, commander of the Great Regiment, the tsar had him told "What folly you undertake! You have no business petitioning over this! I will order a writ drawn up against your father." Sometimes cases were closed when the tsar refused to accept a petition and have it recorded.

Officers of outposts squabbled over precedence no less than commanders. In 1595 Zakhar Liapunov, brother of the later famous Prokopy,[34] not wanting to share command of a garrison with a certain Kikin, deserted the army at Elets. The governor of Riazan received orders to apprehend Liapunov at his military service estate, transport him in fetters to Pereiaslavl-in-Riazan, have him beaten with rods in public, jail him, and then escorted to his post.

Under the year 1586 there is mention of a curious controversy over precedence in urban administration. Yelizar Saburov was appointed commander at Toropets, where Prince Vasily Pronsky already served as governor and commander. Saburov complained that he could not serve under Pronsky. The sovereign resolved the case by having Saburov manage military affairs and Pronsky execute the governor's civilian functions

Finally the records show servitors of the tsar's household quarreling over precedence on the occasion of court festivities. The tsar graced the gentleman of the bedchamber Istoma Bezobrazov and the crown agent Yelizar Stary with seats at his table. Stary complained against Bezobrazov. "Istoma is a gentleman of the bedchamber by way of the tsar's domain," he asserted, "and I am a crown agent attached to the tsar's household. I ought not to sit lower than Istoma, although his office bears more honor than mine." In 1589 Prince Grigory Kurakin refused to appear at the tsar's table because he would not sit lower than Prince Fedor Trubetskoy. When in 1593 Prince Khvorostinin refused to dine at the tsar's table and complained against Prince Turenin, the case evidently became so confused that the tsar neither delivered a verdict nor resolved it by decree.

This period also witnessed the first instances of salaries or subsidies for ambassadors assigned to foreign courts. Thus the conciliar noble Veliaminov, when he rode to the emperor, received two hundred rubles, while Crown Secretary Vlasiev got one hundred rubles. Some noblemen were paid twenty-five rubles, others received twenty-four.

SERFDOM EMERGES

Fedor's reign witnesses a crucial landmark in the history of Russian social classes,[35] the law restricting free mobility of the peasantry. We already have shown repeatedly the roots of this development in Russia's broad expanses and sparse population, in an abundance of land and scarcity of hands to work it. Hence rose the landowners' compulsion to attract and keep as many laborers as possible. As long as the separate principalities existed each principality tried to lure cultivators from the others, seducing them with privileges. Once the separate principalities vanished and the country was united, wealthy and powerful landowners could offer substantial advantages to free peasants and thus draw them away from poorer holders of patrimonies and military service estates. Even as wealthy and powerful landholders strove to entice peasants, they contrived various means of holding those they already had. Under Vasily the Dark the Trinity monastery sought authority to detain the peasants of various districts. How profoundly it distressed any landlord to part with a peasant, to release him to another's land! Some even resorted to violence in order to detain peasants. It can be assumed that such coercion was not rare. However much the most prominent landlords gained by enticing peasants from lesser lords by means of concessions, their interests inevitably conflicted with those of the crown.

The state felt strong and relentless pressure to enlarge its army. This army rested upon the gentry and junior boyars who served in return for military service estates, which provided them the wherewithal to maintain themselves and to serve at the tsar's summons, *mounted, armed and with retainers*, in the parlance of those times. Obviously an estate holder's capacity to support himself and to appear for duty in the prescribed fashion hinged upon the revenue he derived from his parcel of land and, just as clearly, this income depended on the population of the holding. A servitor must possess a permanent labor force on his estate if he was always to meet his service obligations. How might he keep it when his wealthy neighbor lured his peasants with rich concessions? Having bestowed land on its servitor, the crown also must assure him of a constant labor force, otherwise he could not serve.

To appreciate the purpose of the law binding peasants to the soil we need merely consider with what aim and to whose advantage the law gained support later, during the seventeenth century. Poverty-stricken holders of military service estates then petitioned that the wealthy, in disregard of the law, lured peasants away and transported them at once to their distant patrimonies, whence they could not be recovered. This was ruining the poorer servitors. The same question arose much earlier in Lithuanian Rus. How could the peasants be restrained from deserting one landlord for another for the sake of extra benefits? Lithuania's gentry decided to introduce a general statute regulating the conditions under which free peasants might be settled. Anyone daring to entice additional peasants by giving them a better contract became subject to a monetary penalty. Eastern Rus [Muscovy] employed a different method, namely binding to the soil.

Exactly when the peasantry was tied to the soil cannot be ascertained because no surviving decree proclaims the general restriction of peasant movement. We do possess the following decree of 1597. "Pass judgment against and seek out," it said, "those peasants who have fled from military servitors' estates and from patrimonial estates over the five years preceding our current year. In accordance with the judgment against them, bring back the fugitive peasants to where they lived, together with their wives, children and all their property. Render no verdicts against peasants who departed five, seven, or ten years before this decree, whom the military service landholders or holders of patrimonies have not denounced as runaways." Given the sense of this document, a law limiting peasant movement can be placed toward the beginning of Fedor's reign. It cannot be dated earlier because there exists direct reference to a decree of Tsar Vasily Ivanovich Shuisky which identifies Godunov as the perpetrator of such a restriction during Fedor's reign. This source states that Tsar Fedor, swayed by Godunov's influence, spurned the advice of the senior boyars and prohibited peasant departures.

Besides this allusion to Shuisky's decree, another source bears witness to the transformation of the peasantry's status in the first year of Fedor's reign. In a measure which laid the groundwork for restriction and candidly expressed the dominant motive for it, a written resolution of the church council held on July 20, 1584 declared "We have deliberated and we have affirmed that henceforth there shall be no charters of immunity from taxation. The lands of the metropolitan, archbishops, bishops and the monasteries rest under such charters. They pay neither the tsar's levies nor local assessments, yet soldiers and servicemen pay taxes for their lands, wherefore a great desolation has befallen the patrimonial estates and military service holdings of the soldiery. Peasants who have deserted the servicemen live under privilege because of the charters of immunity. Therefore, because of the great want and deprivation of the military men, we have ruled...." and so forth. Clearly this verges on a binding to the soil. Servicemen grew destitute because their peasants were abandoning them in a quest for charters of immunity, hence it was proposed to abolish the charters. The council declared this measure to be provisional, and it turned out to have a short life. Charters of immunity were restored in October of the same year. Consequently a law restricting peasant mobility most probably accompanied the restoration of charters of immunity, for it would have been necessary to provide the servicemen with some guarantee, the need for which the council had declared so solemnly.

Thus Muscovy's first resolution of the problem approximated that method utilized in Western Rus, that is, equalization of benefits attached to all lands. Only such parity might dispel the peasants' motive for transferring from one holding to another. Yet Muscovy soon abandoned this solution because it conflicted with the interest of a powerful social class. To explain this development it must be observed that during this period the Muscovite realm had an extremely low level of industrial development, being purely agrarian. Manufacturing industry was in its infancy. The city as an industrial center did not exist. Towns remained walled villages and their residents engaged in agriculture as if they were the inhabitants of villages and hamlets. In a purely agrarian country the dominant relationship involved landlords and their tenants, the landlords usually attempting to bring the tenants into complete dependence. The principal landlord, the crown, settled its properties with servicemen to whom it felt obliged to supply a fixed population of agricultural labor.

Here the state as landowner clashed with another wealthy holder of landed property, the church. Initially the crown required the church to repudiate charters of immunity to benefit the servicemen. Shortly thereafter neither of these most authoritative landlords, neither the church nor the state, desired to violate the other's interests. The problem was settled in such a fashion that the church kept its charters of immunity and the servicemen retained forever the population of their lands. As for the other landholders, the aristocratic and wealthy owners of patrimonies, binding the peasantry naturally did them no good, for it deprived them of the right to lure to their properties the peasantry of the military service estates. The significance of the aristocratic magnates waned as a result of the struggle of the Muscovite sovereigns with the princes and their retinues. Conversely this contest raised the value of petty servicemen and led the government to elevate their interests to the highest plane. Shuisky's decree, mentioned above, stated that Tsar Fedor heeded Godunov's slanders and ignored his senior boyars when he forbade peasant movement. Obviously Godunov felt no need to spare the interests of boyar magnates who did not acknowledge his primacy, no matter what he conceded. In a struggle with the senior boyars it benefited him to rely upon the clergy and the lesser servicemen, whom through concessions he tried to enlist in his faction. Thus it stands to reason that Godunov promoted this settlement between the clergy and the petty servicemen.

There is no way to determine the precise ratio then prevailing between secular lands, both military service estates and patrimonies, and ecclesiastical property. There remain only bare fragments of a general land cadaster, which demonstrate a very interesting relationship. The Goretov administrative subdivision of the Moscow district in 1586 contained 23,698 chetverts of arable land in military service estates or patrimonies. The crown directly administered 35,420 chetverts of wasteland or land in quitrent, while the church held 38,630 chetverts. Of the fifty-nine military service estates and patrimonial holdings listed in the Goretov subdivision, sixteen changed owners by means other than sale.

A letter conveying an order from Boris Godunov to the peasants of Belsk administrative subdivision provides an enlightening commentary on peasant organization at this time. "Pursuant to the command of Lord Boris Fedorovich," it read, "his chancellery officials (names) decreed to the peasants of Belsk subdivision (twelve persons are enumerated: to Peter Ivanov Diakonov, Nikita Ivanov, and others) the elders and local sworn officials, the hundredmen, the fiftymen, the tenmen and all the peasants of the Belsk subdivision. You besought Lord Boris Fedorovich to remove your tavern from you. You, Peter Diakonov and Nikita Ivanov and your companions who are named in this letter, and the elected judges and elders, and the local sworn officials, hundredmen, fiftymen and tenmen must keep a sharp watch that none among you have drink for sale, nor may you transport wine or any sort of drink for sale. The peasant villagers must not gamble at dice nor engage in theft, and the better *prosperous* peasants, who may keep wine in their homes, must keep it for themselves and not sell it. Whoever has occasion to brew beer and ferment wine for holidays and funeral feasts must give notice of it to you, Peter Diakonov, Nikita Ivanov and your comrades, and to the elected judges, elders, local sworn officials..." and so forth. Here we see that Godunov's estates had elected judges, elders, local sworn officials, hundredmen, fiftymen and tenmen, and twelve particular peasants outranked all these individuals.

Along these lines one of the tsar's charters, issued in 1590, deserves mention. Townsmen of Solvychegodsk and the peasantry of its rural district complained that the abbot of the Koriazhemsk monastery, Father Gerasim, did not join them in providing a subsidy for settlers in Siberia. The abbot countered with a formal accusation that the residents of Solvychegodsk were guilty of unjust deeds. Moscow weighed the matter and charged Maxim and Nikita Stroganov with executing its verdict. The tsar did issue them a charter, but this document makes it plain that the Stroganovs held no administrative post in Solvychegodsk. They were merely the most wealthy and influential residents of that region, and so here the tsar, bypassing the elders and the local sworn officials, addressed his charter to the Stroganovs. "You shall not," he wrote, "allow the townsmen and peasants of the rural district to take from the elders of the Koriazhemsk monastery, from their servants, and from their peasants." These documents illustrate the importance of the district notables and how, alongside the *de jure* administrative officials there existed *de facto* functionaries. This arrangement sharply illuminates the society of that time, to which no present-day categories can be applied.

SLAVES

The restriction on peasant movement during Fedor's reign was accompanied by the binding of free servitors, or their transformation into bondsmen. In 1597 all lords were commanded to bring to the Chancellery for Slavery lists with names of their bondsmen, both those currently serving and fugitives, as well as their contracts of indenture, so that the bondsmen be enrolled as part of a general consolidation of the peasantry. Those who contracted debt servitude since June 1, 1586 now became slaves. They no longer could redeem their contract through payment or appeal, and were handed over to their lords until death. Free men voluntarily serving another were to be registered with the Chancellery for Slavery along with their masters. Subsequent inquiries would fix the length of their contract and determine whether they had consented to debt servitude. Those free men who served for five or six weeks without a formal contract of servitude were given liberty. Those who served for a half year or more were consigned to bondage without recourse to petition because the lord had fed, clothed and shod such voluntary slaves.

MIGRATION

So much land, yet so few hands. Servicemen sank into poverty because peasants fled them, while the already sprawling uninhabited frontier grew steadily. Colonies stretched out southward, into the steppe, and toward the Northeast, beyond the Ural mountains into boundless Siberia. Many have remarked how terribly Spain suffered because its inhabitants migrated into newly opened lands, but did not sixteenth-century Russia, already thinly populated, ceaselessly thrust out colonies? What consequences for the state must this colonization hold? Fletcher says that he observed up to fifty once-substantial villages along the road between Vologda and Yaroslavl now completely deserted. It is easy to comprehend how this sparsity of population must have retarded the evolution of society and hampered every function of government. Conversely lack of population, absence of places where large groups of people might cluster, isolation among relatively populated locales, and the chance to flee at the first physical or moral discomfort to vacant territories without leaving the homeland, permitted the crown to implement with minimal obstacles measures it deemed necessary. Take as an example only one phenomenon from later history, the late seventeenth-century schismatic movement. Doubtless it would have assumed different forms had the numerous fanatics been compelled to stay in their towns and villages, without the option of departing for distant and empty territories, and thereby forced to spare society their presence.[36] Cossack brigands harmed the state, and during the Time of Troubles they were *more coarse* than the Lithuanians and other foreigners, as contemporaries put it. Nevertheless, was not the state's development in peacetime shaped profoundly by the circumstance that individuals inclined to be cossacks fled beyond the state's borders? Obviously, the crown gained force from this exodus of troublemakers.

Empty space already abounded in the Muscovite state when, towards the end of the sixteenth century, it annexed the vast Siberian wilderness. The government seized the Siberian tsardom from the cossacks, especially at the prospect of a treasury overflowing with precious furs. Yet to hold Siberia, Muscovy must populate it with Russians. Filling Siberia's towns with servicemen called for settling plowmen near them, and this in turn meant transplanting migrants from the state's already scantily peopled older territories. In 1590 the town of Solvychegodsk and its district were ordered to select for permanent resettlement in Siberia thirty cultivators with their wives, children and all their property. Each man must bring three good geldings, three cows, two goats, three pigs, five sheep, two geese, five hens, two ducks, grain for a year, a wooden plough, a cart, a sledge and assorted other things. The inhabitants of Solvychegodsk and its district had to donate twenty-five rubles to each migrant.

THE CHURCH

With the extension of the crown's frontiers and the settlement of Russians in new lands came, naturally, expansion of the church's boundaries. Yet even as the church added new members among the foreigners [natives] there, it needed to take steps to insure that its old adherents did not forsake it. Archbishop Hermogen of Kazan[37] informed the tsar in 1593 that in the city of Kazan and in the rural districts of Kazan and Sviiazhsk "newly baptized converts live among the Tatars, Chuvash, Cheremiss and Votiaks, and eat and drink with them. They do not attend God's church, wear the cross, display icons and crosses in their homes, summon the priests or make confessions. Having wed in the church, they remarry before Tatar priests. They eat meat on the fasts and leave their wives for captive foreign women."[38] He, the bishop, had summoned and instructed them, but they rejected his teaching and clung to their Tatar ways. Such apostasy from the Christian faith brought them great grief. Dwelling among infidels far from a church led them to abandon their beliefs and to waver in their Orthodox religious convictions. When other Tatars detected such shallow faith among the newly baptized they not only declined to embrace the Orthodox creed, they even cursed it. Indeed, for forty years after the conquest of Kazan there were no mosques in the Tatar quarter, now one was being constructed within bow-shot of the town quarter.

After receiving this report the tsar ordered the governors that they, having registered every recent convert, must reserve for them a section of Kazan with a church and a full complement of clergy. Of those who would not relocate their households in this quarter, some were to be placed under surety and others jailed. The governors must select a worthy junior boyar and appoint him to oversee the quarter and ensure that recent converts retained the Christian faith, married Russians and gave their daughters to Russians in marriage. Apostate converts must be subdued, jailed, cast in irons, placed in chains or beaten. Others were to be referred to the bishop, who would impose a penance on them. The governors must tear down every mosque.

Hermogen also lamented that many Russians lived among and married Tatars, Cheremiss and Chuvash. Russians likewise resided with Western foreigners in various villages and settlements, either voluntarily or because of debt servitude. All fell away from Christianity, converting to the Tatar faith when with Tatars, and to Catholicism or Lutheranism when among Western foreigners. Fedor instructed the governors to prohibit Russians from living with Tatars and other foreigners, redeem the obligations of those working off small indentures, and assign servants with sizable debts to the newly baptized, exchanging them for Lithuanians and Letts who then would be given to the Tatars and Western foreigners. Henceforth Tatars and other foreigners were barred from indenturing Russians or loaning them money.

In 1597 Prince Vasily Ukhtomsky, commissioned to command the Pustozersk fortress, was instructed to attract the Samoyeds and other foreigners into the Orthodox faith. Pustozersk fortress, Ukhtomsky argued, was too remote for him to draw supplies directly from Moscow, and he owned no villages along the road. Would the sovereign grant him three hundred pails of liquor from the stores at Ustiug, at a fair price? Fedor allotted him fifty.

A MUSCOVITE PATRIARCHATE

During Fedor's reign the Russian church's supreme pastor exchanged his title of metropolitan for that of patriarch. We have noted why the Northeastern Rus church had gained practical independence from Constantinople, although the title of its chief prelate, the metropolitan, still betokened nominal subordination to the patriarch. The Turkish conquest of Constantinople and the dependence of the Eastern patriarchs upon the sultan must have excited in Moscow the urge to achieve full self-government, and also must have eliminated patriarchal antagonism toward the realization of this desire. The rise of a free and flourishing Northeastern Rus church demanded at least its parity with those senior churches groaning under the infidel yoke and needing its assistance. Some in Moscow even thought it dangerous to be tied to a people enslaved by unbelievers, an idea against which Maxim the Greek[39] inveighed. The longing for full independence must have intensified when hostile Catholic movements emerged, when the Jesuits sharply rebuked the Russian church for its dependence upon a slave of the sultan. Consequently the Russian church had to have its own patriarch. Moscow stood to benefit from his presence. It would strike a blow against Vytautas's cause.[40] Moscow would assume indisputable pre-eminence over Kiev, and the eyes of Orthodox Christians in Lithuania could not help but turn to the patriarch of all the Russias.

When Ambassador Blagov traveled to Constantinople he brought a thousand rubles to its patriarch as a memorial offering for Tsar Ivan's soul. As was customary, two Russian youths, Ushakov and Vnukov, resided with the patriarch to study the Greek language. Blagov brought them each a fur coat and ten rubles in cash. The ambassador was to admonish them to study the Greek language diligently and intently, not to carouse, and to heed the patriarch in all matters. The patriarch was asked to instruct the youths zealously, to confine them to his residence as punishment, and to curb their willfulness. Rich offerings also were distributed to the other Orthodox churches, both Greek and Slavic.[41]

Patriarch Joachim of Antioch visited Moscow in the summer of 1586 seeking alms. The details of his reception by Metropolitan Dionisy are interesting. When Joachim entered the Dormition cathedral Dionisy stood at a fixed spot in his clerical regalia, surrounded by prominent churchmen. Having kissed the icons, the patriarch approached the metropolitan, who advanced one sazhen from his place to meet him and blessed him first, only then receiving his blessing. Joachim started to protest in a murmur that the metropolitan should have accepted his blessing first, then he halted. Here, in this confrontation between real importance and nominal prestige, is most clearly expressed the incongruity of the Muscovite metropolitan's relationship with the patriarch. Very possibly it was Joachim's arrival in Moscow and his instructive reception by Metropolitan Dionisy, calling attention to the incompatibility between true authority and nominal rank, which prompted the decisive step.

Whatever the case may be, during Joachim's sojourn in Moscow the tsar suggested to the boyar council a proposal for establishment of a patriarchate. When explaining this action Fedor cited explicitly the lamentable status of the Greek church and the exaltation of the Russian church. "By the divine will, as our punishment," he said, "the Eastern patriarchs and the other ecclesiastical authorities are leaders in name alone. They have been deprived of nearly all their influence. Yet our land, blessed by God, has seen great expansion, and therefore I wish, if it pleases God and the holy scriptures do not forbid it, to place a most august patriarchal throne in Moscow. If you deem this to be improper, speak out. As for me, I find nothing impious in this, only the greater glory of the Christian faith."

The clergy and the high court dignitaries praised the tsar's idea, but added that this must be undertaken only with the assent of the whole Eastern church "lest the Latins and other heretics write concerning our holy faith that a patriarchal throne was raised in Moscow solely by the power of the tsar." These words display Moscow's awareness of movements inimical to Orthodoxy in Western Rus and its sensitivity toward them. When Joachim learned of the tsar's wish he promised to place the question before a council of the Greek church.

In the summer of 1587 a Greek named Nicholas arrived in Moscow with news that the patriarchs of Constantinople and Antioch had convoked a church council, to which they summoned the other two patriarchs, those of Jerusalem and Alexandria. After conferring they would send to Moscow the patriarch of Jerusalem with instructions concerning the establishment of a patriarchate. Within a year, however, in the summer of 1588, the sovereign learned that the senior patriarch, Jeremiah of Constantinople,[42] unexpectedly appeared at Smolensk. This news occasioned a keen reprimand for the commanders there. How did the patriarch land at the wharf without their knowledge? "Hereafter do not behave so carelessly, so that no envoy arrives at the frontier and nobody reaches the of town square without your knowledge." "Should the patriarch beseech the governor to give him leave to worship at the church of the Dormition of the Mother of God," wrote the tsar to the bishop of Smolensk, "we have permitted that he enter there. At that time, you must have convened with great decorum and in large number as many archimandrites, abbots and priests as possible. Greet the patriarch and venerate him honorably, just as you would our own metropolitan." The bailiff assigned to meet and escort the patriarch must "investigate under what auspices the patriarch comes to the sovereign. Does he still hold the patriarchate in Constantinople, or is another in his place? Besides his needs, the charity that he seeks, does he bring for the tsar an edict of all the patriarchs with the council's decision? Revere the patriarch with the highest esteem, like our own metropolitan."

While in Moscow Jeremiah resided at the court of the archbishop of Riazan. His private lodgings were in a large mansion with a suite of rooms. His traveling companions the metropolitan of Monemvasia and the archbishop of Elasson resided at chambers off the Kremlin banqueting hall. The archimandrite stayed in special basement quarters and the elders and servants occupied the basement store rooms. Greeks, Turks, and other foreigners were not authorized to enter this residence, nor could the patriarch's servants leave it. Should representatives of Metropolitan Job, distinguished boyars or clergymen bring provisions for the patriarch, they might enter. When any foreigner sought the patriarch, or if Jeremiah requested an interview with any foreigner, the bailiffs were to refer these requests to the boyars and the crown secretary for foreign affairs, Andrei

Shchelkalov. Tradesmen who came with Jeremiah stayed at the Lithuanian merchants' hall.

Within a week of Jeremiah's arrival Fedor had him summoned for an audience. He was received with the ceremony customary for ambassadors, the sole distinction being that the tsar advanced about half a sazhen from the throne to greet him. After his formal presentation Jeremiah remained at the court to engage in talks with Godunov, on whom he unburdened his woes. The sultan had insulted him, deposed him from his patriarchal throne, and then restored him to it. His church was in a sorry state, despoiled by the Turks. He relayed the knowledge he gained of Lithuanian affairs while on the road. Finally, he gave *secret speeches.* After this the tsar, having consulted briefly with the tsaritsa, advised the boyars "God has ordained that we witness the arrival of the patriarch of Constantinople, and we have pondered whether we ought to establish in our realm a patriarch, whom the Lord God will bless. If Patriarch Jeremiah of Constantinople desires to remain in our realm, he shall rule as patriarch from the primary see, from Vladimir, and the metropolitan will sit in Moscow as before. If the patriarch of Constantinople does not wish to be in Vladimir, a Muscovite council will place a patriarch in Moscow."

Godunov was directed to call on Jeremiah and discuss with him whether he would consent to dwell in the Russian tsardom, in its most ancient capital, Vladimir.[43] "Should it be the will of the great tsar that I abide in his realm," answered Jeremiah, "I shall not disobey it, yet I cannot reside in Vladimir, for patriarchs always live in the presence of the sovereign. What sort of patriarch does not live close by the sovereign?" Fedor then reconvened the boyars and told them "The ecumenical patriarch Jeremiah will not accept a patriarchate of Vladimir and all the Russias, but he does consent to sit at Moscow where our devout spiritual father Job now resides. Yet this cannot be. How can we expel from the see of the Dormition and of the great miracle workers a ruler like unto the great miracle workers, such a man of praiseworthy demeanor as our saintly and reverend spiritual father, the pious metropolitan Job, and create a patriarch of the Greek law, who knows not our native customs and our Russian tongue, and with whom we cannot discuss any spiritual matter without an interpreter."

Godunov, accompanied by the Shchelkalovs, returned to ask Jeremiah to bless Metropolitan Job and invest him as patriarch in the presence of the Russian synod. It was decided at this meeting that Jeremiah consecrate as patriarch of Vladimir, Moscow and all the Russias anyone who met the

sovereign's approval and received his blessing, and that henceforth patriarchs in the Russian realm would be selected from among its metropolitans, archbishops and bishops.

It need not be not assumed that Jeremiah, during his first interview with
Godunov, expressed his personal desire to stay in Moscow as patriarch.
Godunov and others must have sensed the advantages to be gained from
the transfer of the senior patriarchal see from Byzantium to Muscovy.
Even if a new patriarch then was chosen in Constantinople by the sultan's
decree, this would not have cost Jeremiah and his Russian successors their
right to be called ecumenical, their claim to seniority. Jeremiah's accession
in the Muscovite realm would have a pronounced impact upon the Western
Rus church, which long acknowledged its dependence upon him. Conversely the resolution of the question ought not to be imputed solely to the
influence of Godunov, standing to lose by dismissing Job, who was
completely devoted to him. Given the distaste felt towards foreigners and
the widespread suspicion that it strongly promoted, the clear traces of
which appeared everywhere, it must have seemed extremely uncomfortable to accept as patriarch a foreigner, a Greek.

It will not do to argue that unity of religious belief sufficed to overcome
all mistrust, for we have seen how Jeremiah was treated. Not a single
foreigner was permitted to visit him. Our ancestors in that era lived a life
completely dominated by tradition. Consequently, it is understandable
that they were so frightened to have as patriarch a man unaware of Russian
customs, a man of the Greek law. What is more, they had to resolve the
extremely grave issue of rejecting a man whom they were accustomed to
seeing in the exalted station of metropolitan. Unable to devise a higher
honor for Patriarch Jeremiah than that which they rendered Metropolitan
Job, they now must strip the guiltless Job of this very honor, they must
dismiss him! Clearly, therefore, it was not simply Godunov's personal ties
to Job which drove them to insist that Jeremiah reside at Vladimir.

Despite the fact that the tsar declared it impossible to evict Job from the
church of the Dormition of the Mother of God and the great miracle
workers, the usual election was held. The prelates placed three candidates
before the tsar: Metropolitan Job, Archbishop Alexander of Novgorod and
Archbishop Varlaam of Rostov. Fedor selected Job, who was consecrated
on January 26, 1589. Thus the affair dragged on for half a year! A patriarch
must have his metropolitans. This honor was bestowed on the archbishops
of Novgorod, Kazan, Rostov and Krutitsa (in Moscow). Six bishops, those

of Vologda, Suzdal, Nizhny Novgorod, Smolensk, Riazan and Tver were raised to archbishops.

Richly laden with gifts, Jeremiah set forth to Constantinople in May 1589. He carried Fedor's message to the sultan. "You, our brother Sultan Murad," it read, "should keep Patriarch Jeremiah in your land, and ordain that your pashas safeguard him in every way, just as your forefathers long have protected the patriarchs. You should to do this for our sake." When Jeremiah reached Smolensk he received a letter from Godunov asking him to survey the state of affairs in Lithuania. "Concerning Maximilian," he asked, "where is he now, and how does he fare? Is he in the Polish land, or has he been freed? How was he freed, with what proviso? Has the Swedish prince assured his place upon the throne of Poland, and how secure is he, and what are his intentions toward our sovereign? Once you have learned this, write to me in secret and make no mention of your spiritual title, and when you have reached Constantinople send me news of all matters there."

Only two years later, in June 1591, the metropolitan of Trnovo brought to Moscow the charter confirming the patriarchate in Moscow. "We have sent to your holiness the completed conciliar decree," Jeremiah wrote to Job. "You will assume the fifth rank, below the patriarch of Jerusalem. Accept the charter with gratitude and with equanimity, and work on behalf of the metropolitan of Trnovo with both the tsar and the tsaritsa, watching over our blessed and exalted tsar, and render to him every service as befits that oath which you swore at your installation, at your palace. We can rest our hope in none but God and the holy tsar. None but the holy tsar can raise up the patriarchal see of Constantinople and restore it to its former status."

In a letter to Godunov the patriarch sought a donation of six thousand ducats for construction undertaken by his office. The metropolitan of Trnovo brought gifts for Godunov consisting of two gold atlases, a saber of Damascus steel, and two porcelain vessels. Boris declined the presents with the comment "It is not right for us to receive your gifts. We should share with you what God sends." After the metropolitan asked Godunov not to offend him by refusing his offering, Boris took the two glazed vessels. Boris inquired whether the council convened to decide the establishment of the patriarchate in Moscow met with the knowledge of the sultan and the pashas. The council, explained the metropolitan, informed the sultan while meeting. The patriarch's request was honored. Fedor shipped a large quantity of furs and walrus teeth for the construction of a church and a patriarchal residence.[44]

When Saltykov and Tatishchev left on their embassy to Lithuania they were handed instructions. "When questioned about the establishment of the patriarchate," they were commanded, "say 'Patriarch Joachim of Antioch came from the Greek realm to our great sovereign and told the sovereign's brother-in-law Boris Fedorovich Godunov that since earliest times the seven great church councils ruled that a Pope of the Greek faith must be in Rome, and four patriarchs in the Greek state, then the Roman Pope Eugenius convened an eighth council, conceived in arrogance. Thereafter the Roman Popes abandoned the Greek faith. Should a pious Christian tsar rule in the Greek realm, the patriarchs would establish a Pope there. Now they, all four patriarchs, have deliberated with the universal council of the Greek lands to replace the Pope of Rome with an ecumenical patriarch in Constantinople, and in the Pope's stead to create a fourth patriarch, in the Muscovite realm.' If the lords of the council object to the novelty of such a procedure, comment 'You never before had cardinals in Wilno, only bishops. Now the Pope has elevated Jerzy Radziwiłł to be cardinal, and what is so surprising in that?'"

OTHER CHURCH MATTERS

As for other ecclesiastical affairs under Fedor we can note that the new prelates, as stated in the charters installing them, attained office "through the election of the Holy Spirit (at a council) and on the advice of the divinely crowned tsar." A curious event early in Fedor's reign rekindled the ire of the Josephans. Bishop Leonid of Riazan supplicated the tsar. "You showered your grace on me, sire, and invited me to your Christmas table, where Archbishop Yevfimy of Rostov would not let me partake of food from the same bowl with him and disgraced me greatly, even though previously, in your father's time, I ate from the same dish as the archbishop of Novgorod. He calls all us adherents of the rule of Joseph; not Josephans, but Judaizers." It is not known how the dispute was resolved.[45]

In June 1594 at the tsar's command Patriarch Job and the entire consecrated assembly decided to appoint eight deans in Moscow, each aided by four deacons overseeing forty priests. They were assigned offices at the Intercession cathedral, otherwise known as that of Basil the Blessed,[46] where the deans and their assistants were to gather daily. The deans were to guarantee that prayers and masses were offered in every church on certain days. For this purpose they were to distribute a reminder to all the priests. Likewise before each day's mass priests in every church were to chant prayers for the ecumenical order, the welfare of the church, the continued health of the tsar and the tsaritsa, the birth of an heir, the army beloved of Christ, and all Orthodox Christianity. The deans would see that all priests and deacons attended processions of the cross from beginning to end, and report those absent to the patriarch. Priests must serve their parishes in person, not through substitutes, except in cases of dire necessity or some grave sin. They were not to seek compensation for clerical duties from the parish income or the revenue of other churches. Priests without a parish must report to the office for priests in the Intercession cathedral, where the patriarch would find work for them at a rate of one altyn on normal days and two altyns during Holy Week and high holy days. The deans were to watch sharply that these priests earned no more than this and did not trade in the divine liturgy. Black clergy must not be hired to officiate at parish churches.[47] When the liturgy required a requiem ceremony, or on the morrow of funeral masses for the sovereign, the deans and their assistants must issue a memorandum to all churches identifying the books containing the pertinent canons. Priests serving at the tsar's requiem table had to be informed about whom to commemorate, and on which day. If the devout donated alms to preserve their health or find solace, and they wished them divided among the churches, the deans must allocate them. Five archpriests were charged with confirming that the district deans executed this decree.

Concerning proper monastic conduct, the tsar wrote in 1584 to the Solovetsk monastery "A rumor has reached us that some among you sweeten kvass made from honey and then ferment it, and thus alter the old rule of the monastery. You are not thus to ferment kvass, nor violate the fixed monastic order. You must humble those monks who grumble, in keeping with the monastic regulations."

In 1592 two monks appealed against the abbot and cellarer of the St. Cyril monastery at Novgorod, complaining that the latter personally profited by making loans from the monastic treasury without the consent of the brethren, and that they befriended junior boyars and took personal gifts from them. When one of the plaintiffs tried to discuss this with them, they clamped him in double irons and fetters, and beat him for ten days. They contended that this treatment was to satisfy a debt, in fact they were claiming money their victim spent in Moscow on the monastery's business. It did no good to bring an accusation against them, as they were paying bribes with the monastery's funds. Except on Saturdays and Sundays there were never services at the monastery, and it had no priest.

A decree of July 1584 suspended tax exemptions from September 1 until further notice, while the land recovered and the tsar remedied all ills through his personal dispensation. In October of that same year, however, the tsar awarded Metropolitan Dionisy a charter exempting from taxes the Sviatoslavl settlement which Grand Prince Vasily Dmitrievich gave to Metropolitan Cyprian in exchange for the city of Aleksin. Also during July 1584 owners of patrimonial estates were forbidden to donate their properties to the church, but it is clear that this ban either was rescinded or unenforced. In 1587 the subsequently famous Prince Dmitry Mikhailovich Pozharsky, on his father's orders, granted a village from his patrimonial holdings to the Spaso-Evfimiev monastery at Suzdal without the tsar's permission. We shall not list the tsar's own grants of land to monasteries. As always, monasteries exercised their right to engage in commerce, to levy duties on trade in their villages. As always, charters exempted monastic possessions from diverse taxes and obligations. Many such decrees have survived from Fedor's reign, and they appear very early.

As for the relationship between a monastery and those on whose behalf it was built and maintained, there is an interesting charter issued by the tsar in 1595. In the Dvina district, at the mouth of the Lower Morzh river, stood the St. Nicholas monastery, constructed through the efforts of the village community. This monastery's elder complained to the tsar that the metropolitan of Novgorod's tithe collector ruined the monastery with his acts of extortion. Fedor issued a charter to the aggrieved Dvina elder and to the judge of the Kaleisk district court, with jurisdiction over the monastery, charging them to preserve it from harm. In future, should the peasants of the Kaleisk administrative subdivision want to change the elders at the St. Nicholas monastery or audit the monastic funds, or should the monks themselves desire to be replaced and offer an account of the funds, all the peasants of the Kaleisk district, through their four rural communities, must select as elders whomsoever they favored. The peasants would swear in the new elders. Four senior notables from the district must audit the treasury and hand its accounts over to the new elders.

According to old charters of Ivan the Terrible monastic peasants selected their own officials: elders, tax collectors, hundredmen, fiftymen, tenmen and for matters concerning the criminal jurisdiction district,[48] their own bailiffs, district sworn officials and clerks. The monasteries continued to define their relationship with their peasantry through regulatory charters.

Besides the decrees above concerning peasants and bondsmen Fedor's reign left no documented additions to the Muscovite code of laws. The military registers offer an interesting comment on judicial administration, noting that in 1588 the tsar discharged Prince Merkury Shcherbatov from the river guards and transferred him to serve as a judge at Tver.[49]

There exists also this interesting petition to Fedor from the monks of the St. Joseph monastery lamenting the sad fate of their peasants in a controversy with those of the boyar Ivan Vasilievich Godunov. "You, sire, did issue your decree to the districts Kozelsk and Belevsk, to Kuzma Bezobrazov. 'Pick ten of the most worthy peasants of the boyar Ivan Vasilievich Godunov and as many of our most worthy peasants, and provide them with lots. Whosoever drew the lot is to be granted land and forest with an icon.'"[50] Kuzma selected the peasants as ordered and then asked those of Ivan Vasilievich "Will you allot land and forest with an icon, by lot, each in his own boundaries by the chosen order?" "Do not drive Ivan Vasilievich's peasants from the forest and land," a servant of Ivan Vasilievich objected, "and do not draw straws. Let the monastic peasants partition the forest and the land without a drawing." Then the monastic peasants pleaded with Kuzma. "Ivan Vasilievich's peasants need the land and forest of the Immaculate Mother of God and the miracle worker St. Joseph. They swarm from the Belevsk district into that of Kozelsk, across the long standing border between the towns. Grant them the forest with an icon, the land and forest of the Immaculate Virgin, and we will believe them without drawing lots."

"Our dear peasants," continued the monastic petition, "dare not allot their land, and we will not make them surrender the tsar's bounty. Ivan Vasilievich's servants and peasants threaten our peasants, trying to force them to part with our true monastic land. They would defame us, your humble petitioners, bring notoriety upon us and lead us into sin. They would have us sell our peasants and leave our monastic patrimony in ruins. Our good peasants, who suffered constant insults and violence for a quarter of a year, live in terror. O merciful lord tsar! Show your clemency, do without sin what is not being done, have the monastery's holding surveyed with an icon. Have the old cadastral registers and borders brought out. The public witnesses of both towns, Kozelsk and Belevsk, know the boundary between them but dare not utter the truth, for they are being watched by Ivan Vasilievich."

MORALS AND CUSTOMS

We have some idea of the tsar's habits and amusements. He favored one Vasily Usov, giving him fifteen rubles in cash and a good cloth worth two rubles. Usov amused the sovereign by baiting a bear in front of him. Someone called Molveninov released his bear, which carried bread and salt in a quiver, in the presence of a wild bear. Once, when Fedor was enjoying the bears, wolves and foxes on the tsaritsa's estates, a hunter named Glazov was mauled. Fedor awarded him good cloth and two rubles. On August 1 the tsar rode to the outskirts of Simonov for the blessing of the river water, and bathed there (water was poured over him). The court's mourning dress for Tsarevna Feodosia was dark green, purple and blue, without the decorative cowelled collar.

Popular morals and customs can be seen in a pact to which the elders and the peasants of Tarvensk rural district *agreed among themselves* with the blessing of their father confessor. For three years, on holidays and on Christ's Sabbath, they would do no wrong, nor toil on their land, watch over their livestock, work with snares, hunt squirrels, catch fish, pick mushrooms or berries, trace cattle paths or set traps. On Friday they would not pound, grind or strike a spark. They would conduct themselves with purity and love. The women would not sew or take in work on Sunday. Respected citizens would denounce violators of this pact to a hundredman who, under the code of the rural commune, would impose an eight-altyn fine for use in church construction, and two altyns for himself. Anyone who broke eggs paid an eight-altyn fine.

The chronicle for 1595 notes that Prince Vasily Shchepin and Vasily Lebedev hatched a plot to set fires throughout Moscow and then steal the treasures at the church of Vasily the Blessed. Their confederate Baikov, the official charged with keeping locked the lattice work which protected the church during fires, was to leave it open for them. The conspiracy was unmasked, and the main participants were executed.

The chronicle also offers evidence of magic and a deep faith in its power. It is said that Godunov gathered sorcerers and magicians from many towns, employing them to gain the tsar's love. Wizards predicted to Boris that he would rule, but not for long, only seven years.

Even more curious is the chronicle's tale of the Crimean prince, Murad-Girey. His Muslim foes sent sorcerers to cause his flesh to rot. The town commanders of Astrakhan, seeing his grave illness, summoned a Moor,[51] an apothecary. The Moor declared that Murad could not be cured until the sorcerers bewitching him were arrested. He led the Russians into the Tatar quarter, arrested the sorcerers and had them tortured. "If the blood of the sick man has not yet congealed," advised the sorcerers, "he may still be cured." The Moor then forced the sorcerers to produce the tub of blood which they drained from the sleeping prince, his wives and other Tatars, with which they bewitched them. One sorcerer after another addressed the Moorish physician, distinguishing the prince's blood from that of the others and showing that the prince's blood and that of one wife had congealed fully. The prince, it followed, must die, but should those whose blood was not yet congealed be wiped with their blood, they would live.

When Murad died the city commanders reported all this to Fedor. He sent Astafy Pushkin to Astrakhan with orders to torture the sorcerers, learn why they bewitched the prince, and then burn them. Pushkin employed an array of harsh tortures, yet the sorcerers revealed nothing. Again the same Moorish doctor, suggesting that these measures were fruitless, harnessed them to horse bridles and suspended by their arms. He then ordered that not their bodies, but the wall opposite them be beaten, and confessions poured from their lips. After this torture the commanders had the Moor show his skill at burning them. As they burned, a multitude of magpies and ravens flocked together.

A register of gifts from the tsar's treasury to various individuals lists the names of several artists. Posnik of Rostov received cloth worth two rubles and two rubles in cash for creating an icon of the Mother of God of Smolensk. They called him "Posnik the standard-maker" because he earned good English cloth for fashioning the standard, that is, for encrusting with small grained pearls the black velvet pall laid over the coffin of Ivan the Terrible. Fourteen master silversmiths are named as the creators of the shrine of St. Sergius the Miracle Worker. Andrei Chokhov gained fame for casting enormous cannon.

VI

THE END OF FEDOR'S REIGN

THE MISSION OF RIURIK'S DYNASTY

The end of the sixteenth century brought with it the end of Riurik's dynasty. Having followed the activity of Riurik's offspring in two distinct situations, in two different lands,[1] we must take note of a fundamental contrast. We first watched them at work in an enormous and sparsely settled country which before their coming lacked even the semblance of a history. With singular swiftness Riurik's clan subdued vast territories and subjugated the tribes which inhabited them. This rapidity stemmed from the flatness of the land, its convenient waterways, the small number and particularism of the tribes, incapable of any determined and unified resistance because they knew no tradition of concerted action. One by one the separate tribes submitted, providing compelling proof that they lacked solidarity. Only the princes gave them unity, only the princes' activity molded together people and crown.

Even while the princes propagated the Rus land they themselves multiplied in it with robust vigor. This crucial circumstance enabled members of the single dominant family to place their thrones in every corner of the immense land, and let them assume direct control of the most vital sites. They felt no need to delegate large towns or regions to vicegerents who might evolve into a potent aristocracy. Although the princes scattered over a vast country they sensed no separation, for their family ties held them together. In the process this sense of kinship made way for the unification of the land.

Only through constant motion, through their relentless journeys from one far-flung region to another, could the princes forge even weak and tenuous links among the territories. The princes and their retinues provided the vital dynamism which gave the country life, gave it history. Monomakh[2] boasted with good reason of his travels, of the countless journeys he made. Movement, ceaseless movement, was the princes' primary duty during this era. The princes founded towns, populated them, shifted people from one region to another. They initiated new social phenomena, new relationships. Everything new, all that was needed to raise the tribes to a new and superior existence, to a history, sprang from this fluid base, from the princes and their retinues. In their movement they collided with the Greeks, from whom they took Christianity.

The reader wishing to appreciate the creative work of the princes of the house of Riurik and their retinues need only consider a chronicler's account of the appearance of a sorcerer in Novgorod. The bishop asked "Who goes to the cross and who to the magician?" The people, the masses, clinging to custom, drifted to the sorcerer, the representative of the old paganism, whereas the prince and his retinue stood by the bishop. Soon, when depicting the Time of Troubles, we too will portray the crucial role of the commoners as guardians of tradition when movement pushed them down an illegal path.[3]

Thus the house of Riurik played its founding role. Naturally, during an epoch of inaugural activity, when establishing a state in a land previously without history, nothing could be fixed and lasting. All remained embryonic and primordial, the seeds of something, each seed developing by itself without connection to any other. Once each part formed, it sought its own particular existence. Under circumstances of dynamic movement and spaciousness, when flight came easily at the first discomfort, there could be no definition because no foundation can stand on shifting soil.

Freedom to migrate was the most basic of human rights, largely guaranteeing advantageous circumstances to an element of society, to members of a certain social class.[4] This right rested on the possibility of departure and disappeared when that option vanished. Conflicts of interest were not resolved through compromise, rather by breaking off relations through leaving one realm for another where, fortuitously, owing to a particular way of life under a specific government, residence seemed temporarily more convenient. From this flowed the supremacy of the provisional and local, and the ascendancy of personal advantage over the general welfare. Such a relationship necessarily followed from the state's weakness and immaturity.

The state nevertheless grew. It passed from youth to that higher stage characterized by concentration and permanence. This epoch of consolidation is vital for affirming awareness of the state's unity, of its commonality of interest. Here sections, regions and individuals must renounce their detached and exclusive being and submit to the conditions of shared existence. Later, once the prerequisite consciousness of state unity was implanted, regions receive greater or lesser autonomy, self-government. Yet self-government derives from the state's needs and flows directly from the centralizing authority. Thus for example Ivan IV granted tax farming charters which established local control in the rural districts. The relationship between these districts and the tsar in no way resembled that of Novgorod and Pskov with earlier Muscovite princes.[5]

During this epoch of consolidating the power of the house of Riurik new temporal and geographical circumstances (the setting having shifted from the South to the North) compelled the princes to alter their character and steadily to guide society along a new path. Once the progenitors of the land, they now became its gatherers.[6] Formerly Riurik's proud heirs, those bold chieftains of warrior bands eager to carry their honor anywhere, those worshippers of martial glory above all, heedless of moveable or immovable property, were ashamed to accumulate land, preferring to share all with their retinues. Now those sons of Riurik were transformed in the North into thrifty householders most concerned about production and profit, extremely cautious and wary of any decisive battle. In the North during the epoch of consolidation everything assumed a stable and sedentary quality. Consequently those landed relationships which stressed durability came to the fore. Society distinguished the *landed* man, the settled proprietor, from the free wanderer, the symbol of the distant past, relic of a bygone era of chaotic mobility. The anachronistic representative of another epoch found the new society uncongenial. He fled for the open steppe and there awaited his chance to struggle against the new order which he judged to be so hostile. Yet this was the epoch of consolidation, and Muscovy's sovereigns performed their task well. The crown waxed strong, for the vagabond cossack[7] did not overcome the landed man.

BORIS ACCUSED OF DMITRY'S DEATH

Once Riurik's dynasty fulfilled its second mission, that of consolidating the land, it left the stage. Tsar Fedor could not govern alone, and the ruler Godunov appeared. Because earlier sovereigns so concentrated their power and so curtailed the authority of the aristocratic magnates, Godunov easily exploited his intimacy with the tsar to vanquish his rivals. Once supreme, Godunov had to contemplate his future. His prospects terrified him. The higher he rose, the more frightening they grew. Fedor had no son through whom Godunov as uncle might hope to conserve his prominence or at least preserve his honor. The childless tsar's successor had to be his brother

BORIS GODUNOV

Basil Dmytryshyn, *Medieval Russia. A Scource Book*
850–1700

Dmitry, who was banished to Uglich at the time of Fedor's coronation, spirited away "on the advice of all Russia's ranking court dignitaries."[8]

Dmitry grew up with his mother and her relatives the Nagoys.[9] It is obvious what sentiments these disgraced Nagoys harbored towards those who subjected them to disfavor, with what emotions they awaited the end of their misfortune, their exile, and how they viewed Godunov and those nearest him. They imparted these sentiments to the child, who could not hide them. Dmitry not only must live in fear of Godunov, he also must dread all those who owed the fruits of office to the ruler and stood to lose them should the ruler fall. Such men were most numerous. Finally, Dmitry must beware in the future of all whose fate did not strictly depend on Boris's survival, but on whose recommendation Dmitry was consigned to exile. This group included every prominent Russian court dignitary. Now, in May 1591, rumors flew around the country that Tsarevich Dmitry had died[10] at Uglich. He fell victim to violence, they said, murdered by Godunov's paid assassins. Here is how the chroniclers recorded the details of the affair.

THE CHRONICLER'S TALE

At first the assassins[11] hoped to poison Dmitry. They put poison in his food and drink, to no avail. Boris then gathered the Godunov clan and his confidants, the lord-in-waiting Kleshnin[12] and others. Poison, he explained, accomplished nothing. Other means must be found. One of the Godunovs, Grigory Vasilievich, refused to agree to the vile deed. He was excluded from subsequent planning and ostracized. Boris's other henchmen sought out two men they considered capable of murder, Vladimir Zagriazhsky and Nikolay Chepchugov, who declined. Boris lamented that the intrigue went so poorly. Kleshnin consoled him. "Don't worry," he said, "I have many relatives and friends. Your wish will be fulfilled." Kleshnin indeed did discover a man to undertake the task, the crown secretary Mikhail Bitiagovsky.[13] He was sent to Uglich together with his son Daniel, a relative named Nikita Kachalov, and Osip Volokhov, son of Dmitry's nurse. These men had orders to arrange things in the town.

Tsaritsa Maria[14] perceived the hostile intent of Bitiagovsky and his henchmen. She watched over the tsarevich, never letting him out of their house, but for some reason on May 15, at noon, she stayed home while the nurse Volokhova, one of the conspirators, led the child into the courtyard. A wet nurse followed behind, vainly warning Volokhova not to take

Dmitry outside. The assassins already were lurking on the porch. Osip Volokhov took Dmitry's hand and asked "Are you wearing a new decorative collar, sire?" The boy, raising his head, replied "No, an old one." At that instant the knife's blade flashed. The killer fled. He managed only to slash his victim's neck and failed to slit his throat. Dmitry fell to the ground, where the wet nurse threw herself upon him as a shield and started to scream. Then Daniel Bitiagovsky and Kachalov beat her within an inch of her life, tore the child from her and finished him off. Now his mother rushed out and began to shout. The courtyard stood deserted. All her relatives had gone home, but a sexton who witnessed the killing from the church's bell tower locked himself in and began ringing the bell. A crowd flocked into the courtyard. Once they learned of the crime they killed the elder Bitiagovsky and the three assassins. In all twelve persons were slain. Dmitry's corpse was laid in a coffin and carried to the cathedral church of the Transfiguration, while a messenger rode to tell Fedor of his brother's death. The courier, however, reached Boris, who took the message and replaced it with another, stating that Dmitry accidentally cut his throat because of the negligence of the Nagoys. He had this story relayed to the Fedor, who wept for a long time.

Prince Vasily Ivanovich Shuisky, Lord-in-Waiting Kleshnin, Crown Secretary Yelizar Vyluzgin and Metropolitan Gelasius of Krutitsa were assigned to Uglich to bury Dmitry and to investigate the affair. This commission inspected the corpse, buried it, and asked the residents of Uglich how the Nagoys were so negligent as to let the tsarevich kill himself. The inhabitants asserted that Dmitry was murdered by his servants, Bitiagovsky and his companions, on orders from Boris Godunov and his confederates. When Shuisky and the others arrived back in Moscow they reported to Fedor that Dmitry killed himself by accident. The Nagoys were hauled to Moscow and punished savagely. Godunov personally, with the boyars and Kleshnin, attended their torture. Even then the Nagoys professed that the tsarevich was murdered. Tsaritsa Maria was made a nun and cloistered in the Vyksinsk hermitage, beyond Beloozero. The Nagoys ended up scattered about in various jails. Some inhabitants of Uglich were executed, some had their tongues cut out, and some were imprisoned. Many were exiled to Siberia, where they populated the town of Pelym. Thenceforth Uglich became a ghost town.

This story exhibits not a single feature that compels our skepticism. The particulars of the murder, the assassin's prior conversation with his victim, the details of the preparation in Moscow, the names of those who, though chosen, refrained from such villainy, the indictment of Kleshnin as the central figure—all these minutiae do not permit the historian to dismiss this version as a fabrication.[15] Let us now compare this account with a different piece of evidence which aims to prove the opposite, that is, that Dmitry did kill himself.

THE INVESTIGATIVE COMMISSION'S REPORT

Prince Vasily Shuisky, Andrei Kleshnin, and Yelizar Vyluzgin arrived at Uglich on the evening of May 19.[16] They interrogated Mikhail Nagoy. "How did Tsarevich Dmitry die? What illness had he? Why did he, Nagoy, order the deaths of Mikhail Bitiagovsky, his son Daniel, Nikita Kachalov, Daniel Tretiakov, Osip Volokhov and of townsmen, servants of Bitiagovsky and Volokhov? Why, on Tuesday, did he order the collection of knives, arquebuses, an iron club and sabres, which he placed on the dead men? Why did he make the town prefect Rusin Rakov swear to stand by him? Against whom were they supposed to stand?"

The investigators arrived on the evening of May 19 and that very night they questioned Mikhail Nagoy. What did they ask him? Not about the death of Tsarevich Dmitry and the subsequent events, but about the nature of the tsarevich's illness. Why did he, Nagoy, have certain people killed and weapons planted on them? Why did he summon the population and make the town prefect swear an oath? The question arises immediately as to how the investigators could have known all this. Only later does the investigatory report reveal that the commission, having reached Uglich, at once interviewed the town prefect Rusin Rakov, who blamed the Nagoys and attested that the tsarevich killed himself accidentally. Thus a suspicious inaccuracy mars the investigative report from its very beginning. Nothing is said of Rusin Rakov, yet the questioning of Nagoy arises directly from Rakov's testimony!

Mikhail Nagoy replied that Osip Volokhov, Nikita Kachalov and Daniel Bitiagovsky stabbed the tsarevich. The mob then butchered the assassins without Mikhail's order. Rusin Rakov personally laid weapons on the corpses, without Mikhail's knowledge. He, Mikhail Nagoy, did not administer any oath to the town prefect.

Rusin Rakov then referred the commission to Mikhail's brother Grigory Nagoy, and to the servant Boris Afanasiev. They testified that Mikhail commanded that weapons be planted on the corpses. How did Mikhail refute this accusation? We do not know, but we do know for a fact that he did not sign his deposition.

We also know one other odd circumstance. Rusin Rakov and Yevdoky Mikhailov, the watchmen at the crown secretaries' office, vouched that Mikhail Nagoy's man Timofey came to the office that Tuesday. Timofey carried with him a live hen which he killed, smearing its blood on the assortment of weapons which Rusin Rakov then placed on the bodies of Bitiagovsky and his accomplices. Another servant of the Nagoys, Boris Afanasiev, asserted that Timofey had fled for parts unknown by Monday afternoon. Timofey, in fact, was not present for the interrogation.

THE NAGOYS' DEFENSE

Now let us examine what the Nagoys had to say about the tsarevich's death. Mikhail Nagoy, as stated above, testified that Osip Volokhov, Nikita Kachalov and Daniel Bitiagovsky murdered Dmitry. Yet he failed to address a most basic question. Who told him this? He claimed not to have seen the deed, having rushed up only after the sound of the bell convinced him that the palace was in flames.

Grigory Nagoy argued otherwise. The tsarevich cut himself during one of the epileptic seizures he frequently suffered, but Grigory too ignored the vital question. Who informed him of the nature of the tsarevich's death, since he too witnessed nothing, arriving on the run with Mikhail? Grigory's deposition did add the important detail that they found the tsarevich alive and that the boy died in their presence. Yet Grigory omitted crucial details. In what position did they find the tsarevich (the nurse testified that he died in her arms)? Did he have the knife with which he was playing? Was it nearby? The investigators did not inquire.

Grigory Nagoy later stated that when the elder Bitiagovsky appeared and a crowd gathered, *an unknown person* shouted that Daniel Bitiagovsky and his companions slew the tsarevich. Other witnesses identified this *unknown person* as Tsaritsa Maria. Grigory Nagoy, they testified, believed his sister, and at her bidding he clubbed the nurse Vasilisa Volokhova on the sides. What made Grigory Nagoy alter his story? Some contend that he changed his mind when he realized that he and his sister were trapped in their lies. Others hold that he was cajoled and intimidated. The picture remains as murky as ever.

Finally a third Nagoy, Andrei, stated that the tsarevich was in the rear courtyard playing mumblety-peg[17] with some children when suddenly the cry arose that he was dead. Tsaritsa Maria rushed down from above. Andrei, having heard the uproar, left his table and hurried to the tsaritsa, where he saw the boy in his nurse's arms *dead, and they say that he was stabbed.* Andrei did not see who stabbed him. The tsarevich did suffer epileptic seizures. This is a most plausible version of events, but it too contains a curious feature. Andrei Nagoy sat in the palace at his dinner table, hastened after the tsaritsa when he heard the shouts, and discovered the tsarevich dead in the nurse's arms. Grigory Nagoy was dining at the inn, ran up when the bell sounded, and found the tsarevich still alive!

What can be concluded from all this? The fact that, given the apparent contradictions and concealing of vital circumstances, all of it should be suspect and set aside. Perhaps the eyewitness accounts will clarify events more satisfactorily.

EYEWITNESS ACCOUNTS

The nurse Vasilisa Volokhova alleged that the tsarevich, playing with the children with a knife, slit his own throat during a seizure. Tsaritsa Maria then ran from the palace and attacked Vasilisa with a club, refusing to hear any justification. Maria cracked Vasilisa's head in many places and accused her son, Osip Vasilisin, as well as Daniel Bitiagovsky and Nikita Kachalov, of Dmitry's murder. Then the tsaritsa had her brother Grigory beat Vasilisa, whom they left for dead. When the bell tolled at the Savior church the townsfolk came running and Maria had them seize Vasilisa. The townsmen grabbed her, flayed her, and dragged her bareheaded before the tsaritsa. Mikhail Bitiagovsky rushed into the courtyard and tried to calm the people and Mikhail Nagoy, but Mikhail Nagoy and Maria had him killed.

Vasilisa also testified that another nurse, Irina, and a lady of the bedchamber, Maria Samoilova, were with her when the tsarevich died. These women too were interrogated. Quickly and succinctly they stated that Dmitry was playing with the children and slew himself with the knife during an epileptic fit. When questioned, Dmitry's playmates verified this. The investigators asked them who were in the courtyard when Dmitry died, and the children twice pointed out the nurse Irina and the lady of the bedchamber Maria Samoilova, but they omitted Vasilisa Volokhova. The investigators paid no attention to this fact!

Besides these three women and the children, another witness, Crown Agent Semeika Yudin, testified that while standing before his dresser he saw Dmitry stab himself during a seizure. Those were the eyewitnesses. Others testified on the basis of hearsay from unidentified sources. Many of these claimed that the tsarevich was playing with the children and stabbed himself accidentally during a fit.

UNSETTLING QUESTIONS

Besides the misgivings raised above, many dubious circumstances remain. First of all, who was the first to toll the bell at the Savior church, thus drawing a crowd into the courtyard? Mikhail and Grigory Nagoy asserted that they hurried from their inn to the courtyard after the bell alarmed them. Vasilisa Volokhova recalled that Grigory Nagoy was with the tsarevich and beat her before the bell sounded. Grigory Nagoy added that a sexton nicknamed Cucumber[18] first tolled the bell. The sexton of the St. Constantine church, the widowed priest Fedot Afanasiev, called Cucumber, was summoned for an interrogation. He swore that he was sitting at home when the watchman at the Savior church, Maxim Kuznetsov, tolled the bell. Cucumber ran from his house into the town. As he neared the Savior church he met the crown agent of the Office for Provisions, Subbota Protopopov, who ordered him to ring the bell at the Savior church, cuffing him on the neck and forcing him to do it, declaring that Tsaritsa Maria had given the order.

Protopopov gave his statement in front of Grigory Nagoy, who stated that he did not hear Subbota Protopopov order the priest Fedot to sound the bell. That same priest Fedot did tell him that Subbota ordered him to ring it, that Mikhail Bitiagovsky ran towards him and that he closed himself in the bell tower and did not let him in. Subbota Protopopov, when confronted with the priest Fedot, asserted "When he reached the courtyard, Mikhail Nagoy commanded me, Subbota, to ring the bell and summon the community, and I made the sexton Cucumber do so."

So the Nagoys called for the alarm, yet testified that they arrived after it sounded. If they committed perjury, how did they manage to be in the courtyard with the tsarevich? Who told them of the misfortune? The investigators failed to pursue this. Moreover Cucumber declared that he came at the sound of the bell which the watchman at the Savior church, Maxim Kuznetsov, first rang. Why then did Subbota need to shove Cucumber by the neck and have him sound the bell when the alarm already was sounded? Where did Kuznetsov hide? Why did the investigators fail to notice this confusion and summon Kuznetsov for questioning?

The priest Bogdan of the St. Constantine church swore that on that Saturday he was dining with Mikhail Bitiagovsky when suddenly the bell sounded in the city, at the Savior church. Bitiagovsky, taking it to be a fire, sent his servants to investigate the cause of this alarm. When they returned with news of Dmitry's death, Mikhail *at once* rode to the courtyard where he tried to calm the crowd, which killed him. Mikhail Bitiagovsky's son Daniel was at his father's house eating. The priest held that Bitiagovsky was still at home when he learned of the tsarevich's death, and went immediately to the palace.

The dispatch couriers from Uglich testified that Mikhail Bitiagovsky, having heard the clamor, went with his son to the office of crown secretaries. There Mokhovnikov, a crown agent, told him that the tsarevich had suffered an epileptic seizure (just now!) and Bitiagovsky went to the tsaritsa while his son remained behind.

Which of these two accounts is valid? If Father Bogdan's testimony is true, why did Mikhail Bitiagovsky, having learned of Dmitry's death, visit the offices of the crown secretaries for no reason when he should have rushed straight to the palace. Of course interrogation of Yevdokim Mikhailov, watchman at the crown secretaries' office, would have explained these contradictions. He must have known whether Mikhail Bitiagovsky came to the office, how his son Daniel ended up there, and whether Kachalov came with them. The commissioners nevertheless did not see fit to ask Mikhailov about this. They did question Kirril Mokhovnikov who, according to the dispatch bearers, first told Bitiagovsky of the tsarevich's accident. Mokhovnikov said nothing about whether he informed Bitiagovsky. He testified only that when Dmitry stabbed himself and the bell sounded Mikhail Bitiagovsky rushed to the courtyard and found its gates barred, and that he, Mokhovnikov, caught up with Mikhail and opened them. When Mikhail entered the courtyard and tried to pacify the townsmen and others who were there, they set upon Mokhovnikov, nearly killing him and breaking his hands and feet. How could the gates have been locked when a crowd was gathered in the courtyard, and when the alarm was sounded on purpose? Why did they attack Mokhovnikov? The investigators ignored these questions, just as they disregarded Cucumber's assertion that Mikhail Bitiagovsky approached him at the bell tower, but that he shut himself inside.

After all this must we not conclude that the investigators did not act conscientiously? Is it not obvious that they overlooked inconsistencies and the withholding of vital evidence in their haste to pile up evidence that Dmitry killed himself? The Nagoys suffered for inciting the public to kill Bitiagovsky, Volokhov and Kachalov. The inhabitants of Uglich suffered for heeding the Nagoys, yet not a single Nagoy witnessed the calamity. Who first named the killers? Was it Tsaritsa Maria, as Vasilisa Volokhova claimed? The tsaritsa did not see the misfortune. Therefore she either fabricated the story of the tsarevich being assassinated, and the assassins' names, or she heard it from eyewitnesses. Assume that she concocted the tale. Is it not odd that she accused only three men, Daniel Bitiagovsky, Nikita Kachalov and Osip Volokhov? Why not include Mikhail Bitiagovsky, her and her brothers' archenemy? When Metropolitan Gelasius returned to Moscow he told a church council "Tsaritsa Maria, having summoned me, confessed that the murder of Mikhail Bitiagovsky, his son and the residents was a sinful act, a crime. She asked that I bring before the tsar her petition that he show clemency to those poor worms, Mikhail Nagoy and the brothers, in their guilt." Assuming that the tsaritsa said just this to Gelasius, her words make it impossible to infer that she acknowledged her personal responsibility. She called the Nagoys' action sinful and reprehensible. So it was, because the Bitiagovskys and their companions were killed without a trial, illegally. It also bears mentioning that neither the lady of the bedchamber nor the wet nurse nor the children corroborated the governess's testimony that the tsaritsa was first to denounce the killers by name. The chronicle's version speaks highly of the wet nurse Irina Zhdanova. This Zhdanova, like the governess and the lady of the bedchamber, swore that the tsarevich killed himself during an epileptic fit. Yet she, along with the men, later were summoned to Moscow.

RESOLUTION OF THE CASE IN MOSCOW

Notwithstanding all the inadequacy of the investigatory report's findings Patriarch Job declared his satisfaction with it before a church council. "Mikhail and Grigory Nagoy," he said, "and the people of Uglich obviously are guilty of treason before the tsar. It was God's will that Tsarevich Dmitry perish, but Mikhail Nagoy had no just cause to order the murder of the tsar's chancellery officials, crown secretary Mikhail Bitiagovsky and his son, Mikhail Kachalov and other servitors, residents and townsmen, who all stood for the truth. He did so because Mikhail Bitiagovsky often argued on the tsar's behalf with Mikhail Nagoy, and because they quarreled over why Mikhail Nagoy kept the sorcerer Andriusha Mochalov and many other magicians in his household. For such vile and treacherous deeds Mikhail Nagoy, his brother and the people of Uglich already have suffered diverse punishments proportionate to their guilt. This matter, however, concerns the entire land, the towns that God and the tsar rule, all under the tsar's protection. God shall direct the tsar towards execution, banishment or clemency. We must pray God for the tsar and the tsaritsa, for their long life and the calming of domestic strife."

POPULAR OPINION

The council condemned the Nagoys, but the people blamed Boris. Popular memory fondly clings to a particularly astonishing event and connects it to all other important occurrences. It is easy to comprehend the impression Dmitry's death must have produced. Earlier appanage princes perished in dungeons, but they stood accused of treason and the tsar punished them. Now an innocent child had died, not in a civil war, not on account of his father's guilt, not by a tsar's command, but because of a subject. Soon thereafter, in June, a terrible fire ravaged Moscow, destroying the entire White quarter. Godunov lavishly bestowed relief and tax exemptions upon those who lost their possessions, yet rumor held that he had Moscow burned purposely in order to bind its inhabitants to him and make them forget Dmitry. Others said he wanted to make the tsar, then at the Trinity monastery, return to Moscow and not travel to Uglich for the inquest. The people believed that Fedor would not let such a grave matter rest without an inquest, and the people awaited the truth. The rumor spread so widely that Godunov felt constrained to refute it in Lithuania through the diplomat Isleniev, who was ordered "If you are asked about the fires in Moscow, say 'I did not happen to be there at the time. Common thieves, servants of the Nagoys, Afanasy and his brother, were pilfering, as later was revealed in Moscow.' If someone brings up the rumors that Godunov's agents started the fires, comment that some vagrant scoundrel said this, and impute it to the will of an evil man. The Godunovs are eminent, great boyars."

When Ghazi-Girey rode on Moscow a rumor spread through the Ukraine that Godunov encouraged him, fearing the land because of the murder of Tsarevich Dmitry. This rumor circulated among the common folk. A junior boyar from Aleksin reported it against his peasant, who was arrested, taken to Moscow and tortured. He implicated numerous persons. Investigators then sent to the towns seized and tormented many, shed innocent blood and tortured many to death. Many died in prison, and numerous places were depopulated.[19]

Within a year after the Uglich incident a daughter, Feodosia, was born to the tsar, then died in the following year. Fedor was profoundly saddened and all Muscovy grieved deeply. Patriarch Job wrote a consoling letter to Irina, advising her that tears and useless physical exhaustion would not soothe her grief, that she should pray, hope and have faith that God would grant her another child, emulating St. Anna.[20] In Moscow there was mourning and talk that Boris had done away with the tsar's daughter.

FEDOR'S DEATH

Five years after his daughter died, at the very end of 1597, Tsar Fedor fell mortally ill. At one in the morning of January 7, 1598 he died. Kalita's male line ended.[21] Only one woman remained, Martha (Maria) Vladimirovna,[22] the daughter of Ivan's unfortunate first cousin Vladimir Andreevich and the widow of Magnus, the nominal king of Livonia. She returned to Muscovy after her husband's death. Martha cast aside worldly affairs, having taken vows which some argue were involuntary. She bore a daughter, Evdokia, who too died in her youth, according to some by an unnatural death. One man still alive not only carried the titles of tsar and grand prince, he even once actually ruled Muscovy at Ivan IV's behest. This was Simeon Bekbulatovich, the baptized khan of Kasimov.[23] Early in Fedor's reign the service registers still referred to him as tsar of Tver and highest ranking boyar then, the chronicle says, he was removed to the village of Kushalino where he kept few servants and lived in poverty. He finally went blind, a misfortune for which the chronicle indicts Godunov, who did not even escape charges of responsibility for the death of Tsar Fedor.

APPENDIX

DEATH OF TSAREVICH DMITRY

The chronicler's version elicits a range of responses in our historical literature. Above all, some have posed the question as to whether Godunov needed to have the tsarevich dead, and whether his previous conduct showed any proclivity to murder an unfortunate orphan. They argue that Dmitry was the fruit of Ivan's seventh marriage. By contemporary standards he enjoyed hardly any right to the throne, and surely he could make no indisputable claim. We must reply that Dmitry was called the tsarevich. The entire realm recognized him as such, starting with his brother the tsar. His name was mentioned in the church ritual at the litany. He owned an appanage estate with a court. He was advanced as the legitimate heir and

even as his brother's rival. Finally his very exile from Moscow under-
scores how dangerous he was considered.

Others assert that Metropolitan Dionisy, Shuisky and the other high
officials plotted against Godunov. They arranged most humbly to beg the
tsar to abandon his barren wife and remarry, that he might have heirs.
Clearly therefore they did not consider Dmitry an heir. Here close attention
must be paid to the goal of this cabal. Shuisky needed some way to alienate
Godunov from the tsar, and the sole means at his disposal was to separate
Fedor from Godunov's sister. Grand Prince Vasily Ivanovich had divorced his wife and taken a new bride in order to produce an heir. Can it
really be concluded therefore that the grand prince's brother Yury and his
half brother Andrei possessed no right to succeed him on the Muscovite
throne?

The critics go on to say that Boris had not [before Dmitry died] ordered
prayers offered for Dmitry, nor included his name in the memorial liturgy,
meaning thereby to mark him as a tsarevich of illegitimate birth. Why
would Boris have recourse to such superfluous measures if he was bent on
murder? These acts openly would unmask his hostility towards Dmitry,
draw attention to his dissatisfaction with the state of affairs, and later
justified suspicion that he was involved in preparing an assassination.
Surely, we answer, Boris and his accomplices came to this crime only
gradually, having attempted other acts against Dmitry. After the inadequacy of one measure they turned to another, the strongest. Others ask
why, once bent on murder, did not Boris remove from Uglich the Nagoys,
his ill-wishers. Why did he not cut off the subsidy supposedly being
granted the tsarevich? This is easy to explain. Such a course would have
been risky because it would have excited the strongest suspicion.

Equally easily dismissed is the argument that it was excessively prema-
ture of Boris to think of the throne in 1591. Fedor was then only thirty-four
years old. He might still have children or he might in fact enter a new
marriage after his wife's natural death. Why assume that Godunov was
thinking solely of the throne? He and his associates considered it extremely dangerous to wait until the tsarevich matured and undertook to
make good the threats which, reportedly, he was prone to utter in his
childlike way. Fedor *might* have children, he *might* survive his wife and
marry again, but it was infinitely more likely that he would not have
children, and that a sickly husband would not outlive his healthy spouse.

Finally the argument is made that Boris was favored by the clergy and
by a substantial party among the boyars, having attracted people of good

deeds. Really, could he not have known how to arrange matters so that a few days after Fedor's death all Russia would beg on bended knee that he take the crown, bypassing Riurik's many descendants, that all Russia would pray God to inspire him thus? Really, must Boris have feared sharing the throne with a seven- or fourteen-year-old lad unsupported by church, servitors or subjects, a child lacking any positive right? Really, could he not predict that the people would follow the ruler's adherents in rejecting this luckless orphan, especially when Boris's servant Job, patriarch by conciliar decree of the patriarchs of Alexandria, Antioch, Constantinople and Jerusalem, ceremoniously would announce to the crowd, from the platform on the Red Square, that Ivan's son by his seventh marriage possessed no claim to the throne?

Indisputably Boris did enjoy the clergy's favor, did possess a strong following among the boyars, and did win over men of good repute. All this did not mean that Russia, on its knees, would offer him the throne while the tsarevich lived. As evidence, consider only the appearance and success of the False Dmitry. Nevertheless, the critics propose another rebuttal. False Dmitry appeared under different circumstances. He benefited from his alleged innocence, his miraculous survival, and Boris's death. No heed was given then to Ivan's seventh marriage. People could see only Ivan's son, the natural heir, and who could rival him? Young Fedor [Borisovich] was surrounded by the Muscovite boyars, who had not loved Boris.

If False Dmitry was favored by alleged innocence, miraculous survival and Boris's death, nevertheless he suffered the liability of being a pretender, as Patriarch Job assured the nation when he cursed Dmitry as a heretic. The fact that Job was not believed then gives us sufficient basis to argue that his judgment also would have been rejected earlier, had he been inspired to declare that the tsarevich lacked any legal birthright to the throne. Boris understood well that a declaration of Dmitry's illegitimacy would have only the most paltry worth in the minds of the Russian people, who revered the ruling house and inclined towards accepting Dmitry as its heir apparent. This is why Boris brought up Dmitry's illegitimacy in communiqués dispatched to the Polish court, but dared not allude to it in decrees issued for domestic consumption.

We would argue even further that no matter how Godunov might manage to wrest the throne from Dmitry, could he then presume that Dmitry would leave him at leisure to hold the throne? Really, how could Boris not assume that Dmitry, in his contest with him, would gain supporters among the envious? Had not every previous appanage princeling found such backing when struggling against a grand prince? Had not most such princelings enjoyed far weaker claims than those which Dmitry could muster against Boris? How could Boris not fear sharing the throne with the tsarevich, Ivan's son, a natural branch of the ruling tree, when he dreaded sharing power with the baptized Tatar, Simeon Bekbulatovich.[1]

Let us now consider criticisms made of the details of the story of the tsarevich's death. According to the story Boris gathered his relatives and closest associates to contemplate means of eliminating the tsarevich, poison having failed. "Aha!" say the critics. "Boris felt the need to take counsel! What normal assassin (let alone a ruler, future tsar and infamous dissembler) dares announce his impending crime to many people and thus place his fate in their hands? This experienced man of the world leaves himself open to two (or maybe twenty?) men who refuse to do his bidding, and thereby consign themselves to persecution (or even to death?)! How could Boris send away these men (Zagriazhsky and Chepchugov) and sense their aversion to him, in any case a threat? Surely, he must either kill them or reward them boundlessly. Finally he sends to Uglich Bitiagovsky, nominated by Kleshnin, with his son and Kachalov, who also have been awarded with Boris's complete trust.... Isn't this trust of Boris cheap to come by?"

We answer that common murderers can do without accomplices and advisers, but the ruler Godunov could not. He scarcely could ride to Uglich and commit the crime personally! Would it have been sensible for Godunov personally to communicate indirectly with the assassins? Clearly, to deflect even a hint of suspicion, he must act through the most trustworthy agents, as recommended by Kleshnin.

Palitsyn says there were people who, citing the continually present dangers emanating from Dmitry's faction, inclined Godunov to the crime. The story also mentions confederates to whom Godunov did not immediately reveal his intentions, yet to whom he did reveal his failed previous efforts. From this passage it is clear that these advisers participated in the affair from its outset.

Palitsyn's story also most clearly indicates that Boris behaved indecisively, listlessly, that Kleshnin took the leading role. Here Palitsyn, who certainly had no desire to minimize Boris's crime, places greater blame on his confederates. Perhaps Boris might kill Zagriazhsky and Chepchugov but that is easier said now than it could be done then. Boris sought to gain popular affection through mercy, not punishment, yet here he was compelled to kill two men—two innocents! Or he was compelled to reward them in a fashion sure to arouse the suspicions of others, certain to unveil his fear of those whom he rewarded!

We are asked further whether we are to think that Boris lacked the sense to *explain* to the assassins that they commit the murder as quietly as possible, cautiously, at least not during the day, not before witnesses, and least of all in front of a nurse devoted to the Nagoys. It was easy for Boris to explain all this to the assassins; it was another matter altogether for them so to execute his orders. It was most difficult to steal by night into the tsarevich's sleeping chamber (he most probably slept in the same room as his mother). During the day they killed him in the presence of only three women. Did murder by night not require their suborning the guards, the lord of the bedchamber, and so forth, thus leaving far more than three witnesses? On the contrary, the murderers picked a most opportune time. All had left to eat, and the tolling of the bell would be needed to summon them home. Moreover, assuming that the assassins managed to slay the boy at night, how would they, and those who employed them, have explained what had transpired? During the day Dmitry indeed might fall accidentally on a knife during a seizure suffered while playing mumblety-peg, but could it really be argued that the tsarevich played mumblety-peg at night, that he kept a knife in bed with him?

There are those who maintain that the chronicles overflow with absurd accusations of criminality against Godunov and that therefore it must be concluded, arguing by analogy, that the most serious of the crimes, the assassination of Dmitry, is imputed against him out of hostility. Yet we must observe that any important historical character usually is painted in overly sharp colors with both a good and a bad hue. We cannot conclude from such exaggeration that the given historical person lacked either the good or the evil qualities. Think only of Napoleon! In our history, Kurbsky indicts Ivan III[2] for murdering his own son and shutting away his brother and grandson. We know that the first accusation is an absurdity and the second is just. Our image of Ivan has been coated with superfluous accusations of wickedness. Must it be concluded therefore that he never shed a drop of blood?

K.S. Aksakov commented critically on our view of the two accounts of the death of tsarevich Dmitry. "There are absolute inaccuracies in the chronicle's version," he says. "It states that the residents of Uglich testified about the murder of the tsarevich, that the Nagoys were tortured in Moscow, and that under torture they said that the tsarevich was killed. Meanwhile the investigatory commission files contain much testimony by the residents of Uglich, most tending to prove Dmitry's accidental death."

The chronicle, we reply, does speak about the testimony of residents of Uglich, given by the whole town, but it tells nothing about which individuals were interrogated, what they answered and how it was recorded. Ought we really condemn the chronicle as false on the evidence of the investigatory report, which so clearly bore the mark of its composers' carelessness? The critic notes that only Mikhail Nagoy, not in Moscow, but in Uglich, professed that the tsarevich was murdered, and that his two other brothers gave evidence that the tsarevich killed himself. Yes, indeed that was the case in Uglich, whereas the chronicle speaks about something else, about the Moscow tortures, which we have no basis to disclaim.

The critic attacks the chronicle's tale of the earlier poisoning attempts. Had they really occurred the poison should have worked, so perhaps no such poison ever existed. We do not accept this. It is easily explained as the simple result of poor pharmacology.

Our critic also insists on the guilt of Mikhail Nagoy, relying on chancellery clerk Rusin Rakov's testimony that Nagoy ordered weapons placed on the corpses. Boris Afanasiev's deposition, however, contradicts Rakov's story, yet our critic pays no attention to it. Aksakov also stresses Father Bogdan's testimony that he was eating with Mikhail Bitiagovsky exactly when the bell first sounded, and that Mikhail's son Daniel was then also at his father's place eating, but the commission report contains other testimony about Bitiagovsky, contradicting that of Bogdan. Aksakov ignores this. He mentions too the statements of the Uglich children, which testimony we find suspect given the evidence of others present at the murder scene that they twice failed to mention the nurse Vasilisa Volokhova. Such witnesses cannot be trusted."[3]

NOTES

Additional information on personalities and topics found in the text and notes is available in Joseph L. Wieczynski, et al., eds., *The Modern Encyclopedia of Russian, Soviet and Eurasian History* (MERSH, formerly *The Modern Encyclopedia of Russian and Soviet History*); Harry B. Weber, et al., eds., *The Modern Encyclopedia of East Slavic, Baltic and Eurasian Literatures* (MESBEL, formerly *The Modern Encyclopedia of Russian and Soviet Literatures, Including Non-Russian and Emigré Literatures*); Paul D. Steeves, ed., *The Modern Encyclopedia of Religions in Russia and Eurasia* (MERRE, formerly *The Modern Encyclopedia of Religions in Russia and the Soviet Union*); and David R. Jones, ed., *The Military Encyclopedia of Russia and Eurasia* (MERE, formerly *The Military-Naval Encyclopedia of Russia and the Soviet Union*) all published by Academic International Press.

INTRODUCTION

1. S.M. Solov'ev, *Sochineniia. Kniga I. Istoriia Rossii s drevneishikh vremen* (Collected Works. Book I. History of Russia from Earliest Times), I.D. Kovalchenko and S.S. Dmitriev, eds., Vols. 1-2 (Moscow 1988), p. 31.

2. George Vernadsky, *Russian Historiography. A History* (Belmont, Mass., 1978), p. 94.

3. Hellie, p. 44.

CHAPTER I

1. "Gathering of the Russian lands" is a stock phrase of Russian nationalist historians when referring to Moscow's consolidation of its power over the previously independent principalities. The princes' retinues, institutions extending back to the ninth-century Kievan state, naturally reflected the interests of the local princes and had to be displaced along with them.

2. Vasily II ruled from 1425 to 1462. Guile, skill, and luck enabled him to establish a considerable realm which his son, Ivan III, the Great, expanded substantially. His sobriquet stems from his being blinded during the civil wars which accompanied much of his reign. See Hugh Graham, "Vasilii II Vasil'evich," *Modern Encyclopedia of Russian and Soviet History* (hereafter cited as MERSH), Volume 41, pp. 214-217. See also Volume 5 of this series.

3. Ivan IV, the Terrible or the Dread (1530-1584), was the grandson of Ivan III and son of Vasily III. His reign saw territorial expansion in the East, the

conquest of Kazan and Astrakhan, and a series of wars with Poland-Lithuania in the West, largely over Livonia, which began well and ended badly. In domestic affairs the reign began brilliantly with a series of reforms and further development of the centralized bureaucracy, and changed for the worse with the establishment of a state within the state, the oprichnina, or crown estates (see below, Note 22). At Ivan's death the realm was exhausted militarily and financially, as Soloviev notes in Chapter V. For a synopsis see Sergei Zenkovsky, "Ivan IV (Ivan Vasil'evich)," MERSH, Volume 15, pp. 51-60, and works specified in the Introduction to this volume.

4. Tsarevich Ivan Ivanovich was born in 1554, the eldest surviving son and heir apparent of Ivan IV. He participated in a number of his father's military campaigns, as well as in his infamous crown estates policy. He died November 19, 1581 as the result of the quarrel with his father a few days previously, when the tsar struck him on the head with the ferrule of his staff. Rather than a premeditated murder, as Soloviev characterizes it here, the deed resembles involuntary manslaughter. Nevertheless, the death of the tsarevich made the simple-minded Fedor (born 1557) heir apparent.

5. Again Soloviev is speaking figuratively. The cause of the fatal quarrel between father and son, according to some accounts, was the tsar's mistreatment of his pregnant daughter-in-law, which caused her to miscarry.

6. Tsarevich Dmitry Ivanovich, born 1582, was the son of Ivan IV and his last and surviving wife, Maria Nagaia. Soloviev describes the latter as Ivan's fifth wife but according to the commonly accepted calculation she was his sixth or seventh (see following note). The young tsarevich was given the appanage of Uglich, to which he was banished in 1584 shortly after the accession of his half-brother Fedor. It was feared that the Nagoy family was forming a reversionary interest detrimental to the aims of the regent Boris Godunov. When the tsarevich was found dead in the courtyard of the palace at Uglich on May 15, 1591, Boris was suspected of having him murdered. Some time after his death a series of pretenders arose claiming to be the tsarevich who allegedly escaped his murderers and lived in hiding for many years. One such pretender actually occupied the Muscovite throne from June 1605 until May 1606. Soloviev analyzes the evidence for and against Godunov's complicity in Dmitry's death in Chapter VI of this volume. For the pretender's career, see Volume 14 of this series.

7. Ivan's marriages were actually seven in number: (1) Anastasia Romanovna, married February 3, 1547, died August 7, 1560; (2) Maria Temriukovna, married August 21, 1561, died September 1, 1569; (3) Martha Vasilievna Sobakina, married October 28, 1571, died November 14, 1571; (4) Anna Alexeevna Koltovskaia, married April 28, 1572, divorced 1575, died April 5, 1626; (5) Anna Vasilchikova, married 1575, divorced 1576; (6) Vasilisa Melentieva, married 1577, divorced the same year; (7) Maria Fedorovna Nagaia, married September 1580, widowed March 18, 1584, died July 20, 1612. Melentieva is omitted from most official genealogies presumably because the marriage was not consummated. Sobakina also very likely does not count for the same reason. Her mother

gave her a potion to induce fertility, but instead it poisoned her. She was deathly ill at the wedding ceremony and died seventeen days later. If indeed this marriage was unconsummated, Ivan's union with Vasilchikova was canonically lawful, since the Orthodox church permits up to three consecutive marriages. It is to be noted that precise dates are lacking for the tsar's subsequent marriages because the church did not recognize them as legitimate. Soloviev therefore may be technically correct in describing Nagaia as Ivan's fifth wife.

8. Vasily III died when Ivan IV was a child of three, necessitating a regency. Soloviev compares that situation with Ivan IV leaving the realm in a similar state, in which the childlike Fedor ascended the throne and a bitter struggle for power ensued during the brief regency. It culminated, as this chapter shows, in the triumph of Boris Godunov.

9. The Time of Troubles (1598-1613) saw the general collapse into anarchy of Muscovy. The Godunovs and the Shuiskys perished in its storms; the future dynasty was the Romanov. In addition to works mentioned in the introduction to this volume see Volumes 14, 15 and 16 in this series, all translated and edited by G. Edward Orchard and titled respectively *The Time of Troubles. Boris Godunov and False Dmitry* (1988), *The Time of Troubles. Tsar Vasily Shuisky and the Interregnum, 1606-1613* (1989) and *The First Romanov. Tsar Michael, 1613-1634* (1991).

10. The reference is to the Godunov, Shuisky, and Romanov families respectively.

11. Gediminas (1275-1341) called in some sources "king of the Lithuanians and the Rus" ruled as grand prince of Lithuania from 1316 to 1341. In many respects, he founded the Lithuanian state. He spread Lithuanian influence into Western Rus (the current Belarus) and created the vast kingdom of Lithuania, much of which was Western Rus culturally, linguistically, and religiously. Princes of his line and those of his servitors who were Russian Orthodox regularly entered Muscovite service in the fifteenth and sixteenth centuries. See Juozas Jakstas, "Gediminas," *Encyclopedia Lituanica,* Volume II (Boston, 1972), pp. 287-293.

12. Mstislavsky (1530-1586) figured prominently in Ivan IV's campaigns against Kazan and Livonia, and in the defense of Moscow against Crimean attacks in 1555 and 1571. He managed to survive his appointment as a co-ruler in the zemshchina, or domains of the land (see below, Note 23) and a dubious accusation of treason when the Tatars burned Moscow in 1571. See Emily Leonard, "Mstislavksy, Ivan Fedorovich," MERSH, Volume 23, pp. 61-62 and Lloyd E. Berry and Robert O. Crummey, eds., *Rude and Barbarous Kingdom* (Madison, Wis., 1968), p. 264, Note 2.

13. The Patrikeev family traced its origins to Patrikey, a native of Lithuania who in 1408 came to serve Grand Prince Vasily I of Moscow. The Golitsyn and Kurakin families were offshoots of this stem.

14. On Golitsyn's candidacy of 1606, when Vasily Shuisky was elected tsar, and also in 1610, after Shuisky was deposed, see Volumes 14 and 15 in this series.

15. Sviatoslav Olgovich (died 1164) was prince of Novgorod Seversk (1136-1139), Belgorod (1141-1154), and finally of Chernigov from 1154. He assisted

his brother Vsevolod in obtaining the Kievan throne. He tried unsuccessfully to expel Prince Andrei Bogoliubsky from Pereiaslavl. In 1146 he participated in the lengthy struggle for Kiev as an ally of Yury Dolgoruky, whom he met in Moscow in 1147. On this occasion, the first mention in the chronicles of the future capital, Sviatoslav helped Yury gain the grand princely throne. After Yury's death he helped Iziaslav Davydovich become grand prince, receiving as his reward the principality of Chernigov. Here Soloviev uses him to personify the southern branch of the princely clan, as he will use Vsevolod III (see following note) to symbolize its northern branch. For further details see entry by Edward D. Sokol, MERSH, Volume 38, pp. 117-122.

16. Vsevolod III of Suzdal (1154-1212) was the son of Yury Dolgoruky, nicknamed "Big Nest" on account of his large family, eight sons and two daughters. In 1162 he was expelled along with his mother and brother by Andrei Bogoliubsky, and spent the next twelve years in exile at Constantinople. Returning to Russia after Bogoliubsky's death, he helped his brother Mikhail seize the city of Vladimir. In 1176 he succeeded Mikhail as grand prince, having defeated in a civil war his opponents, both princely and boyar. Besides maintaining control over Kiev and Chernigov he was able to establish a series of his nominees on the princely throne of Novgorod, and in several campaigns brought the principality of Riazan under his control. In 1190 the princes of Galich acknowledged his suzerainty. He also conducted successful campaigns against the Volga Bulgars in 1183 and 1186. His main claim to fame is his ambitious building program, monuments of which still remain in his capital of Vladimir, including the Intercession cathedral (1185-1198), the St. Demetrius cathedral (1193-1197), the citadel (1194-1196) and the Nativity cathedral (1192-1195). See Volume 3 of this series.

17. When, in 1263, Prince Alexander Nevsky died, his youngest son Daniel was assigned to rule the then insignificant principality of Moscow; tradition treats him as the founder of the Muscovite line of princes from the house of Riurik. As Soloviev indicates, these petty Muscovite princes came to dominate princes from far more senior lines of that house. See Volume 4 of this series.

18. Patrimonial estate here refers to hereditary property or votchina. Ivan the Terrible forcibly expropriated them during the oprichnina period. See below, Note 23.

19. The battle is incorrectly named here. In January 1564 a Lithuanian army defeated Muscovite troops under the command of Prince Peter Ivanovich Shuisky at the Ulla river. Shuisky fell in battle. His body was brought back to Wilno and buried there with great solemnity.

20. Prince Ivan Petrovich Shuisky first appears in 1562. He was a deputy to the 1566 Assembly of the Land and was promoted to boyar rank in 1574. He served as commander and vicegerent at Pskov in 1573, 1577, 1580-1584 and 1585-1586. He was the effective leader of the defense of Pskov during the siege conducted by Stefan Bathory in 1581-1582, and for his service was awarded the revenues of the city for his own use, at that time a singular honor. After the death of Ivan IV he was named to the regency council, then became involved with the

anti-Godunov faction, and in the autumn of 1586 he was disgraced. Boris suborned one of Prince Ivan's servants to inform against him, secured a condemnation, and had the prince confined to a monastery, where he was put to death unobtrusively on November 16, 1588. See entry by Nancy Shields Kollmann, MERSH, Volume 35, pp. 58-61.

21. The Romanov-Yurievs were one branch of the Romanov clan. For an explanation of their origin see Graham, "Romanova, Anastasia," MERSH, Volume 31, pp. 148-150.

22. For the literature on Boris Godunov see the Introduction to this volume and entry by Orchard, MERSH, Volume 5, pp. 125-131.

23. A crown servitor here refers to an oprichnik, or individual member attached to Ivan IV's crown estates, or oprichnina. In January 1565 Ivan split his realm into two sections, the oprichnina and the zemshchina. The former literally means "separate domain" and describes a state within the state with its capital at Alexandrov village near Moscow. Its independent army and administration, of which Skuratov-Belsky was founder, terrorized the whole country. See Graham's entry "Oprichnina," MERSH, Volume 26, pp. 48-56. Grigory Lukianovich Belsky, better known as Maliuta Skuratov, was Ivan IV's favorite during the latter years of the existence of the crown domain. One of his daughters, Maria, married Boris Godunov, while another, Catherine, married Dmitry Ivanovich Shuisky. Maliuta was killed in action at the siege of the Livonian fortress of Weissenstein on January 1, 1573. See entry by Graham, MERSH, Volume 21, p. 55.

24. Irina Fedorovna Godunova married Fedor in 1580. After his death in January 1598 she retired to the New convent on the outskirts of Moscow, taking the religious name of Alexandra. She died November 5, 1603.

25. Nikita Romanovich (Romanov-Yuriev) was a boyar from 1562, took an active part in the Livonian war and was involved in many diplomatic negotiations. In 1584 he was appointed one of the council of regents, then retired for reasons of health towards the end of the same year. He died in 1586. His daughters married into the Troekurov, Sitsky and Cherkassky families. The most famous of his sons were Fedor (the future Patriarch Filaret) who died in 1632, and Ivan, who died in 1640.

26. The English ambassador Bowes comments that when Ivan died all power passed into the hands of the boyar Nikita Romanovich, whose main adviser was the crown secretary, Andrei Shchelkalov. Boris Godunov exercised no personal power until the tsar's coronation. Nikita Yurievich Romanov died shortly and Boris Fedorovich Godunov replaced him as his successor and ruler. Chronicle of Many Rebellions, p. 7; Chronographs of the Library of the Archives of the Ministry of Foreign Affairs, No. 2 and 14, (Soloviev's note) The editor of the 1959–1966 edition notes that Soloviev's information does not appear in the latter of the two cited sources. Bowes's original account does support Soloviev's argument. See Richard Hakluyt, The Principal Navigations Voyages, Traffiques and Discoveries of the English Nation, Volume III (Glasgow, 1903), pp. 315-329, and particularly pp. 326-327. On Bowes, see below, Chapter III, Note 26.

Soloviev frequently uses the Chronicle of Many Rebellions. On its provenance, see Volume 14 in this series, Chapter II, Note 7.

27. Chronicle of Many Rebellions, p. 5. Accounts of the foreigners Oderborn, Heidenstein and Horsey. (Soloviev's note) The Soviet editor identifies the foreigners as Paul Oderborn, *Joannis Basilidis Magni Moscoviae ducis vita* (Life of Ivan Vasilievich, Grand Duke of Muscovy) (Wittenberg, 1585); R. Heidenstein, *Notes on the Muscovite War* (St. Petersburg, 1889), in Russian translation made after Soloviev's death; "Travels of Sir Jerome Horsey," *Russia at the Close of the Sixteenth Century,* ed. Edward A. Bond (London, 1856), p. 226. The editor also cites a Russian edition of Horsey appearing in 1909. In the cases of Oderborn and Heidenstein the editor again comments that Soloviev's information does not appear in the original as cited. The original title of Heidenstein's work is *De bello moscovitico quod Stephanus Rex Poloniae gessit. Commentarium Libri VI.* (Concerning the Muscovite War which King Stefan of Poland Waged. Six Books of Commentaries) (Basel, 1588). For Horsey and his work, see below, Note 41.

28. Again a comparison is drawn between the situation at the beginning and at the end of Ivan IV's reign. During all the years that Vasily III remained childless the heir apparent was his next eldest brother Prince Andrei Ivanovich of Staritsa, whose hopes were dashed with the birth of Ivan in 1530. He led an abortive rebellion against his nephew and died in prison in 1536. His wife and son, Princess Evfrosina and Prince Vladimir posed a threat, real or imagined, to Ivan IV, who did away with both in 1569. Similarly under the childless Fedor a reversionary interest was building around Tsarevich Dmitry and his maternal relatives, the Nagoy family.

29. Ivan IV married his last wife, Maria Fedorovna Nagaia, on September 6, 1580 and their son Dmitry was born October 19, 1582. At the accession of Fedor most of the Nagoy family were sent to live with Tsarevich Dmitry at Uglich. When the tsarevich was found dead the investigation blamed the Nagoys for inciting the ensuing disorders, and most of the male relatives were imprisoned or exiled. Maria was forced to take the veil under the religious name of Martha. In 1605 she recognized the first False Dmitry as her long lost son, and was installed in luxurious apartments in the Ascension convent within the Kremlin. She retracted her former testimony after the pretender was murdered but since this latest change of mind suited very well the purposes of the new tsar Vasily Shuisky, she remained as dowager tsaritsa in her Kremlin apartments. She died July 20, 1612. Other members of the Nagoy family similarly were restored to favor under False Dmitry I, and also served under Shuisky

30. Oderborn, Horsey, and Petreius (Soloviev's note). The editors, attempting to find Soloviev's sources, comment that Oderborn does not contain this information; they refer to the 1856 edition of Horsey, p. 110. The other reference is to Peter Petreius de Erlesunda, *Historien und Bericht von dem Grossfurtenthumb Muskhow* (History and Relation Concerning the Grand Principality of Moscow) (Leipzig, 1620), p. 256, and its Russian translation, *Istoriia o velikom kniazhestve moskovskom* (Moscow, 1867), p. 167.

31. Bogdan Yakovlevich Belsky was Ivan's last principal favorite and afterwards a partisan of Tsarevich Dmitry. He was also a nephew of Maliuta Skuratov, and hence a kinsman by marriage to Boris Godunov. Despite this, he was exiled during the reign of Fedor, being appointed governor of Nizhny Novgorod. In 1598 he led a conspiracy once again, this time against Boris Godunov, and was appointed to the command of the frontier town of Tsarevo-Borisov. Here his injudicious behavior caused him to be recalled to the capital, where he was degraded and sent into confinement. Restored to favor under False Dmitry, he was raised to the rank of boyar in 1605, but after the pretender's fall again was sent into exile, this time as governor of Kazan, where he was murdered in 1611. See entry by Graham, MERSH, Volume 4, pp. 1-2. See also Volume 15 of this series, pp. 199-200.

32. The Liapunovs were a family of Riazan gentry who were to play a prominent part in the events of the Time of Troubles. See Volume 15, Chapter I, Notes 40 and 41.

33. Junior boyars, in Russian deti boiarskie, singular syn boyarskii, were the most numerous class of military servitors.

34. Powerful crown secretaries, the Shchelkalovs, Andrei and Vasily, acted behind the scenes at major points in Muscovy's sixteenth-century history. Since 1572 they sat on the tsar's personal council of advisers, the boyar council. Andrei directed the Chancellery for Foreign Affairs from 1571 until he died in 1594. Vasily then occupied the post until 1601. Before 1594 Vasily spent seventeen years leading the Chancellery of Military Service and Appointments. Vasily angered Boris Godunov by his role in the election of 1598, but managed to keep his post. After Boris' death he served in a titular capacity under both False Dmitry and Vasily Shuisky, dying in 1610. See entry by Graham, "Shchelkalov Brothers," MERSH, Volume 34, pp. 176-180.

35. Chronicle of Many Rebellions, p. 8 (Soloviev's note).

36. The question mark appears in Soloviev's original text.

37. This probably refers to a dispute over the peculiar and complex system of ranking the nobility, on which see Graham, "Mestnichestvo," MERSH, Volume 22, pp. 8-13.

38. Soloviev does not identify clearly the "one source" mentioned at the beginning of this paragraph. He does cite the "several accounts" in the last sentence as in the *Historica Russiae Momumenta* (Historical Monuments of Russia), Volume II, No. 1 and the Sokrashchennyi vremennik do 1691 goda (Abbreviated Chronicle up to the Year 1691), but without a page reference. The editors cite the latter source as having appeared in *Materialy po istorii SSSR* (Materials Concerning the History of the USSR), Volume 11 (Moscow, 1955), and refer to pp. 148-149.

39. Soloviev does not indicate which chronicler.

40. This may be inferred from the Nikolaevskii Chronicle. "They prayed with tears that there be no delay," but in the Chronicle of Many Rebellions simply "that it be." (Soloviev's note)

41. Jerome Horsey (flourished 1573-1627) went to Russia as a clerk in the service of the Muscovy Company, remaining there for seven years. In 1580 he undertook a mission to England to purchase arms and munitions for Ivan IV. He was detained twice while traversing the Baltic lands and Poland, and each time he convinced his captors he was fleeing from Russia. He returned with the supplies in 1581 and subsequently was employed frequently as an intermediary between the English and the Muscovite governments. It was he who was entrusted with the task of informing Queen Elizabeth of Fedor's accession. At that time he was placed in charge of the Company's house and goods in Moscow. He became friendly with Boris Godunov and on his behalf traveled to Riga in 1585 to persuade Ivan's niece Maria Vladimirovna, widow of King Magnus of Livonia, to return with her daughter to Russia in hope of a suitable marriage for the daughter. They returned, then immediately were cloistered in a Muscovite convent. While in England late in 1585 Horsey was accused by John Finch, an employee of the Company, of having denounced him falsely to the Muscovite authorities. A Privy Council investigation cleared Horsey but later charges against him of trading independently, and of falsifying Company accounts, were taken more seriously. Horsey was obliged to make good at least part of the loss from his own pocket. He returned to Moscow in 1588, but it was evident this time that his credibility was greatly diminished, since he was accused of defaulting on his debts to private Muscovite citizens as well as to the tsar's treasury. He was arrested and deported back to England in the custody of the ambassador Giles Fletcher. Somehow he managed to get himself appointed ambassador in 1590, when the tsar refused him an audience and he left Russia for the last time in 1591. He lived the rest of his life in the county of Buckingham, was knighted in 1604, and served as sheriff in 1610, besides being elected several times as member of the Parliament. He began writing his *Travels* in 1589 as a rebuttal to his accusers, only completing them around 1621. Despite their self-justificatory tone and a number of blatant falsehoods they are a valuable source of information about Russia, especially since Horsey was one of the few foreign observers fluent in the Russian language. The most convenient edition is to be found in Berry and Crummey, pp. 249-369.

42. Soloviev here cites Horsey in English "And all the nobility whatsoever" and quotes Karamzin's interpretation "Probably military men, civil administrators and merchants" and then objects with "But we cannot agree, since by *nobility* [in English] one must understand something other than the service nobility, for Horsey clearly distinguishes *nobilitie* and *cominaltie*." Soloviev refers, according to the editors, to the 1856 Bond edition of Horsey, pp. 269-270 (see above, Note 27) and to N.M. Karamzin, *Istoriia gosudarstva Rossiiskogo* (History of the Russian State) (12 vols., St. Petersburg, 1818–1819), Book III, Volume X, Note 8, col. 5. Bond's 1856 edition of Horsey was reprinted by the Burt Franklin Press in 1963 as Volume 20 of a series of reissues of Hakluyt Society publications. On Horsey, see the preceding note.

43. Dionisy himself had only just become metropolitan in 1584. Soon after the coronation he called a special church council (July 20, 1584) which, in recognition of the sorry state of the national treasury, conceded to Fedor's administration some tax exemptions which Ivan granted to the church. Soloviev describes Dionisy's role in the struggle between the Godunovs and the Shuiskys, his subsequent falling out with Godunov, and his ultimate deposition and exile to the Khutyn monastery in 1584 and where he died in 1587.

44. The reference is to a natural brother, thus to his half-brother Dmitry.

45. The usual rumors flew that the ruler was poisoned. The silence of our chroniclers, who loved to indict Godunov for every crime, witnesses the baselessness of these rumors. (Soloviev's note) Soloviev cites two sources for his assertion that rumors existed: "Versuch einer neueren Geschichte von Rußland" (An Attempt at a New History of Russia), *Sammlung Russischer Geschichte* (Miscellany of Russian History), Volume 5 (St. Petersburg, 1760), p. 36, and Giles Fletcher, *Of the Russe Common Wealth,* p. 27. No other bibliographic data for Fletcher's work is given by Soloviev or his editors, but Soloviev's evidence is easily found in the reprint of the nineteenth-century Hakluyt Society edition of Fletcher and Horsey, edited by Edward Bond, *Russia at the Close of the Sixteenth Century* (New York, n.d.), p. 36. For a biographical sketch of Fletcher, see Bond's extended introduction to the works of Fletcher and Horsey in this same volume, pp. cxx-cxxviii.

46. Soloviev cites Fletcher, pp. 21-22 and Horsey, p. 528

47. Ivan considered the Shuiskys to have been leaders at despoiling and misgoverning the country during his minority. For Ivan's view of his treatment, see J.L.I. Fennell, *The Correspondence between Prince A.M. Kurbsky and Tsar Ivan IV* (Cambridge, 1963). For Soloviev's narrative of the Shuiskys' conduct see Volume 9 of this series.

48. Chronicle of Many Rebellions, p. 9; Morozov Chronicle, Box IV, No. 228, ff. 74 -78v. (Soloviev's note)

49. The monastery of St. Cyril, founded in 1397, was situated near Beloozero, and was by this time one of the richest religious foundations in Russia. It was also a formidable fortress-prison which withstood the Polish siege of 1612-1613. Among its involuntary guests at one time or another were Vassian Patrikeev, Simeon Bekbulatovich, Boris Ivanovich Morozov and Patriarch Nikon. See the entry by Lupinin, MERSH, Volume 17, pp. 27-29.

50. Stefan Bathory, Polish king, reigned 1576-1586. He successfully led the Polish armies in the latter stages of the Livonian War, besieging Pskov from August 1581 until January 1582, when the Truce of Yam Zapolsky brought a suspension of hostilities,

51. The Russian term gosti describes a corporate group of wealthy merchants who enjoyed special trading privileges and easy access to government contracts, favors and monopolies. They prospered under Ivan IV. See Samuel Baron, MERSH, Volume 13, pp. 74-77.

52. The Palace of Facets was constructed between 1487 and 1491 by the Italian architects Marco Ruffo and Pietro Solario. The name is taken from the

eastern facade of the building. The interior contains an audience chamber five hundred square meters in area, with a series of vaults supported by a central column. The chamber was used for ceremonial receptions, meetings of the boyar council and sessions of the Assembly of the Land. See the brief entry, MERSH, Volume 13, p. 99.

53. At the zemskii sobor or Assembly of the Land under Ivan representatives of all classes participated. See entry by Hellie, MERSH, Volume 45, pp. 226-234.

54. The Alexandrov village (Aleksandrovskaia sloboda), on the approaches to the Trinity monastery, is infamous as the headquarters of the crown domains of Ivan IV, who doubtless chose it because of its strategic location.

55. Prince Andrei Ivanovich Shuisky first appears in 1575, and became a boyar in 1584. He was an active participant in the anti-Godunov faction and was arrested in 1586. He died in prison in 1589.

56. Prince Ivan Borisovich Tatev is mentioned first in 1578. It seems that later that year he was restored to favor, since in 1600 he played a leading part in repelling a Tatar attack by intercepting the raiders on the road between Belgorod and Kursk. In 1605 he was appointed governor of Chernigov. Although he remained loyal to Godunov when False Dmitry first appeared, there is suspicion that his appointment to Chernigov was an honorific exile since he is mentioned as one of those in disfavor under Boris but restored to favor under False Dmitry. He assisted at the marriage of Marina Mniszech to Dmitry, was named to the boyar council and to Dmitry's Polish-style senate, and also assumed charge of the Chancellery for Crown Revenues. Early in Shuisky's reign, towards the end of 1606, he was ordered to accompany Prince V.M. Skopin-Shuisky and Prince V.V. Golitsyn to relieve Kaluga, then under siege by the Bolotnikov rebels. He was slain at the battle on the Pchelna river, which was fought May 1-3, 1607.

57. During a general wave of mass hysteria and denunciations around 1600 the Romanov brothers were accused of sorcery on the basis of evidence planted by Godunov. See Volume 14, pp. 58-63.

58. The term here, opala, denotes disgrace arising from the formally expressed displeasure of the sovereign, as well as accompanying punishment. There is a brief entry in MERSH, Volume 26, p. 37.

59. Prince Vasily Fedorovich Skopin-Shuisky was a commander in Pskov, along with his kinsman Prince Ivan Petrovich Shuisky, between 1587 and 1582. He held command posts on the Northwestern frontier, particularly in the Novgorod region, in the early 1580s and again during the main operations against the Swedes in the early 1590s. He died in 1595. His son Mikhail earned fame as the liberator of Moscow in 1610.

60. Chronicle of Many Rebellions, p. 4; *Rerum rossicarum Scriptores Exteri* (Foreign Writers on Russian Affairs), Volume I (St. Petersburg, 1851), p. 150. Petreius says that Godunov, in the process of persuading the metropolitan not to initiate the divorce, raised the argument that if Fedor did have children, civil war between them and their uncle Dmitry would be inevitable. "This is improbable," Karamzin states. "Dmitry would not have any right to the crown if Fedor left

sons." Yet there was no clear evidence that a son's succession to the father was established as immutable law. We saw in Ivan's infancy sedition springing from the appanages, the uncles. When Ivan was ill many wished to enthrone the uncle Vladimir Andreevich instead of the tsar's son Dmitry. The *Tale of How Boris Godunov Unjustly Stole the Throne of Moscow* says that Godunov, in the beginning of the struggle with the Shuiskys, "could do them no evil, only bring abuse and reproach upon himself, and he learned the news of a popular gathering of a multitude of the Moscow citizens. Knowing perfectly well that Boris plotted against them, the Moscow people wanted to stone that accursed one." Then Boris sought a settlement with the Shuiskys. The tale was written in the first part of Shuisky's reign as tsar. The author claims that he was an eyewitness to the False Dmitry. (Soloviev's note) The references are to Karamzin, *Istoriia,* Book III, Volume X, Note 147, column 31; Petreius, *Historien,* p. 259 and, in Russian, *Istoriia,* p. 169. The *Tale* is a manuscript source from the Saltykov-Shchedrin Library, O IV, No. 17, f. 402.

61. The principal suffragan of the metropolitanate was the titular archbishop of Krutitsa, a suburban village of Moscow. Archbishop Varlaam was deposed along with Metropolitan Dionisy in 1586. When Moscow became a patriarchal see in 1589 Krutitsa was elevated with four other archbishoprics to the rank of metropolitanate.

62. Job was the first patriarch of the Russian church, elected in 1588 largely through the support of Boris Godunov. However disinterested his actions in the 1598 Assembly of the Land, Job was perceived as returning a favor in securing the election of Boris as tsar. After the fall of the Godunov dynasty the partisans of False Dmitry seized Job while he was performing the liturgy at the Dormition cathedral in June 1605. They deposed him and exiled him to his former monastery at Staritsa. He was recalled briefly during Vasily Shuisky's reign in an effort to reinforce the proclamations of Patriarch Hermogen against False Dmitry II. He died in 1607 and was canonized in 1652 at the instigation of Patriarch Nikon. See the entry by Nickolas Lupinin, MERSH, Volume 15, pp. 136-138.

63. "How much might Fedor, whose childlike spirit excelled the church elders in piety, have valued in secular affairs an ecclesiastical hierarchy under an ambitious, intelligent and persuasive metropolitan, without Godunov's guidance? But Godunov did not seek government power in order to yield it to monks. He honored the clergy, like the boyars, merely with outward signs of esteem. He listened favorably to the metropolitan and reasoned with him, but remained independent, annoying him with the inflexibility of his will. This explains Dionisy's hostile attitude toward Godunov and close connection with Shuisky." Karamzin, *Istoriia,* Book III, Volume X, col. 45.

64. In 1525 Vasily III divorced his apparently barren wife Solomonia Saburova and married Elena Glinskaia, by whom he had two sons. Solomonia was forced to take the veil at the Intercession convent in Suzdal, manifestly against her will. The divorce was sanctioned by the compliant Metropolitan Daniel but was disapproved by other prominent churchmen, notably Vassian Patrikeev. Division

of opinion on this matter coincided almost exactly with that between the Josephan and non-possessor factions described below, Chapter V, Note 45. See Volume 9, pp. 101-104.

65. Master of the horse (starokoniushii) was one of the ancient household offices of the Muscovite court, allegedly revived especially for Godunov, thereafter falling into disuse. It is commemorated in the name of the Starokoniushennyi Pereulok, a side street in the Arbat quarter of Moscow.

66. Soloviev draws his information from Fletcher, *Of the Russe Commonwealth,* reproduced in Berry and Crummey, p. 144.

67. See Fletcher, *Rude and Barbarous Kingdom,* pp. 236-239.

68. "And thus he flowered like a palm with the leaves of virtue. If the thorns of envious malice had not darkened the flower of his virtue, he might have been in all ways like the tsars of old, who flowered in all piety." J.L.I. Fennell and Anthony Stokes, *Early Russian Literature* (London, 1974), p. 225. See also Volume 14 of this series, pp. xvi-xvii.

CHAPTER II

1. Boris Godunov reigned from 1598 to 1605, Vasily Ivanovich Shuisky from 1606 to 1610. Neither could establish a new dynasty. See Volumes 14-15 of this series.

2. The early stages of the Reformation in Sweden were concerned more with administrative and economic than with doctrinal changes. In 1528 the coronation oath of Gustav Vasa pointedly omitted the pledge to safeguard the rights and property of the church. Georg Norman, the Swedish Thomas Cromwell, actively appropriated church land, and an ordinance passed in 1539 firmly subordinated the church to crown control. The adoption of Lutheranism as the official creed was a process which matured over several generations. "Gustav Vasa's sons were all, in different ways, amateur theologians with pronounced views on matters of doctrine, and the church leadership had several tussles with their royal masters. Erik XIV came under the influence of his Calvinist French tutor Dionysus Beurreus, and urged the clergy to forsake 'papist and ungodly ceremonies.' His brother Johan, in the words of Daniel Rogers, was regarded as 'very ticklish and unconscious in matters of religion, for he causeth many superstitions and popish ceremonies to be reared in the church, which breedeth offense towards many.' Johan was an assiduous reader of the works of the early fathers, and had come under the influence of contemporary syncretist theologians, such as Georg Cassander. The *Nova ordinantia* of 1575, although impeccably Lutheran in its emphasis on preaching and education, also contained elements of Cassander's mediatory theology. Johan urged the clergy to read the fathers in preference to Luther, and in 1576 caused further disquiet with his *Liturgia svecanae ecclesiae,* or the 'Red Book' as it became known. The emphasis placed on ceremony and ritual aroused the opposition of the clergy, many of whom refused to conform and

were dismissed for their pains. Some of those who were dismissed found refuge in Duke Karl's domains, while others went to Germany, from where they showered Sweden with anti-liturgical tracts, denouncing the Red Book as a 'peppered viper.' Johan dallied with the idea of a union with Rome, but the terms on which he was prepared to bring the Swedish church back into the fold were unacceptable to Gregory XIII. By the end of the reign, the anti-liturgists were in the ascendancy, and the brief interlude of catholic teaching at Johan's royal college in Stockholm had come to an end. The endorsement of the Augsburg Confession by the church assembly in 1593 finally gave official confirmation of Sweden's status as a Lutheran land, and subsequent legislation during the reign of Karl IX enforced strict religious uniformity." David Kirby, *Northern Europe in the Early Modern Period. The Baltic World, 1492-1772* (London, 1990), pp. 90-91.

   3. Stefan Bathory, king of Poland, 1576-1586. He successfully led the Polish armies in the latter stages of the Livonian War, besieging Pskov from August 1581 to January 1582, when the war was brought to an end by the Truce of Yam Zapolsky. Apparently he ended his reign at odds with his subjects, whom in his will he berated for their ingratitude. He died without consolation of the sacraments at Grodno on December 12, 1586. It was rumored widely that he was poisoned.

   4. Born a Calvinist on March 19, 1542, Zamoyski converted to Catholicism while a student in Italy. During the interregnum of 1572 he entered public life as ambassador to the newly elected Henri of Anjou (see Note 7, below). During the second interregnum, after initially supporting any Piast (Polish) candidate, he turned to Bathory, who agreed to marry Anna Jagiełłonica, sister of the dead Sigismund Augustus. As Bathory's key adviser and the husband of his niece Gryzelda, Zamoyski served as a counterweight to the other magnates and thus became a favorite of the middle nobility (szlachta). He supported domestic reform and an aggressive foreign policy. In the interregnum after Bathory's death, which Soloviev is about to describe, Zamoyski and Karnkowsi (see below, Note 33) favored Sigismund, whose Austrophile policies later alienated Zamoyski. His proposals to stabilize Poland through fixing the election of kings by law and instituting majority rule in the Sejm received no support. He had a profound cultural influence on Poland, establishing in his private city of Zamość an academy, which he founded in 1580, and to which he imported Italian Renaissance culture. He died on June 3, 1605. Norman Davies, *God's Playground. A History of Poland* (New York, 1984), Volume I, pp. 151-152, 252, 423-426.

   5. Of Martin Zborowski's eight sons the four most famed were Samuel, Jan, Andrzej and Krzystof. Samuel's birthdate is unknown. Soloviev describes his murdering Jedrzej Wapowski during ceremonies crowning Henri of Anjou as king of Poland. Banished, he wandered in and out of Poland, maintaining contact with both the Dnieper Cossacks and the Tatar khan of the Crimea Muhammad-Girey (see below, Chapter IV, Note 1). Soloviev describes his execution, which took place on May 26, 1584. Jan was castellan and hetman of Gniezno, a major figure in suppressing resistance to Polish rule in Danzig. His initial support for

Bathory turned to opposition at his brother's execution. He died in 1604 or 1605. Andrzej also started as a partisan of Bathory, then turned against him even before Samuel's execution, mainly out of dislike for Zamoyski. During the interregnum after Bathory's death he supported the Austrian candidate, and as an adherent of the losing party he lost his court functions and disappeared from sight in 1589. Krzystof spent most of his life in Vienna opposing Bathory and Zamoyski, despite the king's constant requests for his extradition. Of course he also supported the Austrian candidate. He cleared his name at the Sejm of 1591, and died shortly thereafter.

6. All three were active in Roman politics. Catiline was famed for his opposition to Cicero. Clodius Publius took up that opposition at Catiline's death in 52 B.C. Milo supported Cicero but was a demagogue with the Roman mob until his death in 48 B.C. M. Cary. et. al. eds., *The Oxford Classical Dictionary* (Oxford, 1957), pp. 173, 203, 571. Soloviev compares their opposition to the Roman leadership with that of the Zborowskis to Bathory.

7. Henri of Anjou (1551-1589), known in Poland as Henryk Walezy, son of Catherine de Medici, was elected to the Polish throne in 1573, while his brother Charles IX ruled in France. He was quick to return to France in 1574 when his brother died, and ascended the throne as Henri III, the last king of the Valois line.

8. The incident is described in Davies, *God's Playground. A History of Poland*, Volume 1, p. 415. Zborowski challenged all present to a duel, and was insulted when a common soldier serving the Teczyński family took up the challenge. Zborowski then tried to assault Teczyński while the king watched. Wapowski was killed trying to separate them.

9. See the details in Zegota Pauli, *Pamiętniki do zycia i sprawy Samuela i Krysztofa Zborowskich*, (Memorials of the Life and Deeds of Samuel and Krzystof Zborowski), (Lwów, 1846), pp. 1-18. (Soloviev's note)

10. Stanisław Górka (1538-1592) was a major figure in Polish affairs, and the dominant figure in Great Poland during the 1570s and 1580s. Born to a wealthy and powerful family from Great Poland, he lost both parents when he was young. He was raised as a strict Lutheran, attended Wittenberg in 1554, and associated with the Lutheran religious elite, including Melanchthon. In 1565 he commanded troops against Moscow, but warfare did not appeal to him, perhaps because of his poor physique. His Lutheranism and his closeness to Prince Albrecht of Prussia did not prevent him from working closely with Poland's Catholics and maintaining ties to the Jesuit order. At his older brother's death, during the first interregnum, he entered the broader political arena, supporting Henri of Valois. When Henri resigned in 1574 he eventually supported Bathory, yet by 1578 he joined the Zborowskis in opposition. Górka developed a personal following among the szlachta, using as a base his castle in Great Poland. On the national stage, because Zamoyski was his great personal and political foe, Górka drew close to the Habsburgs, especially Archduke Ernst. In 1579 he refused war taxes and rejected the royal summons to take the field, but eventually appeared with his own retinue. In 1581-1583 he became close to Karnkowski (see below, Note 33), whom he

supported in his struggle for the primacy. In 1580-1582 he gained power and property through royal grants, which failed to alter his independent anti-monarchical stance. At dietines held in Poznań and Kalisk in 1582 he was a determined and successful opponent of Bathory's proposed electoral reforms. He and Karnkowski regularly cooperated against Bathory. At Bathory's death he worked in Great Poland together with the Zborowskis for Maximilian of Austria (see below, Note 37). Karnkowski's defection to Sigismund Vasa (see below, Note 52) was a blow to Górka, preventing him from securing all of Great Poland for Maximilian. Moreover, Jan Zborowski also reached agreements with Sigismund's forces, aimed at squeezing out Górka. He accompanied Maximilian's forces at the siege of Cracow, and was captured with them at Byczyna. Górka's fate was not severe. Zamoyski, hoping to gain his allegiance, first intervened on his behalf with the new king, pleading his ill health and then, without the king's knowledge, arranged his release under a good conduct pledge. Much of his estate was restored and he was amnestied in the spring of 1589. Nevertheless he adamantly continued refusing to renounce Maximilian's right to the throne. In his last years he renewed his old alliance with Karnkowski against Zamoyski and Sigismund. He died on October 23, 1592.

11. According to the Statute of 1566 the seimik powietowy was to convene four weeks before the general diet, or Sejm, choose representatives and send them to the Sejm.

12. Mikołaj Zebrzydowski (1533-1620), governor of Sandomir, later was famous as leader of the uprising or rokosz against Sigismund III when Zamoyski died in 1606.

13. Konstantin Konstantinovich Ostrozski or Ostrogski (1526-1608), an enormously wealthy magnate, possessed three hundred towns and several thousand villages, and was famed for his luxurious living and lavish hospitality. Being Orthodox, he was a renowned defender of that faith against Catholicism through his press, schools and the Orthodox brotherhoods. Naturally he was a major opponent of the union of the Orthodox and Catholic churches proposed during the late sixteenth century and partly achieved in 1596. Later he played a major role in launching the career of the first False Dmitry. See Volume 14 of this series.

14. Jan Niemojewski lived between 1530 and 1598.

15. Leo Sapieha (1557-1633) had an illustrious career. He held in succession the offices of secretary for Great Lithuania, deputy chancellor for Lithuania, and chancellor for Lithuania between 1581 and 1589. The Lithuanian Statute of 1588 was implemented by his efforts. He participated in Bathory's wars against Moscow and, as in the case here, was entrusted with several diplomatic missions to Moscow. He was a main instigator of the Polish expedition to Moscow in 1609 (see Volume 15 of this series). In the 1620s he was governor of Wilno and hetman of Great Lithuania.

16. Despite its name, the złoty was a large silver, rather than gold, coin current in Poland-Lithuania in the sixteenth and seventeenth centuries.

17. Alberto Bolognetti (1538-1585) came from a cultured aristocratic family. During the 1570s he was papal nuncio in Tuscany and Venice. In 1581 he was transferred as nuncio to Poland. There he was expected to organize a new crusade against the Ottoman empire, then embroiled in a war with Persia. Muscovy was to be involved, cooperating with Poland-Lithuania in an attack overland, while the Spanish and Venetian fleets executed a joint offensive at sea. This scheme necessitated peace between Poland and Muscovy, which was achieved at Yam Zapolsky, largely the fruit of the labors of the Jesuit Possevino (see below, Chapter III, Note 24), although Bolognetti played a minor role. Bolognetti did begin arranging for cooperation between some Poles and the Habsburgs which, as Soloviev later noted, complicated matters at Bathory's death. When Ivan IV died Bolognetti fell out with Bathory and Possevino, opposing their belligerent stance toward Fedor's Moscow. Bolognetti's policies prevailed, and Possevino's removal was partly due to his efforts. In domestic affairs Bolognetti naturally worked with the Jesuits in the Counter-Reformation and also helped introduce the Gregorian calendar to Poland despite some opposition.

18. On the Cheremiss see the entry "Mari" by Thomas Noonan, MERSH, Volume 21, pp. 99-103

19. See Chapter I, Note 37.

20. Andrei Yakovlevich Izmailov first appears in the service registers as commander at Dankov. Thereafter he served for two decades, and was often involved in dispute over precedence. He is mentioned last as governor of Chernigov in 1598.

21. Here the sense, tense, and context indicate that Soloviev is quoting directly from a source, despite the absence of quotation marks.

22. Pany radnye, in Russian, refers to the lords belonging to the council which advised the grand princes of Lithuania and historically restricted their power. For more details on its background and composition, see Serge Pushkarev, *Dictionary of Russian Historical Terms from the Eleventh Century to 1917* (New Haven, Conn., 1970), p. 82.

23. Sierotka "the orphan" Radziwiłł, born in 1549 to a Calvinist branch of the famous Radziwiłł family, later converted to Catholicism. His military career was cut short early by an injury in 1579. He was marshal of Great Lithuania in 1579, governor of Troki after 1590, and governor of Wilno after 1604. A strong proponent of the Uniate movement (see below, Note 78) he represented the king at the Synod of Brest in 1596. He died in 1616.

24. Michael Haraburda's date of birth is unknown. He died August 12, 1586. He was castellan of Minsk from 1585, a diplomat, and ambassador to Muscovy and the Tatars. He conducted a mission to Moscow in 1586, which ostensibly was unsuccessful, but did lead to further talks concerning peace and union. Moscow maintained its previous policy of concessions at the decisive moment and threats at the first opportunity. The truce, previously negotiated to last until June 3, 1587, was extended for a further two months. S. F. Platonov, *Boris Godunov*. Ed. and trans. by L. Rex Pyles (Academic International Press, 1973), p. 55.

25. Den'gi and zolotye in the original Russian might refer to generic moneys, but here context implies the meaning of the respective national coinages.

26. Prince Fedor Mikhailovich Troekurov appears at the boyar council in 1581 as a lord-in-waiting. He participated in diplomatic missions of the 1580s and in 1585 became a boyar. Between 1588 and 1594 he was the governor of Astrakhan. He died in 1597.

27. The Beznin here is probably Mikhail Andreevich, whom the military registers first list as a captain (golova) against the Livonians and then the Tatars in the years 1559-1560. He then disappears from the records until 1569 when he appears as a commander. He held several commands at this rank between 1572 and 1587, and would have been an experienced officer at the time of the mission described by Soloviev.

28. In both this and the next paragraph the sense, person, and tense of the passage lead to the assumption that these are direct quotes, despite the absence of marks to that effect.

29. The italics are in Soloviev's original text.

30. Andrei Kaskarov and Timofey Teterin were musketeer captains both active in the Livonian campaigns of the later 1550s, and usually are mentioned together in chronicles. Around 1560 Teterin was banished to the St. Anthony monastery on the Sii river, whence he escaped to Lithuania shortly afterwards. Kashkarov helped in his escape and for his pains was executed. See *Prince A.M. Kurbsky's History of Ivan IV.* Ed. and trans. by J.L.I. Fennell (Cambridge, Mass., 1965), pp. 223-224. Ivan IV allegedly wrote a letter to Teterin around 1577. See Edward L. Keenan. *The Kurbskii-Groznyi Apocrypha* (Cambridge, Mass., 1971), p. 70.

31. "One of the Golovins, Mikhail Ivanovich, went to swell the group of political refugees in Poland, imitators of the celebrated Kurbsky." Kazimierz Waliszewski, *La crise révolutionnaire, 1584-1614* (Paris , 1906), p. 9.

32. Information on Novosiltsev is sparse. According to the service registers he was vicegerent of Riazhsk in 1572, attached to the tsar's baggage train and cannon in the Ukraine in 1585, and served as governor in 1588-1589.

33. Stanisław Karnkowski (1520-1603) became bishop of Warsaw in 1563. He was deeply involved in the creation of the elected monarchy, and in the election of King Henri in 1573. In 1577 he became bishop of Cracow. Soloviev describes his activity during the interregnum after Bathory's death. He later played an important role at the Council of Brest, being a proponent of religious toleration. Besides his ecclesiastical and political activity he was an historian and legal theorist.

34. The term here is used interchangeable with the Polish *powiat.*

35. Adashev, one of Ivan IV's closest advisers, was in charge of Muscovy's eastern (and indeed all diplomatic) affairs. A skillful administrator and diplomat, he in particular realized the importance of Kazan to Muscovy in terms of the consolidation of its eastern boundary and, ultimately, the control of the Eurasian steppe. For more information on Adashev, see the entry by Graham, "Adashev, Aleksei Fedorovich," MERSH, Volume 1, pp. 28-30.

36. The position of the Polish crown already was weakened in the fifteenth century under Casimir IV (1446-1492) who made concessions to the lesser nobility to buy support for his territorial designs on Silesia and Prussia. His sons Jan Olbracht (1492-1501) and Alexander (1501-1506) succeeded, not by right of primogeniture, but by elections, for which they had to pay by concessions. Alexander's constitution of 1505, known as Nihil novi ("Nothing new"), in effect gave the council veto power over royal decrees. The youngest of Casimir's sons, Sigismund "the Old" (reigned 1506-1548) in 1530 persuaded the Sejm to elect his ten-year-old son, also named Sigismund, as his successor. In 1539, however, the nobles forced Sigismund the Old to acknowledge the illegality of the 1530 election, and to declare that after the death of the younger Sigismund future kings be elected with the participation of the entire nobility. Sigismund II Augustus (reigned 1548-1572) was too preoccupied with religious problems and the war with Muscovy to pursue the constitutional question. In 1562 he was forced to concede the mandatory resumption of crown lands alienated since 1504, thus depriving the crown of a valuable source of patronage. The terms of the Union of Lublin in 1569 reinforced the legal and economic privileges of the szlachta. Sigismund Augustus, moreover, died without a son to succeed him.

Henri of Anjou, by three documents known as the Pacta Conventa, the Warsaw Confederation and the Henrician Articles, rendered the crown virtually powerless. The third of these documents contained the notorious clause "de non praestanda obedientia" (concerning the refusal of obedience) which stated "If the king act against these laws, liberties, articles and conditions, or does not fulfill them, he thereby makes the nobles free of the obedience and fealty they owe him." The situation was compounded by the failure of Sigismund Augustus's two successors to establish either an Angevin or a Transylvanian dynasty, so by the time the first Vasa king ascended the throne the damage was done. "Poland lay firmly in the dead hand of the landholding minority, robbed of the opportunity of political greatness which its size, wealth and national genius might have made possible had this sixteenth-century conflict between class and nation been differently decided." R.R. Betts, "Constitutional Development and Political Thought in Eastern Europe," *New Cambridge Modern History*, Volume II (Cambridge, 1965), pp. 473-474.

37. "Diplomatic exchanges between the two courts [of Moscow and Vienna] were complex and their purposes were sometimes obscure. They were in close contact after the death of Bathory, because both Tsar Fedor and Archduke Maximilian were candidates for the throne of Poland-Lithuania. But Emperor Rudolf had a further purpose. He was convinced that Tsar Ivan had made provision in his last testament that in the event of Tsar Fedor dying without heir, the house of Habsburg was to be considered first as the source of a new Tsar. The prospect of a dynastic union appealed strongly to the Emperor who saw in it a means of conquering the Ottoman Empire. No such testamentary provision has been found. At the time, however, it gave rise to many rumors. The fact that in the elections to the Polish-Lithuanian throne, Moscow undertook to support the candidacy of Maximilian was taken by many to signify that Moscow favored

union with the Habsburg monarchy." Ian Grey, *Boris Godunov. The Tragic Tsar* (New York, 1973), p. 91. See also Waliszewski, pp. 17-18. A brief recapitulation of the facts is in order. In 1587 there was a double election in Poland-Lithuania. The majority was in favor of Sigismund Vasa, while a minority formed a confederation in favor of Archduke Maximilian. Sigismund landed at Oliwa, near Danzig, in October while Maximilian crossed the Silesian frontier and made for Cracow. Zamoyski secured Cracow for Sigismund and the invading Habsburg army was annihilated at Byczyna on January 24, 1588. The archduke was taken prisoner and spent the next two years in captivity. The Treaty of Bezdin and Bytom was concluded between Rudolph II and Sigismund III on March 19, 1589, but Maximilian continued to be held pending ratification. He then made his escape and fled across the frontier, but refused to swear to observe the treaty, and reactivated the "Austrian" party within Poland-Lithuania. Matters were complicated by a rival Habsburg claimant, Archduke Ernst. Maximilian was backed by Philip II of Spain, who was not a signatory to the 1589 treaty. Ernst established secret contact with Sigismund, promising that if Sigismund relinquished his throne and returned to Sweden, Ernst as ruler of Poland-Lithuania would abandon all claim to Estonia and pay Sigismund an indemnity of four hundred thousand gulden. Sigismund, eager to secure his succession to the Swedish throne, seriously considered Ernst's offer, then in the end decided against it. Maximilian discovered the secret negotiations and in 1592 made them public. As a result Zamoyski at the Sejm later that year denounced the Habsburgs, and even by implication the reigning king, asserting that "foreigners negotiate over us between themselves." Ernst was appointed governor-general of the Netherlands early in 1593 but Maximilian did not renounce his claim until 1598. Although unsuccessful in his quest for a throne, Maximilian from 1590 to 1618 was grand master of the Teutonic Order, which after the secularization of all its Baltic lands still retained extensive landholdings in Southern Germany.

38. "For some considerable time," King Sigismund stated in a memorandum to Stanisław Tarnowski, "abundant rumors have reached us to the effect that the archdukes of Austria are striving to the end that Maximilian, brother of the Holy Roman emperor, replace the present Muscovite ruler, who is less than capable. They also allege that a Muscovite delegation has visited the emperor. Indications are that not only is the Austrian family set on this, there also has been a meeting of princes in Regensburg deliberating what means to employ in order to set Maximilian upon the Muscovite throne." (Translated from the original Latin contained in Soloviev's note)

39. The reference here is to pomestie estates, on which see Graham, MERSH, Volume 29, pp. 29-33.

40. The Russian reference is to the boyar council. See entry by V.I. Buganov, MERSH, Volume 5, pp. 51-53.

41. This reference is to the relative prestige between the two major "historic" centers of the respective states. Haraburda wisely avoids mentioning Kiev, which was more likely than Novgorod to be advanced as a second "historic" center when

dealing with the Poles, who then possessed it. As the text later shows, the boyars were quick to recognize this and put it on the bargaining table.

42. The reference is to the Tatars of the Perekop peninsula, in other words, the Crimean Tatars.

43. That is, tribes of the Cheremiss peoples who were tributary to Moscow.

44. Vytautas (Vitovt) was ruler of Lithuania from 1392 to 1430. See Volume 5 of this series.

45. Pietr Skarga of Powno (1536-1612), an eminent preacher, theologian and apologist for Catholicism, entered the Jesuit novitiate in 1564, having completed his bachelor's degree at Cracow. He studied in Rome from 1568 to 1571, then returned to become a lecturer at the Polotsk college. He went on to found or enlarge various Jesuit institutions of learning, and wrote polemics, theology, hagiography, and sermons. As a missionary he converted some of the Radziwiłł princes and their subjects. His work was influential in bringing about the Union of Brest. After 1588 he was a chaplain at the court of Sigismund III where he became famous as a defender of a powerful monarchy on the Spanish model. Some of the themes of his sermons, with his views on religious toleration and political power in Poland, are summarized in Davies, Volume I, pp. 357-360.

46. After repeated abortive attempts at negotiation the Ukraine under Bogdan Khmelnitsky was united with Muscovy under the terms of the Treaty of Pereiaslav in 1654.

47. Mikołaj Jazłowiecki (1550-1594) possessed substantial estates that provided him the wherewithal to raise private armies. In his youth he served briefly in Moldavia before leaving for Paris, where he lived from 1572 to 1575. He was an emissary to Bathory in the negotiations over his candidacy for the Polish throne, and later held offices under him. During the electoral crisis described here Jazłowiecki staunchly supported Maximilian, even supplying him with soldiers. His inclination towards the Habsburgs was matched by his antipathy towards Zamoyski. "Not only must we defend ourselves against the Tatar and the Turk," he warned the electoral Sejm, "we also must do so against the chancellor, who is the oppressor of our liberty." The failure of the Habsburg cause did not diminish Jazłowiecki's ties to that family. He participated in the coronation ceremony for Anna of Habsburg in 1592. After Sigismund's election he did temper his feelings sufficiently to serve the new king, but his relations with Zamoyski remained strained. During his career he led cossack forces, which made him a natural commander against the Tatars. Jazłowiecki was a beloved patron of Cracow's Jesuits. At the time of his sudden death on August 30, 1595 he simultaneously held the three prefectures of Sniatyń, Czerwonogrod and Sokal.

48. The hetman was the chief commander of the armed forces, the crown hetman being appointed for Poland and a grand hetman for the grand principality of Lithuania. The hetman was one of the great officers of the realm and was chosen by the king, although the king could not remove him. See Davies, Volume I, p. 355.

49. Marcin Liesnowolski (died 1593) entered the Cracow Academy in 1562 and later studied in Italy. In 1573 he carried out a diplomatic mission to France, where he became a strong partisan of Henri of Valois. Later, during the crisis after Bathory's death he supported Maximilian but, as this incident proves, he managed also to maintain close ties with Zamoyski, having participated in the ceremony at his wedding to Gryzelda Bathory. Liesnowolski actively adhered to the new Catholic Counter-Reformation, cooperating closely with Peter Skarga and the Jesuit order. Soloviev's editors erroneously identify Marcin as Stanisław Liesnowolski.

50. Annibale di Capua sprang from an ancient and prominent landholding family which, at the time of his birth in the middle of the sixteenth century, was deeply involved in Neapolitan politics. Some time before 1562, after studies in Padua, he took holy orders. Clerical status in no way diminished his lust for secular pleasures. In an effort to flee the more worldly and less academic temptations of student life he transferred to Pavia, where he earned his doctorate in jurisprudence. In 1576 he served in Prague as nuncio to the new emperor Rudolph II (see following note). In 1586 he was named nuncio to Poland. Bathory died while Di Capua was still in Venice taking counsel with his predecessor, the illustrious Jesuit Possevino. Consequently the new nuncio arrived in Poland at the height of the struggle between Maximilian of Austria and Sigismund Vasa. Di Capua's diplomatic instructions, based on Rome's erroneous but understandable apprehension that the Swedish Vasa might have Protestant leanings, were to support the Habsburg candidate. Moreover his family's ties to the Spanish Habsburgs already so inclined him. Di Capua labored for Maximilian far too overtly and zealously, forgetting diplomatic discretion to the point that even his superiors in Rome grew irritated. Naturally Sigismund's victory left him in a most awkward position. He stayed in Poland until 1591, slowly and painfully attempting to undo the past and restore good relations with the new sovereign. He enjoyed the goodwill of Bathory's widow Anna Jagiełłonica, whose influence proved to be of limited value. Meanwhile Di Capua's numerous relatives and patrons in Italy labored in vain to secure a bishopric there for him. After his return to pastoral duties in his native Naples he frequently alluded to his Polish experience as testimony to the sad consequences of "anarchy and heresy."

51. Rudolph II (1552-1612), Holy Roman emperor from 1576, son of Maximilian II and Maria of Spain. His reign was marked by an erosion of imperial power. In 1606 he was compelled to make considerable concessions to the Hungarian aristocracy, and by the Letter of Majesty of 1609 was forced to grant the Protestants of Bohemia religious freedom. Also by reason of mental infirmity he was obliged to yield the rulership of Upper and Lower Austria, Hungary and Moravia to his brother Archduke Matthias, who succeeded him as emperor.

52. Sigismund Vasa (1566-1632) became king of Poland and grand prince of Lithuania in 1587, and inherited the Swedish throne in 1592. In 1599 he was deposed by a revolt of the Swedish nobility led by Duke Karl of Södermanland, who assumed the regency and in 1604 was acclaimed as King Karl IX. From 1600

to 1629, in addition to his involvement in Muscovy and dealing with domestic revolts, Sigismund was almost continually engaged in war to recover his Swedish throne, to which both of his successors, Władysław IV (reigned 1632-1648) and Jan Kazimierz (reigned 1648-1668) maintained their claim. For an analysis of the abortive union between Poland an Sweden, see Kazimierz Lepszy, "The Union of the Crowns between Poland and Sweden in 1587," *International Congress of Historical Sciences* (Stockholm, 1960), pp. 155-178.

53. The "shameful peace" to which Soloviev refers is the Truce of Yam Zapolsky, concluded in January 1582. By its uneven terms Ivan surrendered to Bathory the territories of Livonia and Polotsk in exchange for some Russian towns in Polish hands. Only the heroic Muscovite defense of Pskov and unrest within Polish ranks prevented the peace from being even more humiliating. See Volume 12 of this series.

54. Here korolevich can mean the son of a king, or a king. Given the date, the reference must be to Sigismund since he became king of Sweden only in 1592.

55. Yelizary Leontovich Rzhevsky (died 1599), a career soldier and diplomat, first appeared in the Livonian campaign of 1556. In 1564, 1572, and 1577 he was a negotiator with the Crimean Tatars. Between these assignments he held field commands and was governor, in turn, of Velizh, Pochep and Orsha.

56. A reference to the terms of the 1569 Union of Lublin whereby the bulk of the Ukraine, which belonged to the grand principality of Lithuania, was attached to the Polish crown.

57. On Timofey Teterin, see Note 30, above. In Rzhevsky's instructions the diminutive form of the forename is used pointedly. The others mentioned here were probably among those who deserted Muscovy in the time of Ivan IV.

58. Mikołaj Radziwiłł probably is cognate with the Sierotka, above, Note 23. For Leo Sapieha see Note 15. Tadeusz Skumin-Tyszkiewicz was governor of Nowogródek and treasurer of Lithuania. He was in Moscow on a diplomatic mission in 1577.

59. The Russian term here is penez. In the context it probably refers to pieniadz, an old Polish term for "small coin."

60. There was a Piotr Czernikowski in Bathory's service, but it is not certain whether this is he. Bogdan Matveevich Oginsky was from the senior branch of a russified Lithuanian family. He was an ardent partisan of the Orthodox church, and was assigned to two embassies to Muscovy, this one in 1587 and another in 1612.

61. The term "gold efimoks" does not really make sense since the efimok was a silver coin. Efimok (plural efimki) is the Russian term for Joachimsthalers, large silver coins minted in the Joachimthal (Jáchymov) in Bohemia and frequently used in other foreign countries. In the absence of Russian silver coins of large denomination efimoks were used in Russia in the sixteenth and seventeenth centuries. In 1655 for a short time they became the official monetary unit called efimki s priznakami (meaning, with marks), as they were overstamped with the Russian crown emblem. Efimoks were received in foreign trade transactions and

then either altered into small Muscovite den'gi or used intact. In the mid-seventeenth century the tsar's treasury accepted one efimok as equivalent to fifty copecks, and issued marked efimoks with a value of sixty-four copecks. Pushkarev, p. 18.

62. Stepan Godunov, like Boris, began his career under Ivan the Terrible. He was governor of Fellin in 1573 and accompanied the tsar on the Livonian campaign of 1576 as a lord-in-waiting. In 1584 he became a boyar. Soloviev describes his diplomatic mission in Poland. Eight years later he led a punitive expedition in Finland. Under the False Dmitry and Vasily Shuisky he was a governor in Siberia.

63. For Troekurov see above, Note 26.

64. On Vasily Shchelkalov, see above, Chapter I, Note 33.

65. Literally, "notice your tsar's groshas." The grosza was a coin of small denomination equivalent to one hundredth of a zloty or a one hundred and twentieth part of a Muscovite ruble.

66. Soloviev's original Russian says that the deputies met v rytsarskom kole. The kolo rytsarskoe was a chamber of the Lithuanian parliament composed of representatives of the middle nobility elected from each district. See Pushkarev, p. 41.

67. The Cap of Monomakh was the ancient Russian crown named for Vladimir Monomakh (1053-1125, grand prince of Kiev from 1113), though in fact it was fashioned in the fourteenth century. Of Central Asian workmanship, it is a pointed sable cap with gold filigrane, adorned with precious gems and crowned with a golden cross.

68. A convert from Calvinism, Jerzy Cardinal Radziwiłł (1556-1600) appears in some sources as a fanatic Catholic who persecuted dissidents, publicly burned anti-Catholic works and closed Calvinist presses. He was bishop in Wilno and Cracow, and cardinal of Cracow after 1586. Rome deemed him one of its most reliable agents in Poland. In fairness, note that Horsey, a Protestant, praised this active, proselytizing clergyman as "...a bouncing princely prelate, loving the company of Livonian ladies, the fairest women of the known world." Berry and Crummey, p. 315.

69. The reference here is to the oprichnina created under Ivan IV (see Volume 10 of this series). The cardinal is rhetorically effective but historically inaccurate, since the crown estates had ceased to exist before Fedor took the throne.

70. Haiduks were Hungarian mercenary foot soldiers in Polish service.

71. Krzysztof Radziwiłł (1547-1603) was among Poland's most talented military commanders, distinguishing himself in Bathory's Livonian campaigns and winning a major victory over the Swedes at Kokenhuoon in 1600. For his feats at arms he gained the sobriquet Piorun ("the Thunderbolt") and was rewarded with the offices of governor of Wilno and hetman of Great Lithuania. A Calvinist, he opposed the persecution of dissidents in Poland.

72. The Piasts were the native Polish dynasty whose descent in the direct male line ended with Sigismund II Augustus.

73. Current, that is, as of 1857.

74. The battle of Byczyna, in German Pitschen, was fought January 24, 1588 (New Style).

75. Ferdinand II (1578-1637) was Holy Roman emperor from 1619. He was educated at the Jesuit academy at Ingolstadt, Bavaria. In 1596 he assumed the rulership of his hereditary lands, and in 1600 married Maria Anna of Bavaria. He avoided taking sides in the quarrel between his cousins Rudolph II and Matthias, then in 1617 secretly negotiated with his Spanish relatives for recognition as heir apparent to Matthias in exchange for Alsace and some imperial fiefs in Italy. The same year he was elected king of Bohemia and in 1618 succeeded also to the Hungarian crown. In 1619 the Bohemian diet deposed him and elected Friedrich V, count palatine of the Rhine, thus setting in motion the Thirty Years War. Ferdinand was able to secure election as Holy Roman emperor and went on to defeat the Bohemian rebels at White Mountain in 1620, but then entered on a troubled relationship with his over-powerful generalissimo Wallenstein. Soloviev here compares Ferdinand to Sigismund III, both of whom were implacable proponents of the Catholic Counter-Reformation.

76. The reference is to Henri IV's willingness to trim his religious beliefs to meet political necessity. "Paris is worth a Mass."

77. Later, during the Time of Troubles, circles in Moscow hostile to Dmitry the Pretender got in touch with Sigismund with a proposal to make his son Władysław tsar of Russia. Such an agreement was reached, in principle, on February 4, 1610, the rights of the Orthodox church being guaranteed. After a revolt which deposed Tsar Vasily Shuisky in July 1610, Hetman Żółkiewski's Polish forces reached the outskirts of Moscow and negotiated on August 17, 1610 a new agreement whereby Władysław would convert. When Muscovite delegates arrived at Smolensk in October to seal the bargain they learned that Sigismund no longer felt bound by it, and intended to assume Muscovy's throne for himself. Soloviev implies that Sigismund's Catholicism stood in the way of his having his son convert, and therefore felt compelled take a position certain to alienate his supporters in Moscow. A later historian, George Vernadsky, argued otherwise. "King Sigismund had never intended to let his son rule Muscovy. He had resolved to obtain the title of tsar for himself and had used Władysław as a decoy in order to incline the Muscovites more toward negotiations." George Vernadsky, *The Tsardom of Moscow, 1547-1682* (New Haven, Conn., 1969), p. 253. See also Volume 15 of this series.

78. On the origins and nature of the Uniate movement see Oskar Halecki, *From Florence to Brest (1439-1596)* (Hamden, Conn., 1968).

79. Andrei Ivanov first appeared as a clerk in 1590. By 1598 he was crown secretary of the Novgorod financial district, a post which he held intermittently until 1615. In 1606-1610 he served as crown secretary of the chancellery for the administration of Kazan. He was assigned several diplomatic missions. In 1590-1592 he was a courier in Lithuania. In 1598 he negotiated with the Austrian ambassador. Under Tsar Boris Godunov in 1601 he accompanied Prince Grigory

Volkonsky on an embassy to Khan Ghazi-Girey of the Crimea, and in 1606 he and the same prince formally notified the Poles of the death of False Dmitry. He last appears as a signatory to documents in 1612.

80. For forty-two years after 1587 Abbas (1571-1629) was shah. After a perilous youth he secured power through a coup and proceeded to build a secure basis for his reign with the support of a personal corps of Georgian warriors, converts from Christianity. During 1589 and 1590 he had to accept disadvantageous agreements with Persia's hereditary enemy the Ottoman empire in order to gain domestic peace and thereby time to execute military reforms expanding the use of the "new weaponry" of his time, cannon and firearms. He then waged two successful wars against the Turks, in 1603-1617 and 1623-1624. He was quick to accept foreigners in his service, and sought especially friendly relations with Muscovy and England. *Encyclopedia of Islam*, 2nd ed. (Leiden, 1960), Volume I, pp. 7-8.

81. See Chapter I, Note 58.

82. Originally a French adventurer from Languedoc, Pontus de la Gardie (1520-1585) served in the French army until the Treaty of Cateau-Cambrésis (1559), when he entered Danish service. When he was captured by the Swedes, Erik XIV of Sweden, recognizing his talents, took him into his service. De la Gardie went on to found one of the great Swedish families of the sixteenth and seventeenth centuries. He fought with distinction in the Livonian War between 1573 and 1576, then was sent to Rome as ambassador. Between 1581 and 1583 he returned to combat in Livonia, where he won a series of great victories. His son Jacob (1583-1652) and grandson Magnus Gabriel (1622-1686) were outstanding servants of the Swedish crown.

83. The agreement of Pliussen, concluded May 26, 1583, arranged a three-year truce between Muscovy and Sweden, the Swedes retaining the towns of Yama, Ivangorod, and Koporie. Both sides agreed to free trade and a prisoner exchange.

84. Soloviev's word for district is piatina (fifth). The powerful republic of Novgorod, annexed to Muscovy in the fifteenth century, contained five administrative districts. Among them was Shelona, a territory between the Luga and the Lovat rivers, and Izhora, later called Ingermanland, along the banks of the Neva.

85. Peter Semeonovich Lobanov-Rostovsky (died 1595) first appeared in service in 1575. He commanded troops in Livonia late in the 1570s and then, in 1582-1584, was named one of the governors of Novgorod. He was reassigned to Novgorod in 1587, when he became a lord-in-waiting and was transferred to a judgeship in the Chancellery for Criminal Affairs. He returned to Novgorod as governor in 1590 and remained there until 1592.

86. Shestunov was a groomsman at the tsar's marriage in 1573 and a member of the tsar's bodyguard between 1577 and 1581. In 1582 he commanded the garrison at Smolensk, and the following year led forces in the field against the Swedes. Swedish affairs busied him for the next few years. Named as lord lieutenant for Beloozero in 1587, he conducted a diplomatic mission to Poland.

He commanded again at Smolensk in 1588, Kazan in 1590, and directed the artillery against Khan Ghazi-Girey in 1591. When, in 1598, the Crimeans again threatened the city of Moscow, Shestunov governed it while the army rode forth to meet the invaders at Serpukhov. He died that same year.

87. Boyar and duma member, governor, commander, lord-in-waiting and treasurer, Ignaty Petrovich Tatishchev held a range of ranks in Muscovy's service. In 1556 he served among the tsar's bodyguard as an honorary "bearer of the full archer's accoutrement," the saadak (see Chapter V, Note 25, below). Crimean sources place him on campaign against them that year, and also name him as a bodyguard of the tsar at Tula in 1559. He then disappears from the records until the last decade of Ivan the Terrible's reign (1574-1584) when he held a number of field commands. During the early 1580s he gained a reputation in the council of boyars for expertise in foreign affairs, especially relations with Sweden and Lithuania. Soloviev describes his diplomatic activity in 1584 and 1585. Under Fedor he held ranking posts in the army. He again negotiated with the Swedes in 1590, and went to Poland on a mission in 1591-1592. After these diplomatic missions he spent 1595 in the construction of frontier fortress towns, among them the future city of Kursk. Between 1595 and 1602 he guided the treasury and coordinated relations with Sweden and Denmark. He died in 1604.

88. Claus Akeson Thott was a prominent Swedish military commander during the reign of Erik XIV, twice taking the field against the Russians. He was named stadholder of Finland in 1576, and died in 1596.

89. Fedor's reference to "eminent" ambassadors was not a simple rhetorical device. He had in fact sent two of his most prominent servitors. Dementy Ivanovich Cheremisinov was a favorite of Ivan IV. His name first occurred in a document dated 1566. In 1571, after Ivan pillaged Novgorod, he commissioned Cheremisinov to gather additional booty from the monasteries there. Cheremisinov is mentioned as treasurer and member of the boyar council during the 1580s. He participated in Ivan's wedding to Maria Nagaia in 1580, and later that year was captured by the Poles at the battle of Toropets. Ivan ransomed him for 4,457 rubles as part of the Yam Zapolsky settlement. He went on an unsuccessful mission to arrange a marriage between Ivan and Mary Hastings, then disappeared from service for some time. The failed mission to the Swedes described here by Soloviev seems to have occurred in 1589. Karamzin gives no date for the failure of this third Russo-Swedish negotiation but places it in the context of late 1589 or early 1590. It must have happened between the summer of 1589, the date of John's letter to Fedor attacking Ivan, and the Muscovite invasion, which Soloviev dates as January 1590. The *Russian Biographical Dictionary*, when describing Cheremisinov, probably errs in dating this embassy in 1594. It also claims 1594 as the year when Cheremisinov was in the South constructing breastworks against a Crimean invasion, which seems more likely. In any case, Cheremisinov was in Astrakhan as commander from 1594 until 1598, and from that town he erected other fortified towns along the Volga and the Yaik rivers.

Prince Dmitry Ivanovich Khvorostinin (died 1591) was, as Soloviev notes later, Fedor's most experienced military leader. The first mention of his service comes in several commands on the southern frontier. After a short service as governor of the frontier town Nizhny Novgorod he served with distinction on all of Muscovy's many military fronts. In 1565 he smashed the rearguard of a retreating Tatar raiding force. The following year he repelled a Tatar army at Volkhov. Transferred north between 1577 and 1582, he took cities in Livonia and won a major victory over Sweden at Lialitsy. Reassigned to his earliest region of service, the Volga valley, he suppressed Cheremiss and Tatar revolts in 1583. These triumphs were rewarded with the rank of boyar and lord-in-waiting and membership in the boyar council. Khvorostinin was in fact, if not by precedence, Muscovy's ranking military commander. He returned to the Volga valley in the late 1580s, and in 1590 defeated the Swedish general Banér (see below, Note 93). He died shortly after Ghazi-Girey's attack on Moscow.

90. Bolshoi polk, literally the "Great Regiment." "The standard division of the Muscovite army in the fifteenth and sixteenth centuries into five large units certainly followed the Mongol setup. These units were known in Russian as *polki*. They were as follows: the center (*bol'shoi polk*, literally the big division); the right arm division (pravaia ruka); the left arm division (levaia ruka); the advance guard (peredovoi polk) and the rearguard (storozhevoi polk)." Vernadsky, *The Mongols and Russia* (New Haven, Conn., 1953), p. 363.

91. According to Fletcher. Following precedence, Khvorostinin was the second commander of the vanguard, while the first was Prince Katyrev-Rostovsky. (Soloviev's note) Soloviev is emphasizing the variance between Khvorostinin's place in the precedence order and his actual talent. For Soloviev's reference to Fletcher see Berry and Crummey, p. 154.

92. Fedor Nikitich Romanov later during the reign of Boris was accused of sorcery and treason and was subjected to involuntary tonsure under the name of Filaret. He later pursued an illustrious career in his new clerical state. Exiled for the remainder of Boris's reign, he was released in 1605 at the accession of False Dmitry and was brought to Moscow where he was honored as a "kinsman" of the new tsar. He was then appointed metropolitan of Rostov and was present in Moscow during the events leading to the overthrow of the pretender. He was commissioned by Tsar Vasily Shuisky to supervise the transfer of the remains of the genuine Tsarevich Dmitry from Uglich to Moscow. At Shuisky's instigation he was passed over for the patriarchate in favor of Hermogen, metropolitan of Kazan. When the forces of False Dmitry II occupied Rostov the rebels proclaimed him patriarch, probably against his will. After the fall of the Tushino encampment he made his way to Moscow, where he was received honorably by the Muscovite government. Shortly afterwards Shuisky was deposed and Filaret was one of the principal figures in the high embassy sent to Smolensk to negotiate with Sigismund III the terms of the proposed accession to the throne of Prince Władysław. When negotiations broke down Filaret, with most members of his mission, was interned in Poland, where he lived in captivity until 1619. Meanwhile his son Michael was elected to the tsardom in 1613. On his return to

Moscow Filaret promptly was elected patriarch, and was the power behind the throne of his inept son for the next fourteen years. For further details see the entry on him by Orchard, MERSH, Volume 11, pp. 126-130.

93. The Banér brothers, Gustav and Sten, were prominent members of the Swedish governing council, or råd. Sten was a participant in the 1566 "skerries meeting," a plot of magnates against Erik XIV in which the king's youngest brother Duke Karl was involved. Sten was taken captive but miraculously escaped a massacre of prisoners ordered by Erik the following year. Gustav was involved in 1572 in a plot to restore aristocratic government as it existed in the fifteenth century, with an innocuous Valois prince as regent. A second plot, to which the first may have had some connection, was led by a country parson called Mauritz Rasmussen with the aim of massacring King John III and his family. In 1587 Sten was one of a commission of four to draw up a plan for the governance of the country in the event of Prince Sigismund being elected king of Poland. This document was known as the Statute of Kalmar. In 1589 both the Banér brothers accompanied King John to Reval, where they tried to persuade Sigismund to renounce the Polish throne and return to Sweden in order to forestall the increasingly manifest ambitions of Duke Karl. In November of that year John and Karl were reconciled, the former sacrificing some of his own key supporters. The Banérs were among those displaced from the råd and deprived of their estates. They were accused in 1590 of a plot to deprive the Vasas of the throne but Sten claimed that the key piece of evidence, the text of the Statute of Kalmar, had been misplaced. As opposition between partisans of Sigismund and those of Duke Karl intensified the Banérs fled the country, slipping over the Danish frontier to seek help from Poland. In 1598 they accompanied Sigismund in his bid to regain power, then when he and Karl came to terms the exiled råd members were handed over to Karl. After a mockery of a trial the Banérs and other supporters of Sigismund were executed at the "bloodbath of Linköping" on March 20, 1600.

94. The reference here is to the Zaporozhian Cossacks, in Soloviev's original Russian cherkasy.

95. Gabriel Wojna held high posts in Lithuania, and carried out diplomatic missions to Sweden.

96. This is the same Dedevshin through whose treason Sigismund took Smolensk in 1611. He already has been noted in the suite of Muscovite ambassador Troekurov to Bathory (Soloviev's note and italics). On the siege of Smolensk, see Volume 15 of this series, also the entry by Orchard, MERSH, Volume 16, pp. 46-53.

97. Peter Nikitich Sheremetev was a prominent figure of late sixteenth and early seventeenth-century Russia, and a close associate of Boris Godunov. Left orphaned when his father was killed at the order of Ivan the Terrible in 1564, he began appearing in service in 1577. By 1581 he had risen to be a ceremonial cupbearer at Ivan's reception of the envoy Possevino (see below, Chapter IV, Note 46). In 1585 and 1589 he held two minor military posts, and while at the court he appeared at the reception for Georgia's King Alexander (see below, Chapter III, Note 7 and Chapter IV, Note 46). In 1589, as Soloviev indicates, he

rose to a higher military post during the campaign against the Swedes, and led campaigns against them in the Novgorod region and along the Neva until 1593. He then disappeared from the service records until 1596. Sheremetev had a reputation for cunning and self-interest. During the 1580s he engaged in a protracted legal struggle with an uncle, Fedor Sheremetev. He exemplified the Muscovite servitor contumacious over his rights in the system of precedence. When he reappeared in the service records in 1596 it was in the context of a serious debate over precedence in which he refused to accept a command against raiding Crimean Tatars despite the dispatch of bailiffs to force him into the field. By the time he took his post under threat of imprisonment the campaign had ended. At the reception of the emperor's ambassador in May 1597 he successfully refused the post of official escort, arguing that it would debase his rights of precedence. Two months later he again protested when summoned for duty against the Crimeans, once more alleging that his post was too low and therefore debased his "honor" in the precedence system. He won again, although the records noted that this was due to his wife's death, not his petition, and thus avoided counter-petitions by other servitors aggrieved by Sheremetev's victory. In 1598 he was sent to investigate criminal accusations against the commanders at Astrakhan.

Sheremetev fared well under Fedor. This was probably because of Boris Godunov, who considered him a personal friend and later sought refuge at his estate during the riots and plague of 1602. This friendship did not avert continued debates over precedence when Godunov became tsar in his own right. When the first False Dmitry appeared in 1604 Godunov entrusted Sheremetev with an important role in repulsing him. Sheremetev's conduct was at best equivocal, and he transferred his allegiance as soon as the pretender's success seemed sure. He continued to serve, with equal self-interest, under Vasily Shuisky. For further information, see Volume 15, Chapter I, Note 29.

98. Born in 1569, Prince Vladimir Timofeevich Dolgoruky entered service as a table attendant and became governor of Pronsk. As Soloviev notes, he was captured by the Swedes in the campaign of 1591 then was ransomed within two years. In 1598 he constructed a fort on the Koisa river, and from 1604 to 1606 he was governor of Terki. Because the Dolgoruky family supported him, Vasily Shuisky made Vladimir a boyar when he took the throne. After Shuisky's fall Dolgoruky represented a faction in the boyar council opposing the accession of Władysław of Poland (see Note 77, above). When the Poles appeared successful, Dolgoruky acted as defender of Pskov and Tver against the Swedes under Jacob de la Gardie (see above, Note 82). He prospered under the rule of Michael Romanov, first as defender of Kazan and then, in 1624, through his daughter's marriage to the tsar. Her death four months later, possibly from poison, shattered Dolgoruky and drove him from public life.

99. The editors identify this Saltykov as Mikhail Glebovich Saltykov-Morozov, a prominent diplomat and lord-in-waiting, and another of Godunov's adherents.

A polonophile, he was involved in negotiations with Poland, and ended residing there after the Time of Troubles. See Volume 15, Chapter I, Note 17, and entry by Orchard, MERSH, Volume 33, pp. 45-49.

100. On Tatishchev, see above, Note 87.

101. In the original Russian cherkess.

102. Karl (1550-1611) was the youngest son of King Gustav Vasa and in 1560 was invested as duke of Södermanland. When his nephew Sigismund III of Poland became king of Sweden in 1592 Karl led the movement against the new ruler's attempt to reintroduce Catholicism. At the Riksdag (parliament) held in Söderköping he was appointed regent, and in 1598 thwarted Sigismund's armed attempt to regain effective rule. The following year Sigismund was declared deposed. Karl continued as regent until officially proclaimed king in 1604, and reigned until 1611 as Karl IX.

103. Sigismund married Archduchess Anna, sister to the future Emperor Ferdinand II, in 1592. She died in 1598, and in 1605 Sigismund married her sister Constantia, who died in 1631.

104. See above, Note 98.

105. The editors identify this individual as Evert Horn. This cannot be, since Evert lived between 1585 and 1616. It must be his father Karl Hendriksson Horn (1550-1601), prominent in the administration of Finland and in wars with Russia at the time of the negotiations described here. Horn participated in the defense of Reval in 1570 and served under Pontus de la Gardie in the campaigns of 1574-1575 and 1580-1582. When not on campaign he was a rural judge, military auditor, and stadholder at Narva. A determined Protestant, Horn opposed the efforts of Klaus Fleming, Sigismund's governor in Finland, to maintain Sigismund's indirect rule of Sweden from Poland during the crisis surrounding the Söderköping Riksdag.

106. Goran Boije (died 1617) negotiated with the Russians in 1583 and again in 1592-1593. During the early 1580s he shared military commands with Karl Horn.

107. Prince Ivan Samsonovich Turenin-Obolensky is an elusive character. He first appeared in the military registers in action around Kolomna in 1553. He died in 1597.

108. Prince Yevstafy Mikhailovich Pushkin rose rapidly in service during the 1570s. By 1580 he commanded at Smolensk, and between 1581 and 1582 he engaged in important negotiations with Poland. In 1588 he commanded forces on the Oka defense line. Three years later he investigated the death of the Tatar prince Murad-Girey. In the 1590s he again engaged in diplomacy, and in 1598 rose to the council of boyars. Godunov exiled him to the post of deputy commander at Tobolsk in 1601. He died there in 1603.

109. The reference is to Sweden's position relative to Denmark under the Union of Kalmar.

CHAPTER III

1. A reference to the fact that Bathory was not of Polish origin, but a native of Transylvania.

2. Lukasz Pauli, known in Moscow as "Lukash Pavlusov, son of Magnus," served in Moscow as resident agent of the Holy Roman emperor from the reign of Ivan IV until 1587, when Fedor sent him to Vienna. He returned to Moscow with Warkotsch (see following note) in 1589.

3. L.P. Lapteva, editor of a Russian translation of Warkotsch's subsequent report to Rudolph, remarks that little is known about the Austrian diplomat. She notes that a Czech historian describes him as a Silesian nobleman from Dobschits, while Russian sixteenth-century sources call him a distinguished royal servitor from Wilmsdorff, of Hungarian descent but related to Bathory. Friedrich von Adelung identifies him as Niklas von Warkotsch und Nobschutz auf Wilhelmdorff, but provides no biographical information. See L.P. Lapteva, "Donesenie avstriiskogo posla o poezdke v Moskvu v 1589 godu (An Austrian Ambassador's Report on his Mission to Moscow in 1589)," *Voprosy Istorii* (Problems of History), 1978, No. 6, pp. 95-112.

4. Sables normally were presented in multiples of forty.

5. Soloviev previously identified Ivan Beloborod as a merchant from Antwerp, John de Wale, trading in Russia's northern ports during the reign of Ivan IV (see Volume 12 of this series). Antwerp was then a part of the Spanish Netherlands, so Beloborod and Warkotsch were both Habsburg subjects. In his reports to Queen Elizabeth the English ambassador Bowes (see below, p. 57) mentioned De Wale as having established a thriving trade through Kholmogory, which Bowes wished to displace. He blamed the Muscovites' unwillingness to do this on De Wale's influence on his powerful patron Andrei Shchelkalov. Richard Hakluyt, *The Principal Navigations Voyages, Traffiques and Discoveries of the English Nation*, Volume III (Glasgow, 1903), pp. 315-317, 469-471, 473.

6. Warkotsch's report of 1589 outlined his and Boris's noble cause, a grand coalition against the Ottoman empire. Muscovy was to attack the Crimean Tatars while generously subsidizing Austria. Habsburg mercenaries in the Balkans were to bear the brunt of the fighting on land. Spain was to harass the Ottoman fleet in the Mediterranean and attack Turkish possessions in North Africa. Persia would reopen its long round of wars with the Turks. The Venetians, Warkotsch observed, probably would enter the fray once they observed the coalition's success. They were not to be invited to participate from the outset since their negative experience in previous anti-Turkish coalitions made them unlikely to join enthusiastically from the very start. Of the coalition's potential opponents, France was distracted by domestic strife and at worst would help the Turk only secretly. England could and would cause trouble for Spain in the Netherlands. Boris told Warkotsch that Zamoyski and Sigismund Vasa were "servants of the Turkish sultan" and urged him to have the emperor redouble efforts in Poland on Maximilian's behalf.

7. Soloviev's conclusion that Austria was only using Moscow may be unduly harsh. In fact Warkotsch's report to Rudolph makes the case that the proposed alliance served both Muscovite and Austrian self-interest. Godunov and his boyars, Warkotsch argued, saw their situation as perilous. Their realm faced two potentially dangerous hostile coalitions: Sweden with Poland, and the Turks with their Crimean vassals. The difficulty of finding mercenaries so far into Eastern Europe and their unreliability once hired meant that even the tsar's substantial treasury (see below, Note 21) could not offset the inferiority of Moscow's native troops. Simultaneous war with both coalitions would prove catastrophic. Under these circumstances, Warkotsch reasoned, Godunov and the boyars knew that they might have to accept permanent peace or even seek alliance with one or the other of these potential hostile coalitions. Neither course was attractive, yet some such action seemed unavoidable. Either course, said Warkotsch, entailed severe consequences for Austria. Permanent peace between Moscow and the Ottoman empire immediately would free enormous Turkish forces for use against Austria in the Balkans, while such a peace would also incline Persia and Muscovy's Caucasian clients to settle with the Turk. Muscovite peace with Poland would expand enormously the power of Zamoyski's party, which had demonstrated its deep dislike for the Habsburgs.

An Austro-Muscovite alliance could solve the dilemmas facing both states. Together they might secure the Polish throne for Maximilian, thereby neutralizing their potential common enemy in the West. The proposed league against the Turk might defeat the Ottomans and free the victors to intervene in Poland. Beyond this, there was Godunov's personal fate which, Warkotsch argued, best would be secured by the eventual accession to the Muscovite throne of a Habsburg prince (see following note). Warkotsch was sure the Muscovites were dealing in good faith, as demonstrated by their efforts to support Shah Abbas of Persia and Alexander of Kakhetia. Austria should press for close cooperation with Muscovy lest it be driven into the arms of Austria's foes.

In Soloviev's defense, an historian's hindsight can lead to the conclusion that the proposed anti-Turkish league was fated to be no more than a paper proposal. The negotiations are remarkable for the ambitious scope of the undertaking—an alliance with Persia, the Papacy, Muscovy, Spain, Venice and the Holy Roman empire against the Turk—and for the caution shown by both sides. Warkotsch reported that the Muscovites questioned him about how Austria could bring itself to negotiate with Zamoyski's Poles, the captors of Maximilian. The boyars also asked about reports from Lithuania of an attempt to strike an understanding which would leave Sigismund on the throne, thereby enabling him to turn against Muscovy. While Warkotsch parried both lines of questioning, clearly the Muscovites did not trust the Habsburgs fully.

Underlying all this was the spread of the militant Counter-Reformation. Moscow must have realized that Rudolph was as staunch a Catholic as was Sigismund. Orthodox Russians then, and to a certain extent subsequent Russian historians, have suspected a "Catholic-Jesuit conspiracy" which equally could have envisioned conquering Russia or using it against the Turks. Both the existence of real papal schemes, sometimes the work of Jesuits like Possevino, and the conduct of the Poles during the Time of Troubles, served to reinforce this view, which makes any Russian historian suspect the seriousness of Catholic proposals. Moreover, circumstances weighed against participation of the other Western states. Lepanto had done nothing to improve Venice's position in the Mediterranean, and the once great naval power remained in decline. Spain had turned its attentions northward, where it had just suffered the catastrophe of the Armada. Asked about this in Moscow, Warkotsch minimized its importance. Still the inquiries may have indicated Muscovite awareness of the importance of England's victory. Persia certainly wanted to cooperate with Muscovy, but was distant. Events which Soloviev describes later in this chapter prove that the Muscovites, who boasted to Warkotsch of their new alliance with Alexander of Kabardia, could not project their power into the Caucasus mountains, let alone beyond them.

8. Platonov observes that this second embassy transpired at a crucial juncture in Muscovite political history. Late in 1593 Fedor's daughter was ill. Her death on January 25, 1594 brought the ruling line to an end. For Boris it opened even wider his path to the throne. Conversely, Boris's opponents realized they must quickly check his drive to power. One way was for them to propose that Maximilian of Austria assume the Muscovite throne when Fedor died. Andrei Shchelkalov, Platonov argues, may well have suggested this succession to Warkotsch on December 17, 1593, when he presented the Austrian with gifts accompanied by a secret oral message for Rudolph. Shchelkalov fell into disgrace in May 1594 not, Platonov argues, because of theft from the treasury as the official version claimed, rather because of his complicity in this cabal against Boris. Certainly there were antecedents for the Austrian interest in the Muscovite succession, as shown by Soloviev's discussion in the previous chapter of the situation at Ivan's death (see p. 21, below). Warkotsch reported to Rudolph in 1589 that Godunov's position would become untenable when Fedor died. Boris, said the Austrian ambassador, had few friends and powerful enemies. Maximilian might succeed Fedor, retaining Godunov in a position of some authority. Pointing to how effectively Zamoyski's Poland might exploit a Muscovite succession crisis, Warkotsch advised Rudolph to act quickly and make every necessary concession if such an occasion arose. The report made it clear that then, in 1589, this "delicate matter" was not discussed, it being best left for the Muscovites to raise it. Perhaps they did so in 1593. See S.F. Platonov, *Ocherki po istorii smuty v moskovskom gosudarstve XVI-XVII vv.* (Sketches on the History of the Time of Troubles in the Muscovite State in the Sixteenth and Seventeenth Centuries) (The Hague, 1961), pp. 212-213, and Lapteva, "An Austrian Ambassador's Report," pp. 109-111.

9. The Russian word here is pominka, which carried the connotative, and here probably denotative, meaning of "tribute." See Pushkarev, pp. 93-94.

10. This probably refers to Chłopicki's cossacks. See below, Note 14.

11. Pope Clement VIII's complex diplomatic efforts to create a grand coalition against the Ottoman empire are described in Paul Pierling, *La Russie et le Saint Siège* (Russia and the Holy See) (Paris, 1897), Volume II, pp. 380-382. Clement's concurrent efforts to abandon the papacy's traditional alliance with Spain created obstacles to this coalition. Like the Austrian diplomacy discussed above in Notes 6-7, papal diplomacy worked towards a grand coalition against the Ottoman empire, but Rome's scheme embraced both Poland and Muscovy, making it even less workable than Vienna's already ambitious undertaking. Pierling, when concluding his discussion of Komulius's mission for the Pope (discussed later in this chapter, pp. 68-69), echoed Soloviev's skepticism about both enterprises. "In the final analysis, save the subsidy recently given to Warkotsch, all of this was still more sweet sounding words and promises, as these projects for a league stayed in the realm of ideals. Cardinal Caetani had scarcely more success in Poland and, some what discouraged, he announced on April 5, 1597 his final return to Italy." Pierling, *La Russie,* Volume II, pp. 367-368. See also entry on Clement VIII by J. Wilkie, *New Catholic Encyclopedia* (New York, 1967), pp. 933-934.

12. Henri IV succeeded to the French throne upon the assassination of Henri III in July 1589. His accession was opposed by the Catholic League, which effectively held Paris, and was assisted by Philip II of Spain, whose incursions from Flanders repeatedly blocked Henri's attempts to occupy his capital. The English were still at war with Spain because the defeat of the Armada blocked the transportation of troops and supplies from Spain to Flanders by the western sea route. About the time of Warkotsch's second mission (1593) Henri IV agreed to accept Catholicism, at the same time buying off the main remaining proponents of the Catholic League.

13. In other words, the Zaporozhian Cossacks.

14. This is the second appearance of the colorful adventurer Stanisław Chłopicki (dates of birth and death unknown) in Moscow. The heir of substantial estates in Podolia and Volhynia, he started his public life unremarkably as bailiff at Stefan Bathory's court. After Stefan's death, in 1585 or 1586, he entered into prohibited relations with Muscovy, for which he was imprisoned at Cracow. Chłopicki managed to escape, only to have the king order his property confiscated. This misfortune impelled him on a career as a cossack in the Ukraine, where he soon rose to be hetman of the Dnieper (Zaporozhian) Cossack host. In this capacity he served Rudolph II, providing Austria with an effective if somewhat uncontrollable mounted force. During 1593 Chłopicki raided the Ottoman empire, riding as far as Adrianople and then returning to the Ukraine, where he dissuaded the Crimean Tatars from a planned raid into Hungary. Rudolph rewarded him handsomely for his services. Soloviev describes his failure to gain similar support from Moscow. Chłopicki's flirtation with Muscovy so alarmed Zamoyski that he urged the Polish Senate to suppress ruthlessly and imprison this freebooter, but his rhetoric cooled in the face of the threat of a cossack uprising. Chłopicki in any case now launched yet another raid, this time into Moldavia. Here he disappears from the historical record.

15. Janusz Zbarażski (died 1608), a famed warrior, defeated the Turks near his estate and under Sigismund waged war against the Crimeans while working with the Papacy at building its anti-Turkish league. This probably explains why Rudolph wrote to him. Had the Austrians been more sensitive they would have addressed him separately. Even worse, Zbarażski also distinguished himself in Bathory's wars with Muscovy and he, along with Albert Radziwiłł and Haraburda, served in the diplomatic mission which ended the war with Muscovy's defeat, facts which should have given the Austrians pause.

16. Mikhail Ivanovich Veliaminov-Zernov was among the less prominent members of the extraordinarily prolific Veliaminov clan. He appears in the service registers assigned to the small Livonian town of Nevel in 1577. He was transferred to Usviat in 1578, where he was promoted to garrison commander in 1580. He is mentioned next on the mission which Soloviev describes here. It is uncertain whether he is the same Veliaminov-Zernov mentioned as Boris Godunov's cupbearer in Volume 14 of this series.

17. Afanasy Vlasiev (dates of birth and death unknown) is first mentioned in connection with the embassy to Rudolph II described here. Between 1596 and 1603 he was one of the officials in charge of the Chancellery for Kazan, and he also succeeded Vasily Shchelkalov as head of the Chancellery for Foreign Affairs, where he served from 1601 to 1605. In the latter capacity he took part in many diplomatic receptions during the reign of Boris Godunov, and was sent to Poland as ambassador in 1601. He was present at an audience between Boris and the Crimean ambassador, and in 1602 received the English agent John Merrick. In the company of Mikhail Glebovich Saltykov he was sent to the frontier to escort Duke Johan, Boris's prospective son-in-law, to the capital. He was the chief negotiator regarding a possible English marriage for Boris's son Fedor. After the fall of the Godunovs, Vlasiev was one of the delegates sent by the city of Moscow to greet False Dmitry I at Tula. In 1605 he was promoted from conciliar secretary to lord-in-waiting. The following month he went to Poland to claim for Dmitry the hand of Marina Mniszech and on November 20 (New Style) stood as Dmitry's proxy at the betrothal ceremony. During the last days of Dmitry's reign, as treasurer, he was virtually in sole charge of crown affairs. It is said by some that it was he who interceded for Vasily Shuisky, about to be executed for treason. If so, Vasily's ingratitude to Vlasiev was exceeded only by that shown to Dmitry himself. He was removed from office and his estates were confiscated after Shuisky's seizure of power, his former house being requisitioned for the incarceration of the Mniszech family. He himself was sent into semi-honorific exile as governor of Ufa. In 1610 he petitioned King Sigismund for the restoration of his estates.

18. Saint Nicholas the Thaumaturge was a fourth-century bishop of Myra, in Southwestern Asia Minor. In 1087 some Italian sailors stole his remains from Myra and enshrined them at Bari. Hence sometimes he is referred to as St. Nicholas of Bari. For some unknown reason he is particularly venerated in Russia, and his feast day is December 6.

19. This war started in 1595 and only ended in 1598. For a brief description see *New Cambridge Modern History,* Volume 3 (Cambridge, 1968), pp. 307-308.

20. This must have been Komulius. See below, Note 25.

21. Warkotsch's report of 1589 observed that Boris Godunov himself assured him of the tsar's vast fiscal reserves. Boris commented that even the extended wars of Ivan IV were less costly than Austria's long wars with the Turk.

22. Pope Gregory XIII (1502-1580), a lawyer and family man, was not ordained until the age of forty. His pontificate, which began in 1572, was concerned with restoring the power of Catholicism. In some areas, such as Poland, he was successful. Not surprisingly, he supported the Jesuit order. His foreign policy opposed Elizabeth of England, Henri of Navarre and the Ottoman empire. Like other Reformation popes, Gregory hoped to bring Russia into union with Rome, like all the others he failed. See entry by D.R. Campbell, *New Catholic Encyclopedia* (New York, 1967), Volume 6, pp. 778-781.

23. Sixtus V (1520-1590) was Pope from 1585 to 1590. A Franciscan preacher of some repute, eventually he became vicar of that order. As a theologian he supported internal reform within the church to meet the thrust of the Reformation. As part of the general plan for a grand coalition against the Turks, embracing Poland and Venice, he supported Maximilian's candidacy for the Polish throne. See entry by Campbell, *New Catholic Encyclopedia,* Volume 13, pp. 273-275.

24. For a short account of the extensive career of this ubiquitous Jesuit visitor to Moscow in the reign of Ivan IV, see entry by Graham, MERSH, Volume 29, pp. 109-114.

25. The Dalmatian abbot Komulius (Alessandro di Comolo), born in 1548, spent some time in the Slavic East as a missionary for the Catholic church. While acting bishop of Wilno he undertook missions to Moscow in 1595 and 1597 as a proponent of an anti-Turkish crusade. They ended fruitlessly. His support for the Brest Union hardly endeared him to the Russians. In the last years before his death early in the seventeenth century, he entered the Jesuit order and proselytized along the Adriatic coast.

26. The embassy of Jerome Bowes (died 1616) to Russia, the pinnacle of an otherwise unremarkable career, became legendary. He evinced contempt for Muscovite ritual, refused to follow customs, and attacked whatever he took to be the slightest denigration of his queen. In the next century both Pepys and Milton approvingly noted his patriotism. See *Dictionary of National Biography* (henceforth DNB) Volume 2, pp. 965-966.

27. Soloviev has discussed and analyzed the operations of the Russia Company with reference to Bowes in the previous volume. See Volume 12 of this series, pp. 57-60

28. Given Bowes' tendency to chauvinism, Soloviev is probably justified in questioning the reliability of his account. See the apologetic DNB entry for Bowes, cited above in Note 26.

29. For a more complete rendering of Bowes's report in the original English, see Hakluyt, *Principal Voyages,* Volume III, pp. 326-327.

30. This is probably Reynold (Reinhold) Beckmann, an interpreter in the tsar's service.

31. Soloviev italicizes the original Russian here: v legkikh gonchikakh. The italicized translation is based on a usage of legkii, literally "light," as applied to diplomatic missions.

32. See Chester Dunning, "Russia Company," MERSH, Volume 32, pp. 27-33, for a description of the English merchants' company in Muscovy.

33. On Horsey, who lined his pockets as the Company's primary agent between 1573 and 1591, see Donald L. Layton, MERSH, Volume 14, pp. 81-82. See also above, Chapter I, Note 40.

34. Robert Jacob (died 1588), Elizabeth's physician, served in Muscovy under Ivan. DNB, Volume 10, p. 559.

35. This is the original English supplied by Soloviev in a footnote lacking any citation. Elizabeth's letter to Boris addressing him thus can be found in Hakluyt, *Principal Voyages*, Volume III, pp. 428-430.

36. In Soloviev's original note Nashu bologodet'.

37. The complete English version of this charter appears in Hakluyt, *Principal Voyages*, Volume III, pp. 347-353.

38. Biographical information on Anthony Marsh is scarce. He is sometimes confused with his relative, the prominent merchant John Marsh. This relationship gained him employment with the Company, of which John Marsh was a charter member. Anthony first appeared in Muscovy in 1579 on a trading expedition to Persia. He only got as far as Astrakhan before being sent back to Yaroslavl on Company business. In 1584 he reappeared as an important man in the English merchants' community in Muscovy. By then he spoke fluent Russian and was acquainted with such powerful Muscovites as Andrei Shchelkalov and Boris Godunov. Their influence, as well as what the Russians later claimed was his obvious association with the Company, allowed him to borrow large sums, particularly during the spring and summer of 1585. When the loans became due the Muscovite authorities attempted to secure payment from the Company, maintaining that Marsh acted as its agent. Given that he was in its employ, lived at its house in Moscow at the time of the loans, and was referred to as an agent, the Muscovite position is easily understood. The Company refused to acknowledge the debts. Marsh, it held, was not its employee but an "interloper," an English merchant trading in Russia despite and around the Company's supposed monopoly. He deceived creditors and others about his standing with the Company, which had warned Russians not to deal with him. Contradictory and confused testimony in both England and Muscovy only clouded the picture of Marsh's activity and his status in the Company. Moreover, members of the Company often supplemented their income through private dealings, thus acting, as it were, as "interlopers." Many of Marsh's debts eventually were settled as a

result of Godunov's efforts. See Samuel H. Baron, "Fletcher's Mission to Moscow and the Anthony Marsh Affair," *Forschungen zur Osteuropäischen Geschichte*, 47 (1992), pp. 107-130, and particularly pp. 118-125.

39. The earl of Leicester was Elizabeth's most influential councilor. See DNB, Volume 6, pp. 112-122.

40. Giles Fletcher the Elder (1549-1611) in his own time was less known as a diplomat than as a poet and historian. Trained in law at Cambridge, he held the office of vicar of Chichester diocese, was elected to parliament in 1585, and was appointed Remembrancer of the city of London from 1587 to 1605. After diplomatic experience in Scotland and the Holy Roman empire he was sent on the mission described here. His account of the journey was suppressed by Lord Cecil (see Note 44, below) at the suggestion of English merchants who feared that the Muscovites might be so offended by its contents as to restrict commerce. See Emily V. Leonard, MERSH, Volume 11, pp. 187-188.

41. The denga coin of the sixteenth century, when minted in Moscow as opposed to Novgorod, was called the moskovka, the term used by Soloviev here.

42. Richardson is called Roman Romanov in Soloviev's text.

43. The polovina zolotaia here is probably a Muscovite coin equal to a half-ruble, and the chetvert' zolotaia may be the chetverets, the same coin under a different name, valued at a quarter-ruble.

44. Cecil (1520-1598) was Elizabeth's most trusted minister. He directed England's affairs through much of her reign. Born to a gentry family, he showed great academic talent and brilliance. He first held important court office in 1550 and the following year was knighted. From 1558 to 1576 he was secretary of state. Robert Dudley, earl of Leicester, appeared during this period as the object of Elizabeth's infatuation. Although the two men were rivals the queen never ceased relying on Cecil as her principal adviser. During 1569 and 1570 he undertook to safeguard the queen against Catholic plots. To this end he persecuted Catholics and created a widespread and intricate spy network. As leader of the Protestant faction he also played an important role in having Mary Queen of Scots executed. Cecil became a baron in 1571 and by then owned impressive estates. In 1572 he was named lord high treasurer, a post he held until his death.

CHAPTER IV

1. Muhammad-Girey ("the Fat") ruled the Crimea between 1577 and 1584. He was dedicated to restoring the balance of power between Muscovy and Crimea, upset in the middle of the sixteenth century when Ivan IV annexed the khanates of Kazan and Astrakhan, both claimed by the Crimea. To achieve his goal Muhammad flirted with all Muscovy's enemies. He sent an embassy to Poland-Lithuania in 1579. Between 1571 and 1583 he received papal emissaries and engaged in correspondence with Pope Gregory XIII, going so far as to feign

interest in conversion. He remained a loyal vassal of the Ottoman Turk until 1584, when tension with Turkey over divergent tactics towards Persia led the Crimean aristocracy to rebel against him. This ultimately brought about Turkish intervention, Muhammad's deposition and his death.

2. Islam-Girey, son of Devlet-Girey, lived his early years as a hostage at Istanbul, where he became Ottoman in tastes and outlook. He then entered a Dervish monastery, and later was called the "Dervish khan." When Muhammad-Girey refused a Turkish request to besiege Kaffa the Turks sent an expedition which placed Islam on the throne. He was a thoroughly loyal and Turkicized ruler, going so far as to have the sultan's name replace his in the evening prayers for the ruler. Aggravated by this, Crimean nationalist elements rallied around Muhammad's sons Saadet and Murad in a civil war described by Soloviev. See Carl Max Kortepeter, *Ottoman Imperialism during the Reformation. Europe and the Caucasus* (New York, 1972), pp. 15, 88, 100.

3. The Nogay, a nomadic tribe, inhabited the steppe to the east and north of the Crimea. See Edward D. Sokol, "Nogai Horde," MERSH, Volume 25, pp. 38-42.

4. The term for "land" here, yurt, can mean a territory, a people or a single encampment. Usage here and elsewhere of the terms for "prince" and "khan," tsarevich and tsar, respectively, is equally loose when referring to the Tatars. While the sense of tsarevich is prince, it clearly connotes a lesser prince.

5. Here and elsewhere pominki, translated as "gifts" or "presents" connotes a meaning close to modern "bribes." Muscovy and its Tataric neighbors based their diplomacy on all parties recognizing that political allegiance and favor flourished only when accompanied by what we would call personal bribery. As Soloviev's text shows, the size of "gifts" was a sure index of the status of the relationship between parties. Such giving or bribery was so pervasive and normal that it would violate the sixteenth-century meaning of the word to translate pominki as "bribes." Tatars and Russians simply did not make our modern distinction between bribes and gifts.

6. Another son of Devlet-Girey, born in 1554, Ghazi-Girey appears in the records as early as 1569 in a Crimean campaign against Astrakhan. He rode in the great attack on Moscow in 1571, campaigned against the Persians in the late 1570s, and was their prisoner between 1581 and 1585. During these campaigns and others in the Caucasus against Kabarda he caught the attention of the Turkish commander Osman-Pasha, who became his patron. After an exile in Thrace between 1585 and 1588 he assumed the throne of Crimea under Turkish auspices in 1588. Except for the years 1591-1594, when he carried out the raid on Moscow described herein, his policies were favorable or neutral. He died in 1608

7 It is difficult to identify this Likharev with absolute certainty, given the lack of information other than a surname. The military registers for the late sixteenth-century show six Likharevs. Only two of them, Boris and Fedor, appear on the registers before or around the time of the mission described, which must antedate 1588 and the fall of Islam-Girey. Fedor Likharev's service started in 1584. He

spent most of his time as commander of the garrison at Riazhsk on the southern frontier or on rivers watch. In 1584 and 1585 he was attached to the Great Regiment of the field army under Prince D.I. Khvorostinin. When in 1591 Khan Ghazi-Girey attacked Moscow Vasily Birkin replaced Likharev as commander from Riazhsk assigned to the Great Regiment. Shortly thereafter, in September, the registers note that Birkin also replaced Likharev as commander at Riazhsk. Likharev was reassigned to the rearguard. This does not seem to indicate demotion. In 1593 he commanded the city of Riazan. By 1595 he was mentioned as a secretary. Thereafter the record grows less brilliant. Fedor Ivanovich's reign ended with Fedor Likharev in the Northwest, at Nevel, near Pskov. Boris Likharev's career started earlier. Nearly all of his assignments placed him in the Northwest, at Govie and Alyst in Livonia and, interestingly, at Nevel between 1581 and 1593. The nature of Fedor Likharev's career, which involved assignments with the field army and at garrisons along the Southern frontier, makes him the more likely Likharev here.

8. This is probably Lukian Borisovich Khrushchov, famous for establishing fortified towns on the frontier and active in military service from 1563 until the 1590s. Soloviev distinguishes him from the Peter Lukich Khrushchov (see below, Note 42), active in Nashchokin's diplomatic mission, discussed later in this chapter.

9. Kirik and Mikhail Yustafievich Ruzhinsky (or Rózyński) were brothers from a Polish szlachta family with ties to the cossacks. They used revenues from their estates in the Ukraine to maintain private cossack bands. In 1593 and again in 1596 Kirik personally led his cossacks in cooperation with the Polish commander Żółkiewski in suppressing other, rebellious, cossacks.

10. Ne krianuli (Soloviev's note). Krianut', a verb from the northern dialects of Novgorod, Tver, Viatka and Olonets means "to budge, to push, or to collide with."

11. The Oka river, Muscovy's traditional frontier with the steppe, was the base for patrol duty against the Tatars, otherwise known as "banks watch."

12. Ivan Feofilatovich Bibikov appears on the military lists as commander at Rylsk in 1587, then commander for siege operations at Chernigov in 1588-1589. After his mission to Crimea he was commander at Zasek Venovsky.

13. This fortification and its role in the general defense plans of the city are described in Karamzin, *Istoriia*, Volume X, col. 88. This type of fortification consisted of wagons drawn into a circle or hollow square. The English word "leaguer," in common usage in the sixteenth and seventeenth centuries, is cognate with the Dutch leger or the Afrikaans laager.

14. Soloviev must be referring to Prince Vladimir Ivanovich Bakhteiarov-Rostovsky, a high-ranking field commander since 1580. Following the defense of Moscow he returned from 1593 until 1596 to Novgorod, a town he had commanded in 1582. After a special mission to the distant Siberian town of Tiumen in 1596, he was sent to command there in 1598. It is unclear whether this change implied a loss of favor in Moscow. At any rate in 1599 he was transferred

to the important border fortress at Tarki in the Caucasus. After passing a year in Turkish captivity he retired from active service until 1610, when he entered the intense political struggles of the Time of Troubles and became a boyar. At the end of the turmoil, in 1613, he was part of the delegation assigned to ask Michael Romanov to take the throne. He then assumed command at Nizhny Novgorod, a post which he held until his death in 1617. See Volume 16, pp. 255-256.

15. Nikita Romanovich Trubetskoy, a boyar since 1584, supported Godunov against False Dmitry I before changing his allegiance to the pretender. He then served Vasily Shuisky before dying in 1608.

16. Timofey Romanovich Trubetskoy served in various commands between 1572 and his death in 1602 or 1603.

17. For organization of the Muscovite army and its ranking of commanders according to formation, see Alton S. Donnelly, "Voevoda," MERSH, Volume 42, p. 210.

18. Ivan Vasilievich Godunov held boyar rank since 1584, appearing at some diplomatic receptions. He died in 1601 or 1602. Stepan Vasilievich commanded at Fellin in 1573 and accompanied Ivan the Terrible on his Livonian campaign of 1576 as lord-in-waiting. A boyar after 1584, he carried out a diplomatic mission to Poland (1586) and a military campaign in Finland (1592). He was named majordomo in 1598, and survived into the Time of Troubles as a commander in Siberia under both False Dmitry I and Vasily Shuisky.

19. Alexander Nikitich Romanov held the rank of carver, a post associated with functions at state dinners. He is mentioned first at a reception for the Lithuanian ambassador Luke Sapieha in 1585. In the late 1580s he assumed posts in the tsar's personal bodyguard. Soloviev describes him in action against Ghazi-Girey in 1591. He again took the field against the Tatars in 1598 under Tsar Boris Godunov, when he became a boyar. Three years later Godunov stripped him of his rank, exiled him and had him killed. See Volume 14, pp. 58-59. Andrei Petrovich Kleshnin, Fedor's uncle and tutor, held high office as long as Fedor lived, then entered a monastery when Godunov ascended the throne. Tradition assigned him a major role in the investigation of the death of Tsarevich Dmitry (see below, Chapter VI). Seventeenth-century chroniclers portrayed him as an intimate co-conspirator with Godunov in the child's murder. Crown Secretary Ivan Timofeev called him Boris's "brother." The veracity of these rumors is suspect, given the controversy surrounding Boris's role in Dmitry's death and the fact that Kleshnin's influence through his relationship with Fedor long antedated Godunov's power. Roman Mikhailovich Pivov commanded in diverse military campaigns between 1578 and his death in 1591. He was garrison commander at Astrakhan from 1586 to 1587 and at Novgorod in 1591.

20. "Kasha" (Ivan Nikitich) Romanov appears as a table attendant, courtier and member of the tsar's bodyguard in the 1590s. He suffered temporary disgrace and exile with the other Romanovs in 1601 and 1602, but False Dmitry made him

a boyar in 1606. After the accession of Michael Romanov he played only a minor role in state affairs, but disposed of vast wealth and engaged in frequent disputes over precedence. See Volume 14, pp. 59-61, 103-103 and for an extensive biographical note, Volume 15, pp. 302-303.

21. Kulikovo was Muscovy's bloody victory over the Tatars in 1380. See entries by Edward Sokol, MERSH, Volume 18, pp. 152-159 and Volume 21, pp. 60-65.

22. In May 1551 Ivan IV constructed the fortress town at Sviiazhsk, from which he undertook the conquest of Kazan.

23. As noted in Note 5, above, the "gift" was pivotal to diplomatic relations. Ghazi-Girey's embassy sought a gift as a sign of the restoration of normal relations. Kazan and Astrakhan were the centers of Tatar lands seized by Ivan the Terrible. Ghazi-Girey was, for the moment, making no territorial claim for them.

24. For a discussion of the office of heir apparent, here the khalgay, the complexities of the Crimean administration, and the little available on Feth-Girey, see *Encyclopedia of Islam* (Leiden, 1965), Volume II, p. 1113.

25. Military registers for 1586 first mention Semeon Vladimirovich Bezobrazov as the crown agent charged with the keys, a courtier's rank. In that year and the next he appears in the tsar's suite on military campaigns. In 1593 he was named garrison commander at Pochep where he remained for the next five years.

26. Merkury Alexandrovich Shcherbatov, an eminent military commander in the late sixteenth century, participated in nearly every Muscovite campaign between 1590 and 1594. Besides field duties with regiments, he commanded key garrisons at Tula (1586-1588) and Novgorod (1588), and briefly served as a judge in 1588. In 1596 he was assigned to the new and distant fortress at Tobolsk, in what was apparently disgrace and exile. He returned to Moscow in 1598 and again led troops in the field in 1600.

27. Soloviev's original text, Nuradinu tsarevichu, indicates the translation given. The editors accordingly index this as a reference to "Nuradin, a Crimean prince." It is possible that the original document referred not to a prince's name but to a title borne by the holder of the post of Nur-ed-Din (Light of the Faith), created in 1584. This office holder stood next in line to the heir apparent or khalgay in the succession, and therefore logically is mentioned here for a smaller bribe. For further details see Kortepeter, pp. 15, 64, and *Encyclopedia of Islam,* Volume II, p. 1113.

28. This rather undiplomatically refers to Ivan IV's conquests of the Tatar khanates claimed by Crimea.

29. Ivan IV constructed Tarki (Terskii gorodok) in 1563 after his marriage to the Kabardan princess Maria Temriukovna (see below, Note 45). A short history of the town in the sixteenth century appears in W.E.D. Allen, *Russian Embassies to the Georgian Kings* (Cambridge, 1970), Volume I, pp. 20-23.

30. Soloviev's Fedor Yakovlevich Khvorostinin is actually Prince Fedor Ivanovich Khvorostinin (1525-1608), whom the *Russian Biographical Dictionary* places on this mission to Livny in 1593. Khvorostinin fought with distinction during Ivan IV's reign, on both the Lithuanian and the Crimean fronts. Ivan favored Khvorostinin for his services in the Livonian campaigns of 1577 and 1579 with the honor of bearing the wedding goblet at the tsar's marriage to Maria Nagaia. Under Fedor, Khvorostinin continued to hold high diplomatic and military posts. By 1588 he was a boyar and member of the tsar's council. When Ghazi-Girey attacked Moscow in 1591 Khvorostinin, initially assigned to Kolomna as commander of the rearguard, was rushed back to command troops arrayed at the center of the battle, and then returned to Kolomna. For this he received the then rare "once and a half gold" award. His mission to Livny in 1593 is described here. In later years he served as lieutenant in Kolomna and engaged in diplomacy with the ambassadors of Persia (1594) and the Holy Roman empire (1597). In 1598 Khvorostinin supported Godunov's candidacy for the throne. He undertook a special mission to have residents of the Volga valley cities swear allegiance to Boris. He survived Godunov's fall from power. Shortly thereafter he took monastic vows, dying as the monk Feodosy.

31. Kaibula was a Tatar from Astrakhan already in the tsar's service.

32. This is probably Boris Petrovich Blagov or Blagovo in the military registers. After this mission he was governor of Velikie Luki, Belaia and Oreshek between 1586 and 1589. Later he was made a majordomo.

33. Murad III, born in 1546, ruled between 1574 and 1595. He remained at peace with Venice and Austria, and treated Bathory as his vassal. During his reign the Ottoman empire intervened successfully in Crimean affairs and waged a lengthy and somewhat fruitful series of wars in the Caucasus. Domestically his reign witnessed the first minor portents of the janissary mutiny and the consequent debilitation of the central authority which greatly facilitated the empire's decline a century later.

34. Selim II (reigned 1566-1574) was Murad's father and predecessor.

35. Kasimov was a Muslim state created in the fifteenth century which generally served as Muscovy's client. Mustafaley (Mustafa-Ali) Kaibulovich became its khan in 1585, earlier having held important field commands in Ivan IV's army during the Livonian War. See entry by Sokol, MERSH, Volume 16, pp. 54-56.

36. A chiaus was a Turkish messenger or emissary.

37. In fact no Russian ambassador returned to Istanbul for six years.

38. Records of the Birkin family date to the early fifteenth century when they served the then still independent princes of Riazan. When Soloviev mentions this Birkin, Vasily Grigorievich, he was starting an eventful decade of military service, largely on the southern frontier. He later gained distinction in the pursuit of Ghazi-Girey's fleeing Crimean forces after the invasion of 1591, described earlier in this chapter. Our last records of him occur in 1593.

39. Grigory Afanasiev Nashchokin began his diplomatic career under Ivan IV with a mission to Bathory in 1580. His performance must have brought favor because a year later he was a guest at the tsar's wedding. In 1581 he led troops with the main army group then vanished from the military registers until this assignment described by Soloviev. He was a tax collector in 1597 and was mentioned last as a fortress commander in the Moscow area.

40. Given traditional Persian-Turkish hostility, this declaration served to warm any chill in relations which might have stemmed from the difficulties that Blagov and his Turkish companion encountered with the cossacks and the subsequent long hiatus between embassies. The same applies to Fedor's reference to the failure of Western efforts to entice Muscovy into an anti-Ottoman league.

41. Three times, in 1572-1579, 1580-1584 and 1586-1595, Jeremiah II Tranos served the Eastern Orthodox church as patriarch of Constantinople. At first he pursued an interest in developing relations between Orthodoxy and Protestantism, which hopes ended in disillusionment. Service so close to the all-powerful sultan had its perils. His dismissals in 1579 and 1585 resulted from the activities of his enemies at the Turkish court. During his third term in office he convened the council which recognized the independent Russian patriarchate (see pp. 129-138).

42. Peter Lukich Khrushchov started his service as a junior boyar at Tula and then commanded cossack hundreds in the frontier towns. This must explain his role in Nashchokin's embassy. Soloviev describes cossack refusal to serve under him. Later, in 1604, Godunov sent Khrushchov to the cossacks to sway them from temptation toward allegiance to False Dmitry. This mission was no more successful since the cossacks took Khrushchov in chains before the pretender. The unfortunate emissary dissimulated, pretending to "see Ivan" in the pretender's countenance and pledging loyalty, for which he later was branded unjustly as "the first traitor." These tactics only gained Khrushchov a respite. In 1605, unable to escape, he publicly exposed the pretender and was executed.

43. Young Prince Mikhail Khromoy-Volkonsky was beginning his career with this mission. Between 1594 and 1598 he held several posts in Siberia. He died a hero's death in 1610 when he commanded the garrison at Borovsk, with its nearby Pafnutiev monastery. See Volume 15, p. 143.

44. The cruel and corrupt reign of Muhammad III (1566-1603) proved disastrous for the Ottoman empire. He assumed power in 1595 during the early stages of the long war with Austria, which lasted until 1606. This war brought some military successes, at great expense. Military expenditures were magnified by the need to suppress a rebellion of the mounted Anatolian cavalry, the spahis. The consequent inflation only increased the pervasive unrest. Muhammad, influenced by his domestic advisers and urged on by both the English and the French ambassadors, continued the war. Consequently, the state of the empire bordered perilously on anarchy when he died.

45. On August 21, 1561 Ivan married Kucheney, daughter of Temriuk (or Temgriuk) Aidarovich, head of one of the dominant Circassian families. She converted to Christianity as Maria, but never was received well at court. Tales of her unbridled "lust" or "passion" circulated, with the inference that she was no fit replacement for Ivan's first wife Anastasia. Perhaps these stories were true. It is equally possible that she encountered the natural hostility of the clergy and powerful families. Certainly it was in the interest of the Zakharins, ancestors of the Romanovs, to denigrate her in comparison with her predecessor Anastasia, their relative. In any case, Ivan seems to have ignored her any infidelity while his own dissolute sexual conduct grew more pronounced than ever. This too may have made Maria a target of those who viewed her a female source of the tsar's degeneracy, even though it surely needed no encouragement. The marital alliance did present him with a justification for expanding Muscovite influence in the Caucasus. The Crimean khan's ambassador's were told that the fort at Tarki "was built for the protection of Prince Temriuk, the sovereign's father-in-law." Maria died childless in 1569. Her brothers established the line of Cherkassky princes in Moscow. [The quotation comes from Soloviev, *Istoriia,* Volume VI, p. 601.]

46. Alexander of Kakhetia (1527-1605) assumed power in 1574 and spent his long reign involved in the maelstrom of relations among Turkey, Iran and Muscovy in the Caucasus, as well as the even more complex interplay among the Caucasian princes. As Soloviev indicates, he flirted with the Russians and found them unable to extend him adequate protection. A Muscovite embassy to Kakhetia was in earshot of events in 1605 when Alexander was murdered on the orders of his younger son Constantine, at the urging of Persia's Shah Abbas. See Volume 14, p. 35; W.E.D. Allen, *A History of the Georgian People* (New York, 1971), pp. 152-157, and Ronald Grigor Suny, *The Making of the Georgian Nation* (Stanford, Cal., 1988), pp. 48-50.

47. The shevkals or shamkals ruled a coastal strip along the Caspian Sea centered around Tarku. Some sources have them originating during the eighth-century Arabic expansion into the region. At one time they dominated much of the mountainous interior. By the sixteenth century the shevkal was elected by a council of his lands.

48. The krym-shevkal in this period appears to have been an office for the heir apparent, similar to the Crimean nur-ed-din (see above, Note, 27). The name Krym did not indicate connection to the Crimea. Here the krym-shevkal was opposed to the shevkal, and sought refuge with Alexander, who provided him with an estate and was using him, as Soloviev shows, as his agent in the power struggle.

49. Soloviev's editors identify this person as Prince Ivan Dmitrievich Khvoros tinin, but Allen (*Russian Embassies,* p. 89) names this commander as Prince Andrei Ivanovich Khvorostinin. Prince Ivan does not appear in the military registers until 1598, while the editors name Prince Andrei as commander of the garrison at Tarki, on special military assignment. Allen must be correct. Andrei Khvorostinin was a famed senior military commander suited for such a distant

and demanding mission. Born in Moscow in the 1520s, he died there in 1604. After entering service in 1544 in the tsar's bodyguard he held a series of field commands, attracting particular notice by his defense of Bolkhov against a besieging Crimean force in 1566. He received new honors at Ivan's court in 1568, and between 1569 and 1580 led forces in Kaluga, Moscow, Tarusa, Novgorod, Kashira and Dedilov. During the Livonian War he commanded the tsar's own arquebusiers, and then defended Pskov against Bathory. In 1588 he first served in the Caucasus, whence he returned to defend Moscow against the Tatars in 1591. Two years later he is again found on the southern frontier constructing fortresses, traces of which survived until early in this century. The expedition described by Soloviev occurred late in Khvorostinin's career, between 1595 and 1597. The old warrior again took the field against the Tatars in 1598. Afterwards he was garrison commander at the new frontier town of Tsarev Borisov, from which ill health forced him back to Moscow, where he died.

50. An Ostiak leader, Karacha was a vassal of Kuchum (see succeeding note). Having ambushed Ivan Koltso, he besieged Yermak in the town of Isker. A sortie ended the siege and cost Karacha his two sons. He fled into the steppe and continued guerrilla warfare until captured by the cossack Chulkov and sent to Moscow in 1587, where he was resettled with estates.

51. A Sheibanid Siberian khan, Kuchum dominated the Irtysh and Tobol river valleys at the time of the Muscovite conquests, although sending tribute to Moscow since 1571. After Yermak's conquest of Western Siberia Kuchum remained active in the steppe, harassing Muscovite cossack forces between 1584 and 1591, when he was driven from Siberia. Although he had aged and was going blind, Kuchum renewed his attacks in 1593 and 1595 only to be defeated again and nearly killed in 1598. He had refused offers, such as the one cited by Soloviev later in this chapter, to surrender and be settled in Moscow, although some members of his family had done so already. This time he ultimately sought refuge among the Nogay, where his enemies killed him. See Volume 14, pp. 36-37.

52. A relative of Kuchum who had helped build his power, Muhammad-Kul also joined him in resistance to the cossacks. His fate differed. Captured in 1583, he was sent to Moscow in 1585 and there was resettled, receiving patrimonial estates.

53. A famous cossack chieftain, Koltso was once a wanted outlaw in the Volga valley with a price on his head, dead or alive. He joined Yermak in the conquest of Siberia, gained a pardon for his services to the tsar, and then returned to Siberia, where he met the fate described here by Soloviev.

CHAPTER V

1. The term here, sosloviia, denotes social groups akin to the medieval and early modern Western estates, as in the French Estates General. See Pushkarev, pp. 137-139.

2. That is, the oprichnina, for which see Chapter I, Note 23.

3. Throughout this section of the chapter Soloviev relies heavily on Fletcher, but cites him irregularly. Fletcher's account of the councils described here are found in Berry and Crummey, pp. 135-138.

4. Soloviev's term for chancellery is prikaz. His word for taxation chancellery is chetvert' or chet'. He is drawing once more on Fletcher. The Berry and Crummey edition of Fletcher observes that Fletcher oversimplified Muscovite reality. Prikazy handled certain types of business and were named accordingly. Chetverti or cheti collected revenues over a broad area of the country. Andrei Shchelkalov was administrator of the Chancellery (prikaz) for Foreign Affairs, but at the same time chief of the Andrei Shchelkalov Chancellery (chet'). Fletcher, understandably confused, also sometimes mixed the terms. In the enumeration which follows, all four offices were prikazy although Fletcher's original calls them chetverti. Soloviev slips into this usage, even though later he makes the proper distinction between them and the prikazy.

5. Sapun, or Vasily Tikhonovich, Abramov served in the Chancellery of Crown Service and Appointments from 1583 until 1605. He became a boyar in 1594, and after 1605 commanded forces in Karelia. See Berry and Crummey, p. 147, and entry on him, MERSH, Volume 1, p. 9.

6. Vyluzgin, a clerk's son, administered the Chancellery of Military Tenures from 1587 to 1601. He served also on the commission investigating the death of Tsarevich Dmitry.

7. This Panteleev, or Petelin in Fletcher's original, is Druzhina or Foma Petelin. He first appears in 1579 among other chancellery clerks accompanying the tsar to Novgorod. The following year he undertook his first of several diplomatic missions, to Wilno. In 1582 he negotiated with the Swedes. Two years later he accompanied Troekurov and Beznin to Warsaw (see Chapter II, above). Later in this chapter Soloviev mentions that when a Prince Bariatinsky was jailed for debating precedence with other princes Petelin delivered his order of incarceration. Petelin also served in the treasury from 1587 until the late 1590s.

8. Berry and Crummey, pp. 147-148

9. Grigory Andreevich Kurakin, Pskov governor, boyar 1584, died 1595.

10. This is the Prince Peter Semeonovich Lobanov-Rostovsky engaged in correspondence with De la Gardie in Chapter II, section "Relations with Sweden."

11. Grigory Vasilievich Godunov was appointed boyar and majordomo in 1584; he died around the time of Boris's coronation as tsar. See Volume 14, p. 16.

12. Soloviev cites Fletcher for these numbers. See Berry and Crummey, pp. 158-168, and particularly their discussion of Seredonin's much lower estimate of revenues in Note 16, pp. 163-164.

13. Despite the absence of quotation marks, both grammar and context indicate that this comes directly from an uncited source.

14. English merchants also enjoyed the privilege and status of gosti as defined in Chapter I, Note 51.

15. Fletcher's original (Berry and Crummey, p. 120) reads "The reason of this abating and decrease of this and other commodities that were wont to be transported in a greater quantity is the shutting up of the port of Narva, toward the Finland Sea, which is now in the hands and possession of the Swedes; likewise the stopping of the passage overland by the way of Smolensk and Polotsk by reason of their wars with the Poles, which causeth the people to be less provident in maintaining and gathering these and like commodities for that they lack sales. Partly also for that the merchants and muzhiki (for so they call the common sort of people) are very much discouraged by many heavy and intolerable exactions that of late time have been imposed upon them, no man accounting that which he hath to be sure his own, and therefore regard not to lay up anything or to have it beforehand for that it causeth them many times to be fleeced and spoiled not only of their goods but also of their lives." (Spelling modernized)

16. Soloviev commented already on the impediments to trade during Ivan's reign. See Volume 12 of this series, pp. 60-64.

17. Literally "four rubles on a hundred rubles, eight dengas on the ruble."

18. Soloviev refers to the statement made by the Nogay when pressed by Muscovite settlements. See above, pp. 89-93.

19. See above, pp. 95-100.

20. The Latukhinsk Book of Degrees says that Godunov, arriving at Smolensk for the foundation of the fortifications there, called this city the necklace of the Muscovite state. "At that very instant Prince F.M. Trubetskoy spoke thus against Boris's speech. 'When he works out the beads on that necklace, he won't be able to survive them.'" (Soloviev's note)

21. Kon constructed solid and elegant fortresses throughout Muscovy during the late sixteenth and early seventeenth centuries. See entry on Kon, MERSH, Volume 17, p. 143.

22. Soloviev here notes that "The Latukhinsk Book of Degrees is correct, not the Chronograph, which Karamzin followed when identifying the builder." His reference is to Karamzin, *Istoriia,* Volume 10, Note 137, col. 29. He supports his assertion with a citation from the published Russian source *Akty istoricheskie, sobrannye i izdannye Arkheograficheskoiu Kommissieiu* (Historical Documents Gathered and Published by the Archeographic Commission), Volume I, No. 230, pp. 436-446. On the work of this commission see the comments in the Introduction. Soloviev's editors comment that the cited information is not found in *Akty istoricheskie.*

23. Although the editors provide no identification other than a surname, context makes this Vasily Andreevich Zvenigorodsky, who served from 1576 to 1616. See Volume 15, p. 338.

24. The siege of Pskov lasted from August 1581 until February 1582, during which the garrison repelled thirty-one attacks by Stefan Bathory's forces. See A.A. Malinovskii, "Pskov, Defense of," MERSH, Volume 30, pp. 61-62.

25. The term here, saadak, denotes the entire accoutrement necessary for the equipment of an archer.

26. Grammar indicates that this segment is a direct quotation, although Soloviev does not set it off.

27. See Chapter IV.

28. The Russian term here, sevriuk, describes cossacks and others hired from the Severian towns for patrol service. See Volume 14, p. 148, Note 23.

29. Afanasy Zinoviev was beginning his career at the time of this mission. He appears often in the military registers after 1589 as a member of the tsar's bodyguard. He also went on other reconnaissance missions. On one, in May 1590, he accompanied Fedor Lihkarev (see above, Chapter IV, Note 7). In May 1593 he commanded troops from Livny in pursuit of Crimean raiders. Apparently he survived the Time of Troubles. He is last mentioned serving as a judge in 1612.

30. Grammar and context lead me to place quotes on this passage. The last parenthetical comment is Soloviev's.

31. See Chapter I, Note 37.

32. Submitting dispatches involved reporting to a superior commander. The three officers conceded that Trubetskoy was their rightful superior, but refused to recognize Khvorostinin as such. To appreciate fully their passion, remember that once they had recognized Khvorostinin their entire family's honor, as accumulated and recorded in the crown registers, would undergo a changed relationship to the honor of the Khvorostinin family. Thus, the reference to being "stripped" of one's father and grandfather.

33. A Danish prince, son of Christian III, Magnus (1540-1583) had spent a decade seeking power in the Baltic for himself and his native Denmark when, in 1570, he arrived in Moscow and married one of Ivan IV's relatives. A Danish connection long had characterized Russian foreign policy, extending back to Ivan III's reign. It flowed naturally from a game of odd and even powers played in the Baltic, given the constant Danish-Swedish hostility. Ivan intended to support Magnus's designs in the Baltic, using them to further Russian expansion there. He proclaimed Magnus as king of Livonia. This brought war with Poland and Sweden. Magnus and his Russian forces fared poorly in three attempts to seize Reval. Feeling the need for a new sponsor, Magnus turned to Bathory in 1578. Ivan celebrated Magnus's wedding with great pomp so as to broadcast and impress others with his marital connection to the "king of Livonia." Such a brilliant occasion naturally held particular interest for those obsessed with precedence.

34. On the Liapunovs, see above, Chapter I, Note 31.

35. The term sosloviia was mentioned in Note 1, above. Concerning the actual existence of this law, see the discussion in the Introduction.

36. Soloviev's biased reference is to the schism of 1667 which tore the Russian church in two and created the Old Believer movement, subsequently persecuted and yet still vital, and re-emerging in contemporary Russia. See G. Douglas Nicoll, "Old Believers," MERSH, Volume 25, pp. 228-237.

37. Hermogen (1530-1612), a monk of uncertain but probably humble origin, fulfilled a role in Russia's history during the Time of Troubles somewhat analogous to that which Joan of Arc played in France's Hundred Years War. Not

surprisingly, the two were canonized within a decade of each other (Joan in 1920, Hermogen in 1913) in the context of their respective nations' surging nationalisms. Here, as described by Soloviev, Hermogen just had assumed the post of metropolitan of Kazan. Earlier, in 1587, he took monastic vows late in life, after the death of his wife and a long career as white or secular clergyman. Hermogen's stewardship in Kazan was characterized by efforts to assure the fidelity of the newly converted population through measures like those described here, and through a program of erecting beautifully decorated churches. Hermogen was named patriarch by Tsar Vasily Shuisky in 1606. Despite this, relations between the two sometimes were strained. His greatness for Russian nationalist historians rose from his epistolary campaign conducted from prison against the would-be Polish tsar Władysław. He was murdered in prison in 1612. See Nicholas Lupinin, "Hermogen," MERSH, Volume 14, pp. 11-13, and for his role in the national renaissance see Volume 15 of this series, pp. 18-22, 92-93, 157-158, 160-163, 204-218 and *passim*.

38. Context and grammar call for a direct quotation absent in the original text.

39. Michael Triboles (1470-1506), known in Russia as Maxim the Greek, spent his youth in Italy where he was an associate of such Renaissance luminaries as Ficino and Pico della Mirandola and from 1502 to 1505 was a Dominican monk. Doubts about the tenets of Renaissance thought and a reconversion to Orthodoxy brought him to Muscovy as a translator by 1516. He became involved in the great controversy between the possessors and the non-possessors. After a trial for heresy in 1525 Maxim was imprisoned in several monasteries and unable to return to Greece, although he continued to advise Tsar Ivan IV on occasion. See George Majeska, MERSH, Volume 21, pp. 26-28, and Volume 9 of this series, pp. 151-153.

40. That is, Poland-Lithuania's dream of using a separate center of the Orthodox church at Kiev from which to attract the Orthodox population of Western Rus. Kiev had never ranked higher than a metropolitan see even when at its glorious eleventh and twelfth-century zenith it was primary among the independent Rus principalities. Since the decline of Kiev and its fall to the Mongols the city had passed into Polish-Lithuanian possession, where it remained until the seventeenth century. Because of its earlier prestige its metropolitan constantly threatened Moscow's influence. First Lithuania and then Poland-Lithuania sporadically cultivated it as an alternative religious center. A Muscovite patriarchate diminished Kiev to inferior status, subordinated it to Muscovite patriarchs, and altered the balance of ecclesiastical and political influence in Western Rus and the Ukraine toward Muscovy.

41. The patriarchate of Jerusalem and its monastery were sent nine hundred rubles, and eighty-two rubles for the eternal flame which burned for the health of the tsar, tsaritsa and their offspring. The archbishop of Mount Sinai got fifty-four rubles. The Serbian Ascension monastery of Milešev, which held the relics of St. Savva the Serb, received two hundred and seventy rubles; the Serbian Annunciation monastery, on the river at Ponarat, got one hundred and twenty rubles. (Soloviev's note)

42. See above, Chapter IV, Note 41 and entry by Theodore Zissis, "Jeremias II," *The Encyclopedia of Religion* (New York, 1987), Volume 8, pp. 6-7.

43. The city of Vladimir dominated North Russia before Moscow's rise from insignificance. It was the seat of the North Russian metropolitans since the decline and fall of Kiev in the thirteenth century.

44. The shipment included forty lots of forty sables each, thirty lots of forty martens each, ten pieces of ermine in winter coat and 542 pounds of walrus teeth. The tsar gave to the patriarch himself an amphora set with pearls, a golden goblet for holy water and a garment inlaid with exceptional pearls. Patriarch Job sent black velvet and forty sables. Godunov sent to Jeremiah, whom he lauded as great lord, sovereign father, spiritual mentor and savior, forty sables, a garment from his wife, and from his son Fedor a gilded silver goblet with a lid. Wares worth five hundred rubles were sent for construction at the St. Panteleimon monastery on Mount Athos. This monastery was renovated by a grant from Ivan IV for its elders to visit Russia for meetings about church construction. A similar grant had been made to the Jerusalem monastery of Blessed Savva. In 1593 Trifon Korobeinikov and Mikhail Ogarkov were sent with salutations and blessings to Constantinople, Alexandria, Antioch, Jerusalem and Mount Sinai. They brought with them 5,534 Hungarian gold ducats and three gold Portuguese coins worth thirty Hungarian ducats, eight times forty sables, large quantities of sable and marten, forty weasel furs, fives of excellent segments from the strong coarse white fur of the spine, and a fox fur cut from the belly. While at Constantinople they were to visit Ivan Kashurin's for the tsar's sables sold to him in Moscow for three hundred rubles, six hundred Hungarian ducats. (Soloviev's note)

45. Soloviev discussed in the beginning of this chapter the crown's problems with supplying both land and labor to its military tenure estate holders. The possibility of expropriating ecclesiastical territories closer to the heartland and less subject to peasant flight toward the frontiers occurred to the Muscovite tsars. Later in the century they may have watched with interest Protestant reformers assailing the church's wealth in the West. The Josephans, followers of a monastic leader named Joseph of Volokolamsk, must be understood in this context. Sometimes also called "possessors," they stood squarely for protecting ecclesiastical holdings from any covetous outside force, including the crown. In return Josephan ideology endorsed the power and influence of the Muscovite tsars, in politics lending vital support to the centralizing tendencies which Soloviev noted in the opening paragraphs of this volume. The Muscovite tsars ultimately found this exchange acceptable, although elements of doubt and vacillation constantly showed in their words and deeds. The religious emotions of the rulers complicated these matters for such tsars as the truly pious Fedor and his candidly sinful and guilty father. Their feelings inspired regular donations of land, tolls, or tax exemptions to the church, even when the state was strapped for resources, as Soloviev has noted pointedly in this chapter. A combination of Josephan domination of the church and crown support for Josephan ideology made life difficult or impossible for such monastic critics as Maxim the Greek (see above, Note 39),

called the "non-possessors." It also made for a suspicious and rigid Orthodoxy which, somewhat like its Catholic Counter-Reformation counterpart, aimed to ferret out heresies, real or imaginary. Among these was the Judaizers' heresy, of uncertain origin but unveiled and eradicated between 1490 and 1504. Here historians of Russia resemble scholars struggling to define great heresies of the Roman church such as Catharism. They must contend with the fact that sources for the Judaizer heresy are often the accusations of the heretic hunters. This makes it improbable that we can ever know accurately the Judaizers' actual beliefs or trace their origins. Considering all this, Evfimy's insult, if in fact uttered, was of a most grave and cutting variety. For speculation about the Judaizers see M. David Goldfrank, MERSH, Volume 15, pp. 143-146; on the Josephans see Joseph L. Wieczynski, MERSH, Volume 15, pp. 140-141; see also in this series Volume 9, pp. 148-151 and Volume 8, pp. 110-119.

46. The colorful onion domes of Vasily the Blessed in Red Square have come to symbolize Russia. The church was erected under Ivan IV between 1555 and 1560 to celebrate the conquests of Kazan and Astrakhan. Originally dedicated to the Feast of the Intercession, in 1580 it was co-dedicated to Vasily, a "fool in Christ" or visionary holy man. Such individuals, it was thought, were divinely graced with madness or folly in a world where what was accepted as "sanity" often brought only evil, sin and grief. See "Basil the Blessed, Cathedral of," MERSH, Volume 3, p. 150.

47. Black, meaning monastic or regular clergy, were celibate in the Russian Orthodox church and lived by the rule of St. Basil. White, meaning parish or secular clergy, married before ordination. Black clergy provided the church's ecclesiastical hierarchy; white clergy provided its parish priests.

48. The reference is to gubnye officials. The guba was a special judicial district for criminal matters created under Ivan IV in 1540. See "Guba Reforms," MERSH, Volume 13, pp. 181-182.

49. On Merkury Shcherbatov, see above, Chapter IV, Note 26. Soloviev is commenting that little in his career prepared him to serve as judge. The reference to the plavnyi rat' or riparian forces is equally interesting. These were the largely river-borne ancestors of the later Russian navy.

50. The expression here is s obrazom. The reference is clearly to a ceremony defining their land, with a sacred icon lending solemnity to the occasion.

51. The Russian term here, Arap, denotes one of black skin and probably African origin. For Soloviev's time, "Moor" rather than "black" seems an apt translation.

CHAPTER VI

1. Soloviev's two different lands are Kievan Rus and Muscovy.

2. Vladimir Monomakh (1053-1125), warrior, lawgiver and folk hero, ruled Kiev as its last great prince. See entry by George P. Majeska, MERSH, Volume 42, pp. 160-164.

3. Here Soloviev compares the inherent paganism of the Kiev Rus population with the deeply rooted Orthodoxy of the people during the Time of Troubles. The commonality rests in conservative adherence to the internalized faith, whether pagan or Orthodox. Nominally Christian, Kievan pagans when pressed spurned Christianity. Centuries later the same population, now truly Orthodox, could not be compelled to follow the novel and "illegal" path of Roman Catholicism.

4. Soloviev's term is sosloviia, defined in Chapter V, Note 1. Here he stresses the importance of the freedom of lesser princes and servitors to depart from the service of greater lords. This right rose logically from that fluidity of society which he considers vital for the house of Riurik's expansion over Kievan Rus. He will argue later that the right of departure meant that within each individual "seed," that is, each small principality, little could be stable and permanent. Soloviev's discourse in these passages is strikingly infused with those nineteenth-century evolutionary models which were then in the air or, to borrow the felicitous term of the French Annales historians, then permeated the mentalité of educated elites everywhere. This volume of Soloviev's history was published in 1857, while Darwin's famous *Discourse on the Origin of the Species* appeared in 1859.

5. Both of these city states were independent for centuries before their eventual annexation to Muscovy in the late fifteenth and early sixteenth centuries. Both also called in outside princes, frequently those of Moscow, on the basis of charters specifying the contractual rights and obligations of both prince and town. Soloviev contrasts this relationship, characteristic of the "epoch of consolidation," with Ivan's grants of self-government after the formation of the mature Muscovite state.

6. For the significance of the term "gatherers of the land" in Russian historiography, see above, Chapter I, Note 1.

7. Soloviev's language here is difficult to convey in translation. Kozak can denote a cossack or connote a wanderer, a vagabond. Soloviev employs the word in both senses to underscore the continual tension between sedentary landed society and the nomadic world of the southern steppe, whether during the Kievan era, when the steppe was the stage for princely activity or later, when it became a largely ungoverned and ungovernable refuge specifically for the cossacks and more generally for any wanderers uncomfortable with the North's stability during the Muscovite "epoch of consolidation." These passages also point forward to the steppe cossacks' role in the coming Time of Troubles, which Soloviev found largely destructive and inimical to what he deemed "natural," in an evolutionary sense, the state-building work of Muscovy's tsars.

8. Avraamy Palitsyn, *Skazanie ob osade Troitskogo Sergieva monastyria ot pollakov i litvy i o byvshikh potom v Rossii matezhakh* (Tale of the Siege of the Trinity-St. Sergius Monastery by the Poles and Lithuanians and of the Rebellions thereafter Happening in Russia) (Moscow, 1821), p. 3. The editors cite p. 101 in a later edition of the same work, *Skazanie Avraamiia Palitsyna* (The Tale of Avraamy Palitsyn), edited by L.V. Cherepnin with text and commentary by O.A.

Derzhavina and E.V. Kolosovaia (Moscow, 1955). See the comments on this work in my Introduction, p. xxvi; also entry by Orchard, MERSH, Volume 26, pp. 195-197.

9. The Nagoy family played an important role in Muscovite politics between the fifteenth and the seventeenth centuries. See V.D. Nazarov, MERSH, Volume 24, pp. 39-40.

10. "As Tsarevich Dmitry flowers with awareness, those around him confuse him over why he no longer sees his brother. He grieves over this and, scoffing and jesting, speaks foolishness about those nearest his brother, about that Boris. Once this is so, the flatterers and the plotters of great wickedness spin a web of tenfold lies, and these reach the magnates, reach that Boris. Thus, the lad is hurled down from perplexity to grief. Thus, unwittingly, they steer him from brilliant youth to eternal rest." Palitsyn, p. 3. In the edition of 1955, pp. 101-102. This is Soloviev's note, which is probably a direct quotation, although he does not mark it as such.

11. The original Russian is in the active voice, but no actors are identified.

12. For Andrei Kleshnin, see above, Chapter IV, Note 19.

13. Mikhail Bitiagovsky (died 1591) was appointed by Boris Godunov to administer funds provided the Nagoy while in exile. They hated him for his frugality, and the townsmen who killed him may have shared this hatred. See "Bitiagovskii, Mikhail," MERSH, Volume 4, p. 190.

14. For Maria Nagaia see Chapter I, Note 29.

15. Soloviev placed here a citation presenting an extended discussion of the historical controversy surrounding the tsarevich's death and Godunov's role in it. It appears as the Appendix to this volume.

16. A thorough examination of the report of the investigative commission is found in George Vernadsky, "The Death of the Tsarevich Dimitry. A Reconsideration of the Case," *Oxford Slavonic Papers,* 5 (1954), pp. 1-19. See also R.G. Skrynnikov, *Boris Godunov* (Academic International Press, 1982), pp. 51-65. For Vyluzgin see Chapter V, Note 6. Vasily Shuisky (1552-1612) alone of the representatives of that great family, managed to secure the Muscovite throne. During Shuisky's struggle with Godunov at Fedor's accession, described in Chapter I, he remained aloof and therefore did not share the fate of some of his relatives. He did suffer a short banishment in the later 1580s, but again was sitting on the boyar council when Dmitry died at Uglich. The boyars clearly appointed Shuisky to the investigatory commission in an attempt to counter the rumors of Godunov's involvement in the tsarevich's death. The Shuisky family being so antipathetic to Godunov, Vasily's presence would seem to guarantee that the commission would be unbiased and thorough. Shuisky attempted to block Godunov's election as tsar in 1598, for which he again was banished briefly. He played a central role in the Time of Troubles, ruling a truncated Muscovite state between 1606 and 1610. He died in exile in Warsaw. See entry by Chester Dunning, MERSH, Volume 35, pp. 61-67 and, for Shuisky's role in the Time of Troubles, Volumes 14-15 of this series.

17. According to the *Oxford English Dictionary*, mumblety-peg, or mumble-the-peg, is a boys' game in which each player in turn throws a knife from a series of positions, continuing until he fails to make the blade stick in the ground. The unsuccessful player is compelled to draw out of the ground with his teeth a peg which the others have driven in with a certain number of blows with the handle of a knife. In Scotland this game is known as "knifie."

18. Ogurets in the Russian.

19. Soloviev notes here "It is interesting that the rumors circulated among the common folk in the Ukraine and the junior boyar reported them among the peasantry." Among the accounts that he credits for his description of the accusations against Godunov is that of Jacques Margeret (1565-1619), a French mercenary captain during the Time of Troubles, which Chester Dunning has translated into English as *The Russian Empire and Grand Duchy of Moscow. A 17th-century French Account* (Pittsburgh, 1983). See also his entry on Margeret, MERSH, Volume 21, pp. 96-99.

20. "Adam, expelled from God and from paradise," wrote Job, "still understood only immortality and paradise, for he had not known the taste of death. Then he saw the death of his son Abel. He cried sitting over the corpse of his son, not knowing what to do, imagining that Abel yet stood before him. Day after day he saw the youth's face and his now fallen goodness. An angel was sent to him to say 'You suffer in vain, O Adam! You sit and sob for a corpse. This is a curse. For it already has been ordained that you have sprung from the earth and to the earth you shall return.' A merciful and loving God will not leave unheeded the prayers of those who approach Him with faith, and the outpourings of those begging of Him, and He will force open the barren and closed marital bed. Such happened in the days of yore to Joachim and Anna. They were fruitless, and for this they were berated by the sons of Israel's twelve tribes, driven from the assembly and kept from making offerings to God. Joachim went into the wilderness and fasted forty days. Anna went into her garden and stood beneath that tree which is called the laurel, which already had blossomed, and there she tearfully prayed God about her childlessness. A tiny bird flew up to her and it landed on the tree's branches. Anna gazed at the tree, hoping to see the bird, and saw it perched in its nest. Anna cried out loudly, lifting her voice unto the Lord, 'O Lord! To whom can I be likened, for I am more wretched than that bird, for that bird has its young. Such is the cruelty befalling me that I am not even like the wild beasts of the earth, for even the wild beasts of the earth bear children. I alone stand childless before you, O Lord! Alas, how wretched I am! I am unlike the waters, for the waters too are fertile for you, Lord, and the waves surge through the rapids, and rejoice in glorifying you, O Lord.' An angel of the Lord stood before her, saying 'Anna, Anna, your prayer has been heard.' So do you see, most gracious and exalted lady, tsaritsa, the power of the prayer of the righteous suffering who are afflicted. Grief, my lady, does no good, only God's mercy. It is no use to pass time in mourning. It only angers God, does your soul no little harm, and purposelessly exhausts your body. No sooner does the devil see one who grieves than he is strengthened. To this end, direct all your prayer, your every hope, your piety,

to God and His Blessed Mother who, seeing the depth of your devotion, will beseech her Son, and He will answer your every request, and your noble loins will be made fruitful, and the vine of your house will bear its fruit.'" (Soloviev's note) Concerning Anna, see Luke 2:36-38.

21. Fedor descended from the Muscovite prince Ivan Kalita or "Moneybag," famed as the first of the line to "gather the lands," supposedly by purchase, and to capitalize on the support of two institutions so vital to Moscow's success, the Tatar horde and the Russian Orthodox church. See entry by Emily V. Leonard, MERSH, Volume 15, pp. 35-40.

22. Maria Vladimirovna was the daughter of Ivan IV's first cousin Prince Vladimir of Staritsa and therefore a second cousin to Fedor and to Dmitry of Uglich. Her parents were murdered at Ivan's command in 1569 although she and her elder sister Yevfimia were spared. In 1573 Maria married Magnus of Denmark as part of Ivan IV's plan to make Livonia a dependent state with that Danish prince as its king. She substituted for Yevfimia, who was betrothed to Magnus in 1570 but died before the wedding. In 1577 Ivan fell out with Magnus, who fled to Bathory, taking Maria with him. Her presence there alarmed some in Moscow who feared that Poland-Lithuania might exploit her as a tool against Fedor's government. In 1585 Horsey arranged that she and her daughter return to Moscow. There Maria, forced to take the veil, lived with her daughter in the Trinity monastery, secluded and absent from the political arena.

23. Among the representatives of the khanate of Kasimov (see above, Chapter IV, Note 35) Sain Bulat (1545-1616) converted to Christianity under the name Simeon Bekbulatovich. In confused circumstances and for reasons still unclear Ivan the Terrible proclaimed Simeon tsar in 1575, whose reign was merely titular and ended within a year. Thereafter he served Ivan loyally, retaining the title of grand prince of Tver. Godunov considered him a potential threat and banished him from his estate at Klushino in 1585. By then he had lost his sight. In 1598 he was entered in the contest for election as tsar, ultimately won by Godunov. He had marital connections to the Mstislavsky family and may have been their tool on this occasion. Boris allowed him to return to his estates, where he remained in relative peace until 1605, when the victorious pretender attempted to secure his endorsement. His refusal to cooperate led to his being tonsured. The next year a triumphant Vasily Shuisky sought Bekbulatovich's recognition and, failing equally, exiled him to the Solovetsk monastery. The Romanovs recalled him from exile in 1613. See Graham, "Bekbulatovich, Simeon," MERSH, Volume 3, pp. 193-195.

APPENDIX

1. On Simeon Bekbulatovich, see Chapter VI, Note 23.

2. The text of the edition of 1959–1966 reads "Ivan IV." Either this is a misprint, or a slip of the pen on Soloviev's part. There is no evidence that Ivan had any but the most affectionate relations with his deaf-mute brother Yury

(1533-1563), and Kurbsky completed his history in 1573, well before the death of Ivan Ivanovich in 1581. Moreover, Ivan IV had no grandson. On the other hand, Kurbsky wrote of Ivan III that he "killed his son Ioann, most excellent and glorious in exploits of valor, who was born of his first wife, the holy princess Maria of Tver, and his grandson Tsar Dmitry, crowned by God, together with his holy mother Elena, the former killed with deadly poison and the latter imprisoned for many years and then strangled." *Kurbsky's History of Ivan IV.* Ed., trans., and notes by J.L.I. Fennell (Cambridge, 1965), p. 169. Fennell (pp. 168-169, Note 5) comments "Ivan Ivanovich died of gout in 1490; it is most unlikely that Ivan III had anything to do with his death. Sofia Palaeologa, 'the Greek,' Ivan's second wife, may have been suspected of having a hand in her stepson's death, as the doctor who treated him had in fact been brought to Moscow by Sofia's brother. Ivan III's grandson, Dmitry Ivanovich (Ivan Ivanovich's son), who was crowned grand prince of Vladimir, Moscow and All Russia in 1498, fell from favor in 1502 and was sent to prison where he died, or was killed, seven years later." The brother referred to was Prince Andrei, "the Elder" of Uglich, Zvenigorod and Mozhaisk, who was imprisoned deservedly in 1491 for repeated rebellion, and died two years later.

3. Soloviev provides three references for this extended discussion: Palitsyn, p. 3; M.P. Pogodin, *Ob uchastii Godunova v ubienii tsarevicha Dmitriia. Istoriko-kriticheskie otryvki* (Concerning Godunov's Role in the Murder of Tsarevich Dmitry. Critical Historical Commentaries) (Moscow, 1846), pp. 271-305, and K.S. Aksakov, *Polnoe sobranie sochinenii* (Complete Collected Works) Volume I (Moscow, 1861), pp. 241ff.

INDEX

Grey, Ian, historian, 178
Grodno, 24, 172
Gryzelda, niece of Stefan Bathory, 72, 180
Guba reforms, 211
Gustav Vasa, Swedish king, 171, 189
Gvozdev, Prince, table attendant, 120

Habsburgs, 38, 42, 177-178, 191
Habsburg empire, xx
Haiduks, 37, 182
Hakluyt Society Collection, xx, 196
Halecki, Oscar, historian, xix
Hanseatic towns, 112
Haraburda, Michael, Habsburg emissary, 17-18, 21-24, 175, 178, 194
Hasings, Lady Mary, proposed bride for Ivan IV, 185
Hegel, Georg Wilhelm Friedrich, philosopher, xii
Heidenstein, Reinhold, Prussian narrator, xxvi, 165
Hellie, Richard, historian, xvii-xviii, xxii-xxiii, 169
Henri of Navarre, later King Henri IV of France, 183, 193, 195
Henrician Articles, 177
Henryk Walezy, king of Poland, later King Henri III of France, xx, 13-14, 172-173, 176-177, 180, 193
Hermogen, archbishop of Kazan, later patriarch of Moscow, 128, 170, 108, 109; compared with Joan of Arc, 209-210
Hetman, 179
Holland, Dutchmen, 114
Holy Roman emperor, 20-21, 36, 62, 94, 102, 178
Holy Roman empire, 58, 197, 191, 202
Horde, 2, 32
Horn, Evert, 189
Horn, Karl Hendriksson, Swedish ambassador, 54, 189
Horsey, Jerome, English narrator, xxv, 5, 71, 103, 167-168, 182, 196, 215
Household guards, 115
Hundred Years War, 208
Hungary, 32, 62, 87, 91, 180 183, 190, Hungarian gold, 53, 85; Hungarian land, 66

Iberia, 102
Ibrahim, Turkish emissary, 94
Ingermanland, 184; see also Izhora.
Ingolstadt, 183
Interregnum, 172, 176
Iran, 204
Irina Fedorovna, consort of Tsar Fedor, sister of Boris Godunov, xxvi, 3, 4, 7-8, 11, 20, 141, 153, 155, 167
Irtysh river, 103, 105-106, 205
Isker, fort, 103, 205
Islam-Girey, Crimean khan, 78-80, 92, 198
Isleniev, noble, ambassador to sultan, 100, 153
Istanbul, 198, 202
Italy, Italians, 28.172, 180, 183 194
Italian Renaissance, 172
Ivan Ivanovich. son of Ivan III, 216
Ivan Ivanovich, tsarevich, son of Ivan IV, 1, 161
Ivan III "The Great", grand prince, 158, 160, 216
Ivan IV "the Terrible", tsar, xiii, xiv xvii, xx, xxiii, xxv, xxvi, 1-8, 13, 15-19, 28, 43, 49 69, 74, 76, 86, 93, 101, 103, 105, 107, 109, 111, 114, 130, 137, 140, 143, 154, 160-163, 167-168, 170, 175, 177, 181-182, 185. 187 190, 195, 200-204, 209, 211, 215, 216
Ivan Kalita, grand prince, 154, 215
Ivan Timofeev, crown secretary, chronicler, 200
Ivangorod, 44-47, 49, 55, 112, 184
Ivanov, Andrei, 183
Ivanov, Nikita, 125
Ivanov, Senka, Russian captive, 91
Izhora land, 43, 184. See also Ingermann-land
Izium burial ground, 115
Izmailov, Andrei Yakovlevich, Muscovite ambassador, 16-18, 175

Jacob, Dr. Robert, gynecologist, 71, 196
Jan Kazimierz, Polish king, 181
Jan Olbracht, Polish king, 177
Janissaries, 81, 202
Jaworowo prefecture, 14

Livonian war, xiii,164, 1168, 172, 176,
181-182,184, 202, 205
Lobanov-Rostovsky, Prince Peter
Semeonovich, deputy governor of
Novgorod, 43-44, 184, 206
London, 71
Longworth, Philip, historian, xxi
Lopasnia, 83
Lopatnichi, village, 8
Lords of the council (pany radnye), 34-35,
39, 49-50, 68, 175
Lovat, 184
Lower Austria, 180
Lower Morzh river, 137
Lübeck, 68, 112
Luga, 184
Luguy, Ostiak prince, 105
Lukash Pavlusov, foreign merchant, son of
Magnus, 57-58, 190
Lukomski, Prince, Polish noble, 53
Lutheranism, 129, 171-173
Lvov, 27

Magnus, king of Livonia, 119, 154, 167,
208, 215
Maliuta Skuratov-Belsky, 3, 164, 166
Mamay, 85
Mamonich, Luke, rich Lithuanian trader,
30
Mansurov, Muscovite commander in
Siberia, 105
Margeret, Jacques, French mercenary,
xxvi, 214
Maria Anna of Bavaria, wife of Emperor
Ferdinand II, 183
Maria Fedorovna Nagaia, tsaritsa, widow
of Ivan IV, 165 1, 3, 145-146, 161,
165, 185, 202, 213,
Maria Grigorievna, daughter of Maliuta
Skuratov, wife of Boris Godunov, 164.
See also Kucheney.
Marina Mniszech, wife of False Dmitry,
194
Maria of Spain, consort of Emperor
Maximilian II, 180
Maria of Tver, first wife of Ivan III, 216
Maria Vladimirovka (religious name
Martha), kinswoman of Ivan IV, 154,
167, 215

Marsh, Anthony, English interloper, 73-
74, 76-77, 196-197
Mary Queen of Scots, 197
Master of the Horse (starokoniushii), 171
Matthias, archduke, later Holy Roman
emperor, 180, 183
Matvey, ataman, 117
Maxim the Greek, 129, 209-210. See also
Triboles, Michael.
Maximilian, archduke, candidate for
Polish throne, xx, 21, 24, 28, 33, 36-
41, 56-60, 68, 134, 173-174, 177-178,
190-192, 195
Mazovia, 40
McNeill, William H., historian, xxi, xxiii
Mediterranean, 190, 192
Medveditsa river, 116
Medyn, 7
Melancthon, 173
Melentieva, Vasilisa, Ivan IV's sixth wife,
177
Merrick, John, English agent, 194
Meshcheriak, cossack ataman, 103
Meshchersky, Prince, 18
Michael Fedorovich Romanov, tsar, 186,
188, 200-201
Mikhailov, Yakov, cossack leader, 103
Mikhailov, Yevdokim, watchman, 148-
151
Mikoshinsky, Bogdan, hetman, 64
Mikulinsky, Prince, 119
Milo, 13
Mishuk, cossack bandit, 117
Mishurin, courier, 80-81
Mniszech family, 194
Mochalov, Andrei, 179, 193
Mochalov, Andriusha, sorcerer, 152,
279,183
Moldavia, 32, 87
Molkhovnikov, Kirril, crown agent
Molveninov, bear trainer, 139
Monasteries and convents: Ascension
(Moscow Kremlin), 165; Caves
(Pskov), 58; Danilov (Moscow), 83;
Donskoy (Moscow), 85 ; Intercession
(Sudal), 170, 211; Khutyn (Novgorod),
168; Koriazemsk (Solvychegodsk),
126; New Convent (Moscow), 164;
Serbian Annunciation (Ponarat), 209;

THE EDITOR AND TRANSLATOR

Wayne David Santoni presently is chairman of the History Department at Southern Illinois University at Edwardsville, where he has taught for twenty-nine years. A graduate of the University of Maryland (B.A., M.A.) and Kansas University (Ph.D.), he has devoted most of his career to teaching. He received SIUE's all-university teaching award five times, and was nominated for a Carnegie Award for teaching in 1995. His research interests include P.N. Durnovo's activities in suppressing the Revolution of 1905, on which he wrote his doctoral dissertation, and the militarization of labor in the Allied countries during the First World War. He, his wife Lana, and his twenty-one year old cat Socks live in Edwardsville.

FROM ACADEMIC INTERNATIONAL PRESS*

THE RUSSIAN SERIES

1   S.F. Platonov **History of Russia** **

2   **The Nicky-Sunny Letters, Correspondence of** Nicholas and Alexandra, 1914-1917

3   Ken Shen Weigh **Russo-Chinese Diplomacy, 1689-1924**

4   Gaston Cahen **Relations of Russia with China...1689-1730**

5   M.N. Pokrovsky **Brief History of Russia**

6   M.N. Pokrovsky **History of Russia from Earliest Times**

7   Robert J. Kerner **Bohemia in the Eighteenth Century**

8   **Memoirs of Prince Adam Czartoryski and His Correspondence with Alexander I**

9   S.F. Platonov **Moscow and the West.**

10 S.F. Platonov **Boris Godunov**

11 Boris Nikolajewsky **Aseff the Spy**

12 Francis Dvornik **Les Legendes de Constantin et de Methode vues de Byzance**

13 Francis Dvornik **Les Slaves, Byzance et Rome au XIᵉ Siecle**

14 A. Leroy-Beaulieu **Un Homme d'Etat Russe (Nicholas Miliutine)...**

15 Nicolas Berdyaev **Leontiev (In English)**

16 V.O. Kliuchevskii **Istoriia soslovii v Rossii**

17 **Tehran Yalta Potsdam. The Soviet Protocols**

18 **The Chronicle of Novgorod**

19 Paul N. Miliukov **Outlines of Russian Culture Vol. III Pt. 1. The Origins of Ideology**

20 P.A. Zaionchkovskii **The Abolition of Serfdom in Russia**

21 V.V. Vinogradov **Russkii iazyk. Grammaticheskoe uchenie o slove**

22 P.A. Zaionchkovskii **The Russian Autocracy under Alexander III**

23 A.E. Presniakov **Emperor Nicholas I of Russia. The Apogee of Autocracy**

24 V.I. Semevskii **Krestianskii vopros v Rossii v XVIII i pervoi polovine XIX veka**

25 S.S. Oldenburg **Last Tsar! Nicholas II, His Reign and His Russia**

26 Carl von Clausewitz **The Campaign of 1812 in Russia**

27 M.K. Liubavskii **Obrazovanie osnovnoi gosudarstvennoi territorii velikorusskoi narodnosti. Zaselenie i obedinenie tsentra**

28 S.F. Platonov **Ivan the Terrible** Paper

29 Paul N. Miliukov **Iz istorii russkoi intelligentsii. Sbornik statei i etiudov**

30 A.E. Presniakov **The Tsardom of Muscovy**

31 M. Gorky, J. Stalin et al., **History of the Civil War in Russia** (Revolution)

32 R.G. Skrynnikov **Ivan the Terrible**

33 P.A. Zaionchkovsky **The Russian Autocracy in Crisis, 1878-1882**

34 Joseph T. Fuhrmann **Tsar Alexis. His Reign and His Russia**

35 R.G. Skrynnikov **Boris Godunov**

36 R.G. Skrynnikov **The Time of Troubles. Russia in Crisis, 1604-1618**

38 V.V. Shulgin **Days of the Russian Revolutions. Memoirs From the Right, 1905-1907.** Cloth and Paper

39 A.E. Presniakov **The Formation of the Great Russian State.**

40 J.L. Black **"Into the Dustbin of History"! The USSR From August Coup to Commonwealth, 1991. A Documentary Narrative**

41 E.V. Anisimov **Empress Elizabeth. Her Reign and Her Russia, 1741-1761**

42 J.K. Libbey **Russian-American Economic Relations, 1763-1999**

43 Nicholas Zernov **Three Russian Prophets. Khomiakov, Dostoevsky, Soloviev**

44 Paul N. Miliukov **The Russian Revolution** 3 vols.

45 Anton I. Denikin **The White Army**

55 M.V. Rodzianko **The Reign of Rasputin—An Empire's Collapse. Memoirs**

56 **The Memoirs of Alexander Iswolsky**

THE CENTRAL AND EAST EUROPEAN SERIES

1   Louis Eisenmann **Le Compromis Austro-Hongrois de 1867**

3   Francis Dvornik **The Making of Central and Eastern Europe** 2nd edition

4   Feodor F. Zigel **Lectures on Slavonic Law**

10 Doros Alastos **Venizelos—Patriot, Statesman, Revolutionary**

20 Paul Teleki **The Evolution of Hungary and its Place in European History**

FORUM ASIATICA

1   M.I. Sladkovsky **China and Japan—Past and Present**

REFERENCE SERIES

The Modern Encyclopedia of Russian, Soviet and Eurasian History 60 vols.

The Modern Encyclopedia of East Slavic, Baltic and Eurasian Literatures 50 vols.

The Modern Encyclopedia of Religions in Russia and the Soviet Union 30 vols

Russia & Eurasia Military Review Annual

Russia & Eurasia Facts & Figures Annual

Russia & Eurasia Documents Annual

USSR Calendar of Events (1987- 1991) 5 vol. set

USSR Congress of Peoples's Deputies 1989. The Stenographic Record

Documents of Soviet History 12 vols.

Documents of Soviet-American Relations

Gorbachev's Reforms. An Annotated Bibliography of Soviet Writings. Part 1 1985–1987

Military Encyclopedia of Russia and Eurasia 50 vols.

China Facts & Figures Annual

China Documents Annual

Encyclopedia USA. The Encyclopedia of the United States of America Past & Present 50 vols.

Sports Encyclopedia North America 50 vols.

Sports in North America. A Documentary History

Religious Documents North America Annual

The International Military Encyclopedia 50 vols.

Nationalities and Ethnicity Terminologies. An Encyclopedic Dictionary and Research Guide 2 vols.

SPECIAL WORKS

S.M. Soloviev **History of Russia** 50 vols.

SAFRA Papers 1985-

*Request catalogs. Sample pages, tables of contents, more on line at www.ai-press.com